THE DISQUIETING DEATH *of* EMMA GILL

THE DISQUIETING
DEATH
of
EMMA
GILL

ABORTION, DEATH, AND CONCEALMENT
IN VICTORIAN NEW ENGLAND

MARCIA BIEDERMAN

CHICAGO
REVIEW
PRESS

Copyright © 2024 by Marcia Biederman
All rights reserved
Published by Chicago Review Press Incorporated
814 North Franklin Street
Chicago, Illinois 60610
ISBN 978-1-64160-856-5

Library of Congress Control Number: 2023940022

Typesetting: Nord Compo

Printed in the United States of America
5 4 3 2 1

To the people of Bridgeport, Connecticut, past and present.

CONTENTS

Prologue. 1

1 Before Henry Met Nancy. 7

2 Creating a Doctor 17

3 Lynn, Lynn, City of Sin 31

4 Lethargy. 49

5 The Salem Trials 71

6 New Haven, Hotbed of Abortion. 93

7 Road Trip 119

8 Coming Home to Her Funeral 141

9 Link by Link. 161

10 Transcontinental Dragnet 179

11 A Much-Persecuted Woman. 201

Afterword 217

Acknowledgments. 223

Notes. 225

Index. 241

PROLOGUE

THE EXPERTS SAID A WOMAN couldn't have done it alone, and they were right. The family had done it together, as they'd always done things. They'd jointly made a mess of it. All their efforts at concealment were undone in a moment. It might have been comical if it hadn't been criminal.

It happened in early September 1898, on one of those last summer vacation days when children tend to bore easily. On this warm Monday at four o'clock, three boys had spent the day doing nothing in particular. As they walked home over a bridge, two white bundles on the mudflats below caught their attention. Another boy and some men joined them. The carefully shaped objects—one round and one rectangular—made a sharp contrast with the muck of nature. It was strange.

The adults seemed content to marvel, but a boy decided to investigate. Johnny Jackson descended from the bridge and found a long stick. Another twelve-year-old, Stephen Kelly, came to assist. The objects lay close to the shore of Yellow Mill Pond in Bridgeport, Connecticut. Although called a pond, it was a tidal inlet, filling and draining in delayed synchronization with the ocean's ebb and flow.

The family had thrown the packages off the bridge at high tide, painstakingly weighting them down with stones to sink them in six feet of water. Now, at low tide, almost the entire pond floor was exposed. Anyone who lived here could have explained that would happen, but the family didn't live here, at least not in the way other families did.

The stones, at least, had worked as intended. Applying the stick to the larger package, the rectangular one, the boys couldn't make it budge. One of the boy's uncles, a blacksmith, lived near the bridge. Recruited to the effort, the uncle spliced the stick to a rake handle, attaching a hook to the end. Now properly equipped, the team retrieved its quarry. Cord held the cloth covering

1

together. As if handling a Christmas present, the children brought the bundle onto the bridge for unwrapping. Complicated knots threatened to slow their progress, but one boy lent a knife.

The heavy white cloth fell away, "and I saw a foot in it," Johnny later told the coroner.

Perhaps shamed by all this juvenile initiative, an adult retrieved the second package. In his retelling, a head "rolled out" with blue eyes open, but that was probably an embellishment. The neck was still attached, down to the third cervical vertebra, making free rotation unlikely. Long auburn hair indicated that these were the barely decomposed remains of a young woman.

At this point, the amateur detectives of the Seaview Avenue Bridge summoned the police, who found that the package with the foot contained both legs, severed below the knee. The four dissected parts of the lower limbs were bound together neatly in linen, apparently ripped from a man's undergarment.

Cloth was also bound around the dead woman's mouth, suggesting to some that she'd been gagged before being murdered, but the police never seriously considered that theory.

It was too late for the evening edition of the papers. With sixty-five thousand inhabitants, Bridgeport was one of New England's largest cities. Nevertheless, word spread quickly, all the way to the North End. A search began for the missing body parts. As the waters rose, boaters were placed on alert, and volunteers in hip boots scoured the pond.

As they searched, journalists and thrill-seekers flocked to the private funeral home that served as the city morgue. The police had placed the head on display, hoping someone could identify the victim, described in one paper as having an "aquiline" nose and in another as possessing a "wealth of hair." It was a spectacle worthy of the showman P. T. Barnum, formerly a mayor of the city.

As night fell, correspondents and illustrators from the big New York papers queued up at the morgue, eager to see the head in a bucket. Just blocks away, a phaeton drawn by a hired team of horses rolled down a street, preceded by a cyclist.

It was the family again, oblivious of the commotion around the corner from their home at Cullinan's Funeral Home. The phaeton headed for a lonelier part of town. All was quiet on the bridge, where the search parties had paused their work when the tide came in. Again, two bundles splashed into six feet of water, and the family separated. The cyclist pedaled east toward Stratford and New Haven, and the hired carriage returned to the stable.

The police had planned to dredge the pond, but that proved unnecessary. In the early hours of Tuesday, a young man delivering newspapers saw the two parcels in shallow water. Guessing their contents, he and a friend rowed out for them. Unwrapping again proved irresistible. By the time the police arrived, most of the torso had been found in one package, with arms still attached. The other contained the lower section of the body's trunk. All internal organs had been removed except the lungs and heart. Fatefully, a small bit of uterus had survived the disembowelment.

By Wednesday, the national press was all over the story. Bridgeport's city prosecutor, V. R. C. Giddings, had several announcements. By now, thousands of local men and women had viewed the head, but no one recognized it. From this, Giddings concluded that the victim must have been an out-of-towner.

He said it was now clear that the mutilation was intended to cover up the consequences of a "criminal operation," by which, as everyone knew, he meant abortion. Citing the medical examiner's findings, he said the woman succumbed to sepsis after an illness of several days.

In an exclusive that ran in the sensationalist New York *World* under his byline, the prosecutor asked the public to help find the culprit. According to Giddings, the person who committed the crime was knowledgeable about anatomy and autopsies. More importantly, this was someone who could handle a knife and saw. That led him to another significant conclusion.

"A woman . . . though she be a midwife or a physician, would, in my opinion, not be skilled sufficiently to make the clean cuts found on the various portions of the body," Giddings wrote. He added, "No old resident of Bridgeport had anything to do with it." The locals wouldn't have picked Yellow Mill Pond as a place to hide evidence of murder.

For it was murder, or at least it could be prosecuted as such. The headline over Giddings's words said, DEATH RESULTING FROM CRIMINAL PRACTICES IS MURDER IN CONNECTICUT. If a jury found it to be first-degree murder, the penalty would be death, he added.

As the story continued to fascinate, many medical experts would chime in. Not all would share Giddings's high opinion of the cutting and sawing. At best, the perpetrator had experience in butchery, some would say. A journal of forensic medicine would pan this crude dissection of a body into seven sections, contrasting it with the masterwork of a man who reduced his wife's body to 153 morsels. Sliced that finely, a corpse couldn't easily be identified, and there might even be the question of whether all parts came from the same body.

In the Bridgeport case, the two batches of body remnants were easily fitted together. They formed the corpse of a 105-pound woman around twenty-five years old, five feet one in height, with long arms and slender fingers. Raising the dead was a matter of easy assembly.

Distrusting newspaper sketches, people across the nation formed their own versions of the face. A parade of parents, husbands, and lovers insisted it was their absent daughter, wife, or romantic partner. Described as "slender and graceful in figure," the reconstructed form became an American Everywoman. Within weeks, the Bridgeport police received more than three hundred letters from people believing they knew the person she once was. Only one-third were mailed from Connecticut. Hundreds of people in dozens of places thought someone they knew might seek an illegal abortion.

The murderer was a fool to leave the face intact instead of pouring acid on it, said a Bridgeport police detective. Speculating why the body wasn't minced more finely to hinder identification, the *Medico-Legal Journal* credited the "impelling force of fear," typical in cases "in which the victim dies, not from murderous intent, but as the result of some illegal act, as rape or abortion."

There was fear of detection, to be sure, but also the fear of separation. A daughter and a son, both embroiled in this, had been torn from their mother in childhood. As adults, both were devoted to her. There was a father—violent, philandering, and, at this critical time, imprisoned. He stood by the others, at least publicly.

They were the typical crime family of modern-day television and film, loving one another while wreaking havoc on society—except that dismembering a body wasn't a serious crime, and many of their neighbors weren't sure that abortion should be either.

Nancy Alice Guilford didn't know the waters of Bridgeport, but she'd been seeing women patients there for years. Dozens of ads for Dr. Guilford listing her Bridgeport office hours had appeared in Connecticut papers and even a public-library bulletin. Naming her specialty as "diseases of women," the ads were barely encrypted. They also gave her address: 51 Gilbert Street in the center of Bridgeport, near city hall and police headquarters.

This was no back-alley operation. A brownstone with bay windows on the second floor and dormers on the third, it was judged by the press to be a handsome dwelling. Cleaned by a live-in housekeeper, it defied the stereotypes of abortion-parlor filth and squalor in the era before *Roe v. Wade*. Indeed, police noted later that the hallway had a strong odor of carbolic acid, an antiseptic favored by germ-theory pioneer Joseph Lister.

When finally cornered, after a chase spanning two continents and three countries, the midwife threatened to expose the names of her four hundred Bridgeport patients, many known to the "best society," and twice that number in New Haven, from which she'd come. She promised revelations that would shake the "pillars of the courts, the clubs, and the churches." Or so said the newspapers, and no one doubted it.

After all, Nancy Guilford herself was said to "move in the best society," and her husband's roots stretched back to the American Revolution. Indeed, the story that ended with a head in a pond began with baptismal waters, as a young evangelist set forth to save sinners.

1 | BEFORE HENRY MET NANCY

FOR ONE YOUNG EVANGELICAL, the early months of 1840 were heady times in northern New England, even if the cold had frozen a dead man to the ground. As twenty-two-year-old Henry Pittman Guilford paid visits to the people of Kittery, Maine, he "appeared to be sent of the Lord," an older clergyman noted.

Religion was taking hold here, nearly as popular with some people as alcohol was with others. Suddenly, a backload of prayers were being answered, or so said many at church when the spirit moved them to testify, often rambling on about mundane matters just to get them off their chests. Shipyard workers lined up for baptism in Kittery, hundreds braved snowy roads to attend a New Hampshire chapel dedication, and quiet meetings erupted into raucous revivals all along the coast.

Amid this joyful noise, young Guilford became Rev. H. P. Guilford, ordained on the New Hampshire island of New Castle. Preparation for pastoral duty was a casual matter in Guilford's branch of Protestantism, which called itself simply the Christian denomination or sometimes the Christian connection. "We make no boast of a learned ministry," wrote one official of the loosely organized church. "Some pastors have only a common education," he added, "while others have educated themselves."

H.P., as he signed himself, was in a category all his own. The son and brother of Massachusetts shoemakers, he nonetheless met the high standards for clergy set by his religion's leading newspaper. Less tolerant than the church itself of the common touch, the *Christian Herald and Journal* favored a literate voice from the pulpit. Its editors embraced Guilford, printing his overwrought letters, praising his work, and charting his frequent moves on the preaching circuit. They also made him a sales agent, paying a commission for each sub-scription sold. Thus, the paper encouraged H.P.'s twin interests, in business and religion, that he maintained throughout life. His firstborn son would join him in the first interest and spectacularly reject the second.

But child-rearing still lay in the young minister's future. As he wrote his first letter to the *Christian Herald*, he'd been married only a few months. His bride was Lucy Ann Wells, a native of Hampton Falls, New Hampshire. It's not clear where they met, but her village was in Rockingham County, on the route of his evangelical travels. At age twenty, Lucy was nearly three years younger and probably no taller than her shorter-than-average husband. Whether or not marriage had anything to do with it, H.P. seemed flushed with excitement as he took up his pen.

Since arriving in Portsmouth fresh from ordination, the minister had roamed its streets in wonder. "Religion appears to be the general topic of conversation," he wrote, noting approvingly that few spoke of anything but this "blessed theme" in public or private. Here to assist an older pastor, he'd postponed his planned departure date. A highly charged atmosphere agreed with him.

Lengthy stays were not in H.P.'s nature nor suited to his dual professions. Soon the enterprising pastor was on the move again, armed with scripture and a subscription ledger. In New Hampshire, he'd briefly led the congregation that had witnessed his ordination, but he took a step back after Portsmouth. Returning to his native Massachusetts for several years, he assisted other pastors but had no flock of his own. At home, too, he and Lucy had lighter tasks than most. Four years into their marriage, there were still no babies.

They'd eventually have eight children, not unusual for the era. Given their religious beliefs, their late start on parenthood was probably not by choice. Still, other women of the time may have envied the childless young Lucy. Many, whether married or unmarried, used pills and herbs to try to reverse menstrual "stoppages," as early pregnancies were viewed. Until fetal movement or "quickening" was felt, usually in the fourth month, pregnancy didn't seem definite. Few people cared if a woman managed to terminate it.

However, as H.P. and Lucy began their married life, more effective abor-tions—involving physicians, instruments, and overnight stays—were gaining popularity and drawing legal scrutiny. For the most part, churches stayed out of the fray, but the Christian connection thought the procedures immoral.

Covering the widely discussed case of Mary Rogers, whose body was found in a New Jersey pond after a physician-assisted abortion, the *Christian Herald* called her "a voluntary criminal" who "came to her death by endeavouring to hide her shame."

As the young pastor sold subscriptions to that paper, Lucy experienced quickening. She was carrying her first child, whose name would someday be connected with another pond, another abortion, and another body—this time sawed into sections.

Meanwhile, Lucy's husband became a "voluntary criminal" of sorts. Not satisfied with selling religious papers, he decided to publish one himself. It would be a bold new magazine for Sunday schools, a substitute for the dusty books that had bored children for generations. Through boundless enthusiasm and extravagant sales projections, H.P. enrolled subscribers before even one line had been printed.

Predictably, it went bust, leaving printers unpaid and subscribers disappointed. Still, H.P. couldn't leave the gaming table. Changing the name of the publication and switching to another printer, he deepened his "embarrassments," as debts were called. However, he wasn't too embarrassed to publish a plea for financial help in the *Christian Herald*, ready cash preferred. Presenting his failure as noble, he blamed it on factors beyond his control. His firstborn would borrow from that playbook.

If H.P.'s open letter didn't clear all his debts, it at least brought a job. The North Christian Church of Swansea, Massachusetts, made him its pastor. He was there for the community's late August clambake, a tradition started by Native American people and appropriated by the churches. Wearing ribbons that signified their religious affiliation, children marched from the churches to a shoreline oak grove.

Now four years old, Henry M. Guilford likely marched with the smallest scholars. In his family's first year in Swansea, he and a younger sister, Ellen Eudora, were joined by a brother, Lester. Like their deceased grandmother and many others, Lucy would continue having babies at this rate throughout her childbearing years. At the same time, her church took some small steps toward gender equality. Its Sunday schools enrolled girls, unlike those of some other denominations, and women could preach in certain circumstances.

Lucy's son Henry would grow into a man who attracted women but abused them. Any thought he gave women's issues, including his mother's pregnancies, was probably in marketing terms. As the century advanced, white Protestants would increasingly seek to limit family size, sending married women to his practice. Meanwhile, industrialization drew single women from farm to factory, a social shift that not infrequently produced unintended pregnancies.

Henry grew up like a modern-day military brat, always relocating. When he was about six, the family left Swansea for a rural river town in western New Jersey's Alexandria Township. Uprooted from New England for the first time, the Guilfords were far from friends and family.

Over the next seven years, the preacher's family would leave the quiet of New Jersey, where their daughter Annie was born, for the bustle of New York City. There, H.P. moved the Second Church of Christ into a building on West Twenty-Seventh Street near Ninth Avenue, where he served as minister, with the times of his sermons announced in a city newspaper.

The family next appeared in Danbury, Connecticut, only fifty miles from New York yet in an entirely different world, with its white buildings surrounded by picturesque hills. They were finally back in New England, albeit the southernmost portion of the region. The only mark they left here was the birth of a third Guilford son, Frank. A history of Danbury that traces the growth of its Christian denomination fails to mention H.P., suggesting that he was but one of many preachers who revolved through its doors.

As a clergyman in an evangelical religion, H.P. could hardly have expected to stay in one spot. But now, he and the church were changing. The young preacher, once enraptured by the revivalist spirit of Portsmouth, was now a middle-aged father of five. The Christian denomination in Danbury had arisen from a similar impulse; the town historian described it as "a small struggling band of adherents" to "a simple faith." But around the time the Guilfords arrived, its appearance was acquiring more polish, moving from the fringes to the center of town and occupying a church formerly owned by the Methodists.

Some well-heeled donors embellished the new quarters with memorial windows and a pipe organ. Although the deed indicated that the remodeled building would be called the Church of Christ, it opened as the Disciples of Christ. Elsewhere, too, the denomination was undergoing name changes amid disagreements about its future direction. In Danbury, the church was enjoying its new financial security. Founded by lay preachers, then reliant on visiting preachers, the Disciples could finally employ their own ministers.

H.P. was not one of their long-term hires. He soon moved the family to Maine, where their sixth child was born. This son was named Millard, most likely for David Millard, one of the Christian brethren who'd preached alongside H.P. in the days before stained-glass windows and church organs supplanted revivals and testimonials. But as the new baby came into the world, his father had returned to a secular cause. The 1856 presidential campaign was on, and the new Republican Party was rallying behind John C. Frémont, staunchly opposed to the western expansion of slavery. In one of the last weeks of summer, Frémont supporters organized a clambake in Manchester-by-the-Sea, Massachusetts. A crowd estimated between six thousand and ten thousand gathered on a bluff of land jutting out into the sea.

This clambake was no Sunday-school affair. A carriage arrived carrying young women representing the various states. They wore white for the free states and black for the slave states. One woman wore red to symbolize Kansas—Bleeding Kansas, as it was then known—the scene of violent battles between pro- and antislavery factions.

The clear day afforded a stunning view of surrounding harbors, islands, and picturesque towns. But storm clouds were gathering over the nation as Kansas bled. Frémont did not appear, but a half-dozen speakers presented his antislavery positions. Among them were a senator, an ex-governor, a newspaper editor, and one H. P. Guilford of Maine.

For the first time in decades, the title *Reverend* didn't precede H. P. Guilford's name. He was taking a break from clerical duties. In fact, he had left the Christian denomination altogether. When he next used the title, he'd do so after ordination as a Baptist.

It was a startling sea change for a man who'd taken visceral delight in his former denomination, devoted his life to spreading word of it, and, at his lowest point, thrown himself upon its mercy. Thanks to Southern support, James Buchanan was elected president. His supporters fought a dirty campaign, lumping Frémont supporters like H. P. Guilford with "free love" advocates, supporters of women's rights, and other undesirables. Soon after the inauguration, the US Supreme Court's decision on the Dred Scott case galvanized antislavery sentiment.

In the spring of 1857, as the national mood darkened, a Baptist newspaper ran a brief item:

Rev. H. P. Guilford, formerly a minister with the Christian Connection, but who recently united with the Baptist church in Eastport, has
taken the pastoral charge of the Baptist church in Fredericton, N. B.

Fredericton was the capital of New Brunswick, then a British colony but
familiar to many in the American clergy. It was an optional extra stop on preaching tours of New England. However, for the Guilfords it would be home for
the next seven years, as the rumbles from their country intensified and civil
war began.

Two more Guilford children were born in New Brunswick, where the
family eventually left Fredericton for a small lobstering community. When
the first shots were fired at Fort Sumter, seventeen-year-old Henry was still
living with his family. The New Brunswick census, taken that year, gave his
occupation as "farmer" while all of his younger siblings were "at school."

As the war progressed, the Guilfords were undoubtedly aware of the inevitable consequences for a family with sons. Even men born in New Brunswick were volunteering for the Union Army. In 1863 the family returned to
their divided country, and H.P. took charge of a makeshift church in Maine's
Aroostook County.

A year later, Henry was in Boston, volunteering for the Union Navy. It
was hardly surprising that a son of Rev. H. P. Guilford, adamantly against
slavery, had entered the fray. Yet young Henry's choice of branch, navy over
army, suggests that he planned to expose himself to a minimum of danger.
Enlisting a few months before becoming conscription-eligible at age twenty,
he chose port blockading over land battles.

Three years into the war, romantic notions of battle had faded. Newspapers
daily listed the dead, and veterans with amputated limbs were a common sight
on village greens. Some men still volunteered for ideological reasons or from a
sense of duty, typically choosing the army as their branch. They marched off with
others from their towns or villages and fought beside others from their states.

The navy was different, often recruiting near urban taverns. Volunteers for
this branch of the service were often immigrants or native-born discontents
seeking food, shelter, and risk mitigation. The Confederacy's weak naval force
made sea battles relatively rare. Most sailors passed their time enforcing the
Union blockade and hoping to catch vessels that dared to penetrate it. Captur-
ing blockade-runners brought big prize money, or so the recruiters promised.

Henry M. Guilford felt drawn to this milieu. The prize money might have appealed to the gambling instincts he shared with his enterprising father. Enlisted as a "landsman" because of his lack of nautical experience, the former farmer did well. He learned to handle himself among the tough urban "jacks," as the Union sailors were called. Indeed, he flourished.

His first ship was the USS *Massasoit*, a gunboat propelled by steam. On a sidewheeler like this one, tinkerers counted for more than old salts, and Henry's farm work would have made him handy. Within months he became a petty officer, a boatswain's mate, overseeing men older than himself in the endless cleaning of the ship and maintenance of its hundred-pound guns.

Like other ships enforcing the Union's blockade, the *Massasoit* patrolled the North Atlantic, scouting for ships bearing supplies for the Confederacy. The task involved long stretches of monotony punctuated by hectic chases. Frigid night watches on the deck would have been part of Henry's duties, but there were rewards, too. He and the other petty officers would have shared a cook and mess, eating apart from the sailors. They would also have been attended by one of the *Massasoit*'s stewards. Among them was at least one formerly enslaved person or "contraband."

Blockading was not without its hazards. The raiding vessels fired back and laid mines. One of the *Massasoit*'s targets was a deadly rebel ship, the CSS *Tallahassee*, which had been sinking Union craft along a long stretch of coast.

The preacher's son must have acquitted himself well. Soon he was promoted to master's mate and transferred to the USS *Dumbarton*, also a steam gunboat. At age twenty, Henry Guilford wore a star above the stripe on his uniform, signifying that he was in the line of command. Full charge of the ship could fall to him in the absence of senior officers.

The river gunboats saw more action and were generally more effective than the coastal blockaders. In addition to intercepting rebel boats, they transported personnel and fortified ground troops in battles. An ensign who'd served in the squadron on a James River gunboat a year earlier wrote of enjoying oysters, fresh fruit, and daily newspaper deliveries. He also remembered drilling endlessly to prepare for action. When rebels attacked a badly outnumbered army brigade on the Virginia shore, the crew nearly instantly swung the guns into position, and the cooks left their pots to pass the ammunition. Meanwhile, the ensign wrote, the ward-room has been converted into an hospital, and there stands the surgeon and his steward with their instruments spread out on the dining-table, ready to make a clean job of any jagged limb that may have been roughly amputated by a cannon ball.

Such scenes might have become familiar to the future Dr. Henry M. Guilford, encouraging him to take up the scalpel himself, or at least making the thought of it less daunting. The steward, after all, must have been trained on the fly. Other events on the river could have also affected Henry's life. Asked to transfer soldiers to naval duty on the shorthanded gunboats, Ulysses S. Grant sought "unruly men," including those who'd been court-martialed. Master's Mate Guilford learned at an early age how to tame rough men, even cutthroats. That skill would later serve him well in prison.

As the war drew to a close, the sound of an approaching gunboat terrified white Southerners. Slaveholders fled, and enslaved people escaped. Guerrilla ex-Confederates, unwilling to surrender, boarded Union ships in the guise of refugees and murdered sailors. Retaliating gunboat crews didn't always heed the rules of war. At least on some boats, discipline was thrown to the winds. Theft of cotton was also commonplace.

Even after civility was restored and the world made shipshape, Henry would choose the laws he cared to follow. Military service had also taught him how to use firearms, which he'd keep handy in civilian life.

The war hardened Henry, but it didn't spare him a personal loss. A few months after his enlistment, his brother Lester joined the Maine Sixteenth Infantry Regiment. Private Lester Guilford died in February 1865, three months after his sixteenth birthday. He was buried just a few miles west of the James River in a cemetery for soldiers fallen during the siege of Petersburg, Virginia. Army records show he'd lied about his age.

As Lester was buried with members of his Maine regiment, his parents and siblings were in Reading, Massachusetts. Now pastor of a Baptist church, H.P. said a prayer at the dedication of a soldier's memorial erected there, one of the first in the nation.

Of the forty-eight names engraved on the Reading memorial, only fifteen died in action. The others succumbed to wounds or illness. H.P.'s eldest child, Henry, would have known of the nation's acute need for trained physicians. Because a master's mate bunked close to other officers, he undoubtedly knew his ship's surgeon and, perhaps, that man's income and status in civilian life. Henry could have borne that in mind as he planned his postwar future.

He didn't immediately return to civilian life. Henry remained in the navy until March 1866, almost a year after the war's end. Now a mate in the regular army, he finally earned full salary for his rank.

Had he left with the other volunteers, his service would have wreathed him in glory. Instead, he was dismissed, a less than honorable discharge for officers. In some way, he'd violated the code of military discipline. After the chaos of the war's final months, the rulebook was back in force, but not for Henry.

But now, where to? As the son of a wandering evangelical, he had no home to return to, no longtime neighbors to inquire into his whereabouts.

Over the course of Henry's remarkable life, the public and the press would grow intensely curious about him. Nobody looked into his military record, but inquiring minds wondered how he became a physician. His answer never changed. He said he'd graduated from Geneva Medical School in 1867. The American Medical Association and a regional medical directory duly noted this in listings issued for the public.

The school, located in Geneva, New York, was an interesting choice for Henry's real or mythical education. Two decades earlier, it had been the first American medical school to enroll a woman, Elizabeth Blackwell. For men, the standard for acceptance was much lower. Medicine did not yet enjoy high social status or necessarily command high salaries, and Henry M. Guilford's patchwork education would not have necessarily excluded him, although his dismissal from the navy might have. Most American medical schools of the era accepted nearly any male who could pay tuition.

Geneva Medical School required a two-year course of study for the medical degree. Henry's presumed graduation date followed his dismissal from the army by only one year. Blackwell, admitted after having studied medicine elsewhere, nonetheless had to complete two full years at Geneva.

During Henry's lifetime, at least one newspaper claimed to have authenticated his diploma. "It has been found that one Henry Guilford graduated from Geneva University [sic]," wrote the paper, without citing the source of its information. But neither that name nor an alias that Henry adopted appears in the lists of Geneva Medical College's 1867 graduates retained by the alumni association of Syracuse University, into which Geneva merged. Nor does his name, real or assumed, appear in the records of Hobart College, with which Geneva was once affiliated.

It seems improbable that Henry completed the requirements for a medical degree. If he studied medicine, he let his knowledge languish for a decade, never advertising his services during that period as he later did incessantly. Eventually, he was licensed to practice in one state through a statutory fluke. For the most part, he was a highly convincing impersonator.

But as he left the navy under a cloud, his patients would have to wait. The same steam that had powered his gunboat was driving the machine belts of Lynn, Massachusetts, where he'd get a legitimate job in the shoe trade and put his own illicit stamp on it.

2 | CREATING A DOCTOR

DAYS IN POST-CIVIL WAR Lynn began with the shriek of factory whistles and continued with the whir of stitching machines, the thrum of machine belts, and the percussion of steel rolling over leather. Cutting rooms in the city's red-brick factories were all-male domains, but the stitching rooms were full of women. Those not operating machines were at the tables, doing the eyeleting, embroidery, and buttonholing not yet mastered by machinery.

Orders for satin gaiter boots, dancing slippers, and other feminine footwear confections kept Lynn's factories humming. Each manufacturing corporation employed traveling salesmen, called agents, to take orders and note trends. When *Demorest's Monthly Magazine* declared that shoes are no longer worn the color of dresses, an astute agent would alert his employer to stock up on black and white kid.

One such agent was Henry Melancthon Guilford. After his many years away from Massachusetts, the 1870 US Census found him in Lynn, age twenty-six. He gave his occupation as "trader." He was living with a woman, Helen M. Guilford, age twenty-five and born in Maine. The census lists her as his wife, although they may never have wed. As Henry's life would abundantly illustrate, he didn't care much for the sacrament of marriage.

There was another addition to the Guilford family. The census counted their infant son, Herbert, born on February 3, 1870. In the city register marking the birth, Henry's occupation appears as "agent." There can be little doubt about what industry he was in. Nearly all the other fathers registering births in Lynn that day were shoemakers. Three years after his supposed graduation from Geneva Medical College, Henry was selling shoes.

According to the census, Henry P. and Henry M. Guilford had done well for themselves, each estimating the value of their personal estates at one thousand dollars. Rev. H. P. Guilford, especially, was in robust shape, with an additional six thousand dollars' worth of real estate.

Few of their neighbors—leather cutters, carpenters, and the like—could match their assets. Another property-owning minister on the street fell slightly short of the Guilford mark.

H.P.'s early experiments with business had finally borne fruit, and he no longer relied on the church for his livelihood. In the census and for several years in city directories, he's described as an insurance agent, not a minister.

The two family men, father and son, were often absent from home. In middle age, H.P. and Lucy were still living with six children, ranging in age from nine to twenty-four. The adult children worked, and the little ones went to school. Both of Henry's daughters were music teachers. When pupils came to them, the house must have rung with wrong notes and struggling voices.

It's small wonder that H.P. sought chances to escape this charming domestic scene. Soon after burying his son Lester and memorializing the other war dead, he resumed his antebellum work of selling magazine subscriptions. Retracing a route taken in his evangelical days, he headed to Fall River, Massachusetts. The reverend had formed lasting friendships in that textile-producing city. Fall River would always have a place in his heart.

However, the city was not eager for magazine subscriptions. While not giving up on the road-trip dreams entirely, H.P. returned to his home and the staid insurance business. Another minister had taken the reins at the church in Reading, and he'd spend the next five years on matters more material than spiritual. With children still at home, the clergyman-entrepreneur stayed by the hearth. But he had his finger to the wind, waiting for the right opportunity.

Meanwhile, the holy man's firstborn was leading a distinctly unholy life. Henry lost interest in his wife, Helen, a few years after the birth of the son. Apart from the name, age, and birthplace recorded in the 1870 census, she is a cipher. There are no Massachusetts records of their marriage. When her son, Herbert, applied for his marriage license, he gave her birthplace as Massachusetts, not Maine. On Herbert's death certificate, her birthplace is "U.S.A.," and her maiden name is left blank. The grandson who helped prepare the certificate knew nothing more.

It didn't take long for the relationship between Henry and Helen to sour. Later, Henry said she'd sought a legal separation. She had ample reason to do so. Henry's footwear sales ventures took him to a western New York village, where he fathered two more children by another woman.

Several years after giving birth to those children, this second woman would become Henry's wife. She'd also become his accomplice in crime.

It began as romantically as it could, given the circumstances. His name, Guilford, became hers without benefit of matrimony. Like law-abiding brides, she had a new monogram, which she'd someday snip off handkerchiefs and scratch off purse clasps to avoid detection.

When he met her, she was Nancy Alice Brown, blue-eyed and described as "comely," at least when she met Henry. She was about twenty then, a school-teacher in Wellsburg, a suburb of Elmira in New York's Southern Tier, just north of the Pennsylvania border. One paper went so far as to call her the town "belle," although that was scarcely a distinction. The town had fewer than six hundred inhabitants. Farm families comprised most of the town, along with carpenters, carriage makers, and blacksmiths. A funeral director and a hotel operator rounded out the mix.

Nancy may have taught at the public school that she'd attended, reciting a piece called "The Rabbit" at an evening of music and declamation. Wellsburg also had a private school, operated by a townswoman. Besides these establishments, the village boasted a mill, a store, a post office, a wagon shop, a blacksmith shop, and a few houses.

The couple's meeting was described as having "a tinge of the romantic," although there were conflicting reports of how it occurred. In one version, Henry spotted the lovely lass returning on a train from a circus and followed her home. Feigning thirst, he asked her for a drink of water. She obliged, lowering an oaken bucket into her family's well, and it was love at first sight.

The two were nearly matched in size. Measuring five feet and five inches, Henry had inherited his father's slight stature. Nancy, often described as tall, was one inch shorter. Her thin lips are barely smiling in a photograph taken years later. Her eyes, downturned at the corners, were said to be pale blue. A newspaper sketch of Henry shows a high and wide forehead balanced by broad lips and a cleft chin. It could have been drawn from a photograph, although both he and Nancy avoided studio portraiture. By conventional standards, he was the better-looking of the pair. With thick necks, both Henry and Nancy look slightly pugilistic.

As fit for family consumption as the charming stories of H.P.'s Sunday-school magazine, this first-date story had various versions. Nancy may have been returning from a fair, not a circus. Henry either followed her off the train or spotted her at the station. The refreshment offered to the thirsty stranger might have been milk, not water.

In the most reliable telling, Henry first stopped at a grocery store near the train depot and asked the owner if there were any "nice girls" in town. The storekeeper replied by pointing to Nancy Brown as she walked toward the post office. Henry stalked her home from there, then feigned thirst to ask for a drink.

That account, printed in a Baltimore paper, names the storekeeper: Miles Roberts. The anecdote is not attributed to him, but he's quoted elsewhere in the piece, indicating that he was the source. Roberts was a longtime resident of Wellsburg who lived near the Browns and did business with them for years. As Roberts told it, the meeting was not merely serendipitous. Henry was on the hunt for a woman.

Nancy's father, Horace, farmed forty acres and was also a tanner. In real estate and other assets, he was H. P. Guilford's equal. In pedigree, too, they were well matched. Henry let it be known that he was the son of a minister from an old New England family. Shoemakers aside, H.P.'s great-grandfather, Samuel Marble, had fought at Lexington with the Minute Men. Horace couldn't top that, but his father, Stephen H. Brown, was among Wellsburg's early settlers, coming there from Orange County, New York, in 1806.

Genealogy didn't warm Horace's feelings toward Henry. "He did not like him," wrote the paper that had interviewed Roberts, their neighbor. Henry was, after all, eight years older than Nancy and a stranger. But in Wellsburg, where the only other excitement was Brother Clark's Temperance Sociable Dance and an occasional church lawn festival, the farmer had no way to stop the relationship. At any rate, his wife had no objections to it, so Henry's frequent visits to their daughter continued.

Henry seems to have told Roberts, his matchmaker or procurer, that he had a first wife who'd filed for separation from him. Such frankness wasn't characteristic of Henry. He might have sensed that discovery was inevitable, or perhaps he was bracing Wellsburg for the appearance of his eldest child, Herbert, whose name was written in the Brown family bible.

About a year after meeting, Henry and Nancy went off on a brief trip that they claimed was an elopement. In truth, the couple wouldn't legally wed until 1879, when they already had two children. Later, Nancy would count the years of their married life from 1871, eight years before her wedding in Massachusetts. The "elopement" became as real to her as to others.

Wellsburg swallowed the story, and Henry and Nancy lived there as man and wife. It was said that Henry set up a shoe store in the village to give her something to do. Apparently, he was frequently absent. Henry's job in footwear must have called him back to Lynn, at least at the beginning. He could also have visited Herbert, who lived for a time at his parents' house but later came to live with him and Nancy.

Eventually, though, Wellsburg came to regard Henry as a doctor with an out-of-town practice. Some thought that Henry maintained an office in Barton, New York, twenty miles to the east in neighboring Tioga County. If so, no records of that have survived. However, a new health craze was sweeping the country, and Henry's father had bought into it.

The Reverend H. P. Guilford was promoting a new kind of gym in his beloved Fall River. All it lacked was an in-house physician. He made Henry a doctor by advertising him as one.

The year was 1876 when gyms in many cities offered a new body-building contraption targeted at the middle class. A weight-training machine had been designed for use in standing position, promising busy working people a quick yet complete workout. They didn't even have to take their clothes off. One model was designed for women in full skirts.

Marketed by competing companies under various names, these partial-lift machines were generally known as the "health-lift." The phrase became so familiar that it was used in a word-puzzle clue.

Fueled by the craze, a new breed of health facilities cropped up in major cities. Workingmen's gyms, with their medicine balls and dumbbells, stank of sweat. Health-lift centers exuded a medical aura. The press was smitten. A wellness magazine recommended the device for "sedentary and anemic young ladies, as well as bankers, dignitaries, and other kinds of brain-workers."

Chief popularizer of the craze was George Barker Windship, a Harvard-trained physician who mesmerized audiences with his weightlifting demonstrations and lectures on fitness and nutrition. Windship opened a Boston gym that included a medical office. The New York–based Health-Lift Company and other machine makers followed his template elsewhere. It's doubtful that the "doctors" of the copycat salons could match Windship's impressive medical credentials.

Alert to trends since the Sunday-school boom, H.P. seized on this one. He became an agent for the Health-Lift Company. It was a radical departure from his other lines of work, both spiritual and material.

Rev. H. P. Guilford was back in Fall River. Once, he'd been an activist clergyman here, encouraging parishioners to fight for a shorter workday. Now, he assisted gentlemen during daytime hours at the health-lift salon on the third floor of the new elevator-equipped Borden building. A woman helped the ladies in a separate room. Upholstered chairs and carpeting created an air of propriety. Perspiration seemed impossible.

Ads for the Fall River facility were dense with testimonials from physicians. What's more, it boasted of having an on-site doctor. "To those who cannot come during the day, Dr. Guilford, the manager, is in attendance from 7 to 9 each evening," promised the newspaper ads. Whether or not Henry ever stepped into a medical school classroom, now he had his degree.

Henry also provided part of the capital to open the facility. He owned the Fall River gym in partnership with Charles Rossiter. A mechanic and engineer, Rossiter may have been in charge of machinery maintenance. But he stayed in the background as the Guilfords bought ads and worked the press.

Vital to the operation was H.P., who'd maintained friendships in the area. A local paper, obviously benefiting from the gym's heavy advertising, praised it on its editorial pages. "The Rev. Mr. Guilford, the agent, we have known for years, and the patrons may be assured of his capability in conducting the business," an editor wrote. As for "Dr. Guilford," the reverend's son, the piece found him "a very intelligent and courteous gentleman, who explains in a clear and courteous manner the principles of the system." The repetition of *courteous* indicates that no stronger adjective suggested itself.

Henry didn't seem to spend much time at the gym. In late July, the Fall River paper ran an announcement: "Dr. Guilford returned this morning from New York and will again give his personal attention to his patrons at the Health-Lift rooms." He must have paid at least a flying visit to Wellsburg, where Nancy was caring for their eighteen-month-old son. Named Henry Brown Guilford but called Harry, he'd been born with a noticeable spine curvature. Harry would have a physically active life as a bicyclist and sailor, but he'd need to endure the gaze of a world that labeled him a hunchback.

Henry's personal attentions didn't last long. He soon left Fall River, returning in August. H.P. was absent, too, but only to move another health-lift facility to bigger quarters in New Bedford, where it had scored a hit.

Then everything nearly unraveled. On September 12, 1876, George Windship Barker died of a massive stroke at age forty-two. Many attributed his death to the regimen he'd promoted. The health-lift movement suffered a heavy blow. Frightened consumers turned to other activities, like outings on the new "safety" bikes that had replaced high wheelers. Lifting machines went on the scrap heap.

Three months after Windship's death, Henry bailed out of the business. A few lines in a newspaper announced the dissolution of his partnership with Charles Rossiter "by mutual consent," adding that Rossiter intended to continue "in the same rooms." That proved impossible, however. A few months after Henry abandoned the enterprise, it shrank to half its size. Only the suite for women remained operational.

Soon Rossiter was out of the picture too. The *Fall River Daily Evening News* announced that a local woman would "control the business entirely." But a salon dependent on the income of nineteenth-century women was doomed. Henry had chosen the right moment to fold his cards.

Not as instinctive as his son in these matters, H.P. hung on longer. He managed to open a health-lift facility in Cambridge, Massachusetts, the one place where the Windship name was still magic. The deceased strongman had been a fourth-generation student at Harvard and its medical school. But that marked the end of H.P.'s fitness venture, with hopes dashed yet again. He and Lucy would grow increasingly dependent on younger members of the family, including Henry and Nancy.

For Henry, it was a perfect time to explore other avenues for quackery. Earlier in the century, state medical societies licensed physicians, including graduates of apprenticeships who'd never attended medical school. For a while, some states let unlicensed doctors practice but permitted only the licensed ones to sue for fees. However, as medical education advanced and the old licenses lost prestige, those laws were revoked, and states exited the licensing business.

Sectarianism in medicine also clouded the picture. Members of the Massachusetts Medical Society were forbidden to consult with homeopaths while the New York Medical Society declined to impose this restriction. A contributor to a medical journal wrote that it was possible to reject the scientific basis for homeopathy while recognizing the competence of some of its more "flexible" practitioners.

"Yesterday we bled everyone . . ." this medical doctor reminded his readers. "The pendulum swings back and forth."

Certainly, the press and the public seemed open to doctors other than the "regulars," as MDs were known. Bloodletting was not yet ancient history, and memories of other useless panaceas were still fresh. The regulars had once prescribed calomel, a dangerous mercury derivative, for every imaginable ailment. People had grown wary.

Under the heading of "Physicians," an 1878 New England directory offers many alternatives. All names except those of the regulars are annotated with the names of their sect. Most common are homeopathic and eclectic practitioners, some of them educated in respected schools. The directory also lists officers of their medical societies, which they'd formed to distance themselves from quacks.

Nevertheless, quacks abounded. These practitioners formed no societies but instead competed with others of their sects. So-called Indian and botanical doctors used roots and herbs as therapeutics. "Electrical" practitioners exploited the contemporary fascination with science, and "clairvoyant" clinicians profited from the hunger for spiritualism. All were represented in the New England directory.

One notation stands out. Among the physicians of Providence, Rhode Island, is John P. Brooks, followed in parentheses by "health-lift." Henry M. Guilford's name isn't in the directory, but evidently, he wasn't the sole diplomate of that short-lived sect.

Now, however, it was time to choose another. As a guest of the Fall River's Narragansett Hotel, Henry would have been exposed to a cornucopia of quackery. A host of charlatans rented the hotel parlors by the week, promising to cure the incurable. "The Lame Walk! The Blind See! The Deaf Hear!" promised an ad placed by Dr. Henion, said to use "magnetic operations" in place of medicine. Henry would soon relocate, taking bits of this bunk for future use.

However, he couldn't run a roadshow like Henion's. There were many such miracle workers in the nineteenth century, dazzling new audiences, then leaving before the novelty wore off. At thirty-three, Henry had responsibilities. He was preparing to reunite with Nancy and the baby. His older son, Herbert, was to live with them. Around this time, Nancy became pregnant again.

Reinvented as a physician, he also sought a life as a family man. Although he was still not married to Nancy, she became indispensable to his plans. He was about to enter a medical specialty that required the participation of a trusted woman partner.

He started small, as if testing the waters. He rented a modest space for his residence and medical office in Worcester, a city in central Massachusetts near the Connecticut border. With fifty-eight thousand inhabitants, it was, for Henry, a throbbing metropolis. He might have known Worcester from his days as a shoe agent, or his father could have suggested the location. As an insurance agent, H.P. sold policies issued by a Worcester company.

Here, however, he was not Reverend Guilford's son or even Henry. Leaving his first name in Fall River, he emerged in Worcester as Melancthon Guilford, without even the initial *H* as a link with the person he'd been—disgraced naval officer, shoe agent, and exercise-salon physician.

His first tentative ad in the *Worcester Spy*, so small as to be almost invisible, called him simply Dr. Guilford, offering special attention to "complaints peculiar to females." Abortion providers commonly used this phrasing. However, it was also used in advertising for patent medicines targeted to women, like the popular tonics and compounds produced by Lydia Pinkham in Lynn. Or it could merely indicate a medical doctor focused on obstetrics and gynecology, although the "regulars" of the profession generally advertised only their names and addresses if they placed ads at all.

Advertising abortion services in Massachusetts could result in a prison term of up to three years and a fine of up to one thousand dollars. Abortion itself, either by medication or instrument, was punishable by a prison term of five to twenty years if it caused death. If the woman didn't die, imprisonment of the practitioner could range from one to seven years with a maximum fine of $20,000.

Perhaps out of fear, but more likely for other reasons, Henry quickly changed his advertising strategy. Larger and utterly preposterous, new ads for "Dr. Guilford, Psychomatic [*sic*] Medicine," featured the image of a hand emerging from clouds and emitting magnetic waves. Promising to cure the incurable, he listed so many specialties that no known malady seems to have been overlooked.

Henry M. Guilford. *Boston Sunday Post*

Quoted in some ads was a rousing endorsement from the *Worcester Evening Gazette*. It assured readers that Dr. Guilford "is not a traveling quack or cheap lecturer, but is a regularly educated physician and surgeon, and differs in practice from other regular physicians in the application of magnetism which he claims to possess to a high degree of a healing character."

Henry's days in the shoe industry melted away as he professed to have ten years of experience as a physician (or twelve years, depending on the ad). The *Gazette* endorsement seems to have been his first public boast of an earned medical degree.

As he prospered in Worcester, the ads contracted. Magnets and "psychomatic" powers were mothballed, and the medley of maladies yielded to the phrase "chronic illnesses." But the appeals to female patients resurfaced. Beginning as a jack-of-all-trades, Henry would close his Worcester chapter by advertising himself as a "physician, surgeon, and accoucheur," available for obstetrical house calls.

Henry's brief retreat from women's services, followed by a return to them, tracks with his youngest child's birth. On January 8, 1878, Nancy delivered a baby girl. She was named Eudora, the middle name of Henry's beloved sister. New York didn't register births at the time, but the date of birth is noted in the Brown family bible, and Eudora would always name New York as her birthplace.

It seems that Nancy and the children moved to Worcester with Henry. His initial ad appeared one month after Eudora's birth. But if Nancy had intended to help him with female patients, as she did through most of his career, it might have been too early. Harry was three, and Herbert, who joined them in Worcester, had just turned eight.

But she soon recovered. Eventually, they hired a live-in servant. Within months, Henry was back to advertising for female patients. Eudora may have started to talk around this time, mispronouncing her name as "Dodie," which became her family nickname.

Nancy had come to Worcester with a new name, too. She called herself Alice Guilford, substituting her first name with her middle name, as her husband "Melancthon" did. They had come to a new place with new names, apparently prepared to court danger.

Less than a year after arriving in Worcester, they were ready to expand. Their first quarters at 211 Main Street were inadequate for housing patients overnight, often a necessity for abortion.

In the fall, when Eudora might have begun crawling, Dr. Guilford triumphantly announced a move. He and his practice were relocating to a fifteen-room house at 35 Lincoln Street. The first floor, "newly and elegantly furnished," included a reception area, examination rooms, offices, laboratory, and an operating room. "Good boarding accommodations" were offered on the upper level. In effect, he and "Alice" had opened a private hospital.

Evidently, he anticipated a flood of out-of-towners. The ads gave train directions from various compass points. From the north, passengers could debark at Lincoln Square Depot, just steps from the new facility. From Union Depot, horse-drawn streetcars could deposit travelers right at his door.

Within a few months, he added a satellite office downtown open to "persons of either sex" in the mornings. It was now made clear that the fifteen-room doctor's "residence," as he called the Lincoln Street infirmary, was strictly for women.

"Afternoons devoted to lady patients," said the notices. With two locations, overnight patients, long hours, and house calls, Dr. Melancthon Guilford's practice was busy and, undoubtedly, lucrative. While promising that all fees were "moderate," he routinely offered to arrange monthly payments, which suggested the opposite.

Outfitted with elegant furnishings and desirably located, the Lincoln Place infirmary was no backstreet operation. In New York, one male abortionist reportedly charged ten dollars for the entire procedure, often paid on installment. Ten dollars, worth about $300 today, was Henry's minimum for a house call.

Lodgings also brought in income. More importantly, they were essential to the business. Abortions of the era were often achieved by dilation of the cervix, followed by the introduction of an irritant or instrument. Patients might need a bed for up to five days until the contents of the uterus were expelled.

Other practitioners had to make arrangements with boardinghouse owners, who often demanded substantial fees. Henry, on the other hand, had Nancy to help with both the medical and hospitality sides of the business. This is the glue that kept them together.

After Eudora, there were no more children. Nancy would never become like her mother-in-law, Lucy Guilford, perpetually pregnant into middle age. Never having lived in a crowded household, Nancy had one biological sibling, Stephen, and an adopted sister, Maggie.

It's impossible to know whether Nancy took steps to control her childbearing, as did so many of her peers, a point repeatedly made by disapproving regular physicians. "The married woman . . . seeks the abortionist, and by the outlay of a few dollars shirks the high destiny of a mother," wrote a doctor, one of many involved in an antiabortion crusade, begun before the Civil War but only now bearing fruit in the form of convictions. Tongue-clucking in high gear, the writer added, "The luxury of an abortion is now within the reach of the serving-girl."

That was not news to Henry, who'd arranged monthly payments for his services. He'd just left Fall River, where a woman named Naomi Clair was on trial for performing abortions on five women, including one who was married. Clair, who advertised herself variously as a "physician and surgeon" and an "Indian doctor," had much in common with Henry. Indeed, Henry and Naomi Clair had the same alma mater. She'd once worked for a health-lift facility. And like him, she'd chosen to stay in one community, renting prime real estate—in her case, over a popular department store—and advertising treatment for "female diseases."

The new legal perils of abortion were made plain in the trial of Naomi. (News reports avoided calling her "Mrs. Clair" or "Dr. Clair," not taking the implied clairvoyance seriously.) No fatality or complications had brought her to court, and the press showed little interest in her patients, who were not criminally charged. However, a prominent local surgeon had been indicted along with Naomi, charged with referring patients to her. Caught in the snare by a state police officer—local law enforcement would have left him alone—the eminent surgeon doomed Naomi by testifying against her.

In the end, Naomi was sent to prison for five years—a light sentence, in the opinion of a paper published in Boston, where the press took a stronger stand against abortion. Charges against Dr. Charles C. Terry, respected throughout New England, were dropped. Many years later, when a governor proposed naming Terry to a state hospital board, a political candidate objected, reminding the public of Terry's associations with abortion.

Ultimately, the doctor declined to be considered for the hospital post, but not before letters of support for him had flooded the governor's mailbox. Among the Fall River citizens attesting to Terry's "high moral" and "Christian" character were a judge, a postmaster, and three Protestant ministers.

Henry, with his fake name and questionable credentials, wasn't in the same class as Dr. Charles Church Terry with his impeccable medical degrees, including one from Harvard, and many publications. Still, consciously or not, Henry roughly followed Terry's pattern, including the esteemed physician's use of a female accomplice. Naomi, involved with a wealthy Fall River developer, was not Terry's romantic partner. But the prominent surgeon seems to have groomed Naomi to help him provide abortions.

The same would be said of Henry and Nancy. The exact date of her initiation remains elusive. Indeed, no court records show that they practiced abortion in Worcester, although their subsequent history, their aliases, their boardinghouse, and the meteoric rise of their fortunes all point to it. They would soon leave town, one step ahead of law enforcement. In another place and another time, a prosecutor would tell a courtroom about Henry's sudden departure from Worcester under cover of night.

Before that, Henry and Nancy interrupted their outlaw life to become lawful man and wife. During their Worcester period, years into their intimate relationship, they traveled a few miles east to Framingham. There, the pastor of the First Baptist Church united the son of a Baptist minister to the daughter of a Baptist church trustee. Assuming their discarded first names, probably to coincide with birth documents, they were married as Henry Melancthon Guilford and Nancy Alice Brown. They gave false addresses, though, both naming Wellsburg. They seemed eager to cover any tracks pointing back to Worcester.

But they were not so eager that Nancy could refrain from boasting of Henry's thriving practice. One month after the delayed wedding, she went to

Wellsburg, where people thought she'd married years before. Traveling three hundred miles for a brief visit, possibly to show her parents the marriage certificate, she encountered an Elmira newspaper's local correspondent. The result was an item for the gossip page:

> Mrs. Dr. Guilford, the accomplished daughter of our townsman Mr. Horace Brown, is spending a few days at home. We regret very much that her stay is so short, but owing to the many patients under the Dr.'s care she returns this week.

"Accomplished daughter" was no special compliment. The Wellsburg scribe routinely used the phrase to describe village offspring. While omitting the name of Nancy's return destination—perhaps because Nancy kept it vague—the item made one thing clear: Nancy was an essential part of Henry's practice.

Indeed, she'd soon graduate from "Mrs. Dr." to "Dr." Henry would have not only a wife but also a partner. If he'd converted her, he'd done a hell of a job. Whether for mercenary or ideological reasons, or the first with a dash of the second, she was determined to provide abortions. As her daughter and husband would discover, there was no stopping her now. Henry had created a sorcerer's apprentice.

Nancy Alice Guilford. *New York Journal*

3 | LYNN, LYNN, CITY OF SIN

HENRY AND NANCY TOOK the three kids and moved from Worcester to Lynn. It had taken years to build up their practice there, but only days to abandon it all: the downtown medical office, the plush boarding hospital, and the Turkish baths. That last investment, obviously Henry's idea, was the most foolish of all, inspired by his pipe dreams. He was always telling Nancy to slow down and find another line of work.

Nancy would have none of it. She complained to a friend about the costs of supporting Henry's aging parents. Under the circumstances, how could she afford to go legitimate? There was also the cost of decorating Nancy's fingers, throat, and ears, on which she habitually wore "a profusion of diamonds," as one observer noted. Henry, too, took pains to present himself as what he called a "gentleman of culture." It was all part of the advertising, like the signs on Lynn's busy Market Street announcing the presence of MRS. DR. ALICE GUILFORD, PHYSICIAN FOR FEMALES, as Nancy billed herself in Lynn, using her middle name as her first.

"Flamboyant" signage, as city residents described it, marked her location at Market Street above an apothecary and a frame shop. An understated shingle couldn't have competed with the images of dentures grinning from dentists' windows. After trying various locations along this bustling strip, Nancy had settled into No. 39½—the fraction reflecting the red-hot pace of commercial development, with new buildings jammed into every available space.

Thriving in a booming city, on some days Nancy had an "immense number of callers," according to another occupant of the building. Most were married women.

At one end of Market stood city hall, where the city marshal supervised the police department. At the other was the depot of a narrow-gauge railroad that made frequent hops between Lynn and Boston, where Dr. Horatio Storer was celebrating the outcome of his crusade against abortion.

With the American Medical Association's support, Storer had persuaded state legislatures across the nation to pass or tighten laws against the procedure. Yet less than fifteen miles from the city where Storer had issued his screeds—including a warning against allowing women to practice medicine—Nancy brazenly touted her services.

In the rear room of her second-floor office on a street lined with milliners, picture galleries, and pool halls, Nancy examined female patients with a speculum, often arranging to end pregnancies on a subsequent visit. Depending on the case and need for concealment, the patient might return home to await the voiding of the uterus. In many cases, though, she would need a bed and nursing. As in Worcester, the Guilfords had established a lying-in hospital, presumably for maternity services. They'd had to start over again.

The first year in Lynn was particularly difficult, with neither downtown office nor infirmary. Nancy's first ads directed patients to the family's rooms at a seaside hotel called the Glen House, on Lynn's border with Swampscott. There, among the bowling alley and stables, she set up shop, surreptitiously offering pelvic exams, pregnancy termination, and post-abortion services—all at a travelers' inn.

As the practice grew, she added the downtown office, an ideal location for business transactions as well as medical procedures. On a thoroughfare bustling with picture galleries, pool halls, and pharmaceutical suppliers, Dr. Alice Guilford rented three rooms. Visitors entered an elegantly furnished reception area staffed by a young woman. Two exam rooms were in the rear.

Nancy spent her weekday afternoons here. Mornings were for tending to family and inpatients at home, if that was the word for it. The Guilfords had left one seaside hotel, the Glen House, for another on Sachem Street called the Ocean Cottage. But they hoped to leave these temporary quarters, desolate in the winter months, for a place where they could settle in.

Henry wasn't always in town. Having left Worcester under a cloud, he had gone underground. Nancy took charge in Lynn while Henry practiced elsewhere under various aliases. One of his bases was Brockton, south of Boston on the route to Fall River, where his father had often fled from family duties. On call when truly needed but frequently absent, Henry was replicating that pattern.

In Brockton, Henry's mail came addressed to Dr. Ford, Dr. G. Ford, Dr. F. Ford, Dr. Frank Ford, Dr. Frankford, and Dr. Bamford. In Salem, a medical practice called Brown & Co. listed Henry's real surname in the city directory. Nancy was also named as a member of that practice, along with "Dr." Stephen Brown, a new honorific for her younger brother. Dr. Brown's home address was also listed, presumably for urgent cases, in Elmira, New York, four hundred miles from Salem.

Nancy, in close communication with her brother at the time, seems to have initiated him into her trade. When in New York, he lived near their parents with his new wife. In Massachusetts, he could have found a new source of revenue that eclipsed his earnings from tanning and farming. Henry, who held his brother-in-law in warm regard, might have shown Stephen the ropes.

Stephen's soiree into criminal activity could have been brief. He eventually ran a prosperous tannery near his native village. But for Nancy, recruiting Stephen was a smart move that would prove to be useful. Having formed a criminal partnership, however temporarily, they could trust one another entirely.

Whether Henry could be trusted was another question. He was said to gamble, not successfully. While Nancy's business thrived, her husband racked up debts to innkeepers, newspaper advertising departments, and druggists. Those seeking him at the offices of Brown & Co. in Salem never found him in. In Brockton his frequent moves between hotels and offices frustrated his creditors. Among them was a sympathetic housekeeper, who'd lent Henry every penny left by her late husband, assured of quick repayment. Conned, and perhaps also smitten, the woman never saw the money again.

For someone trying to keep a low profile, Henry generated quite a bit of salacious talk in Brockton. One report described him as "a well-dressed, rather good-appearing man" whose liberal advertising and "reputed success" in Brockton had attracted "a vast amount of lady patients and but few of the other sex."

Iva Marsh, age twenty-two, was a former domestic servant with no nursing training. Nonetheless, Nancy decided to try her out in the spring of 1884. In addition to tending to patients, Iva sometimes looked after the children, a boon for Nancy as she packed up to leave Ocean Cottage. The family had finally found a permanent home. In the fall, they would occupy a large house in a pleasant residential part of Lynn, where they could run their business behind a picket fence and try to blend in.

Satisfied with the young woman, Nancy retained her until the summer. The Guilfords planned to spend the first weeks of summer on Onset Bay, a seaside retreat at the gateway to Cape Cod. They left Iva on good terms but on her own, without a promise to rehire her on their return in August. The young woman found a service position with a Lynn family, but now trained in nursing, she hoped someday to return to it.

The job with the Guilfords had suited Iva despite its criminality and quirks. Certainly, it paid better than housework. It also gave Iva an important role. For some patients, abortion required induced labor. They needed a nurse's care to get through the process. But there were less savory parts of the job, like handling the expelled uterine contents.

Then, too, there were live births, whether planned or otherwise. For these, Nancy had an arrangement with a woman in Brighton, now part of Boston. At times the infants' screams could be heard beyond the walls of the house, and tales spread about babies left untended on cupboard shelves. Whether those stories were true or not, Iva Marsh would have known they were circulating. Still, none of this prevented her from hoping to resume work at the Guilfords' should she be needed in the fall.

Until then, the busy Dr. and Mrs. Dr. Guilford had the summer to spend with their children. Herbert, Henry's older son, was now an adolescent. Harry, Henry's second son and Nancy's first, was now about nine. As for six-year-old Eudora, both parents worshiped at her altar.

Boating may have been one of Onset's attractions for the family. Henry, the disgraced former naval officer, would have found ample opportunity to take the family sailing on the bay. Coached by his father or learning in some other fashion, Harry also acquired the skill. The spinal difference that drew strangers' stares didn't stop him from becoming an accomplished sailor.

For the parents, a five-acre island in Onset Bay offered a chance to mix business with pleasure. At her Home for the Infirm on Wicket's Island, Dr. Abbie E. Cutter taught classes in such subjects as the use of electricity "as a therapeutic agent in all diseases." Life-sized mannequins were available for dissection, and there was also the occasional séance. Calling herself an eclectic physician, the doctor also dabbled in spiritualism. Indeed, the building where she conducted her medical training eventually became a home for mediums.

Less a hospital than a spa, the Home for the Infirm advertised medi-cated baths and electrical treatments along with sea bathing and delightful views. There is no way to know for sure if the Guilfords availed themselves of Dr. Cutter's cures or classes. But it's likely that both Guilfords had heard of Cutter before vacationing in Onset. The three self-styled physicians had much in common.

In the months before the Guilfords' vacation, Cutter had given a series of lectures in Boston for women only, charging twenty-five cents per session. The topics could have interested Nancy—among them were "Parturition Without Pain" and "Cause and Cure of Nervous Prostration in Women." The venue was Boston's Tremont Temple, just a streetcar ride from Lynn. Moreover, Cutter's ads for her spa-like infirmary promised access to her medical library, a tempting attraction for Nancy, whose own collection of medical literature would later draw the notice of the Lynn police.

Henry would have been curious about Cutter's promotion of electrical therapy, which he would later dabble in. Around this time, he was considering ditching abortion and reverting to quackery, at which he had considerable skill. Cutter's electric panacea harked back to Henry's early days in Worcester when he had promised cure-alls to patients of all genders. It was said that Henry had begged Nancy to abandon abortion, but she resisted. More likely, he had been trying to keep his own hands clean—training women in Brockton and elsewhere to do the operations and, if necessary, take the fall.

If he had begged Nancy for anything, it would have been to banish patients from beds in their house, where he couldn't distance himself from them entirely. But any such pleas would have come to nothing. With his parents, her parents, and their children dependent on her, Nancy could scarcely quit her lucrative practice to rely on Henry. She was devoted to her work and her independence despite all the risks.

As for quackery, Nancy might perform illegal operations, but she never promised to relieve all ills with some faddish pill or procedure. She had left that to Henry, who in Worcester had claimed to cure hundreds of people of afflictions ranging from pimples to paralysis, including cleft palate and clubbed feet. The intensely competitive arena of medical quackery demanded charisma and showmanship—qualities that Nancy lacked but Cutter had in abundance; she staged her husband's funeral as a theater piece, with "spirit forms" popping out from black draperies. Henry didn't try to raise the dead, but he made other extravagant promises. As later became evident, if he didn't study under Cutter, he at least tore pages from her playbook.

By early August, their seashore idyll was over, and Nancy's face again appeared at the window of her downtown office. Mornings and evenings were devoted to the family and the inpatients on Lewis Street, where not every neighbor was pleased by the comings and goings at no. 70. For every patient arriving in a private carriage, at least one was deposited by the Lynn Railway streetcar. Among the latter group was Jennie Peters, who by age thirty had scrubbed floors, made boots, and waited tables in half a dozen Massachusetts cities. Now she was working for a Lynn couple named Hall. More than just an employer to Jennie, Margaret Hall took an active interest in her single friend's life. The two women had met five years earlier in Brockton, where Margaret and Charles Hall had rented a room, and Jennie had been their boarder.

Born into poverty, like Jennie, Margaret was barely literate. However, marriage had boosted her up the social ladder by a rung or two. Charles Hall could read and write, but as became evident, he didn't always apply those skills for entirely wholesome purposes. Employed at a Lynn hardware store, Charles felt he deserved more money than he was getting.

Always looking out for her less fortunate friend, Margaret had recently found Jennie a housekeeping job in Danvers. When that ran out, Jennie came to Lynn for a brief position with one of the Halls' neighbors. That ended, and she moved in with the Halls again, helping Margaret with laundry and other heavy housework in what had to be a temporary arrangement. She could count on Margaret's friendship and kindness, but Charles was less charitable.

Accustomed to job insecurity, Jennie found herself with a bigger problem. Margaret Hall noticed that a man had been "paying attention" to Jennie since her arrival in Lynn. In early September 1884, Jennie realized that she was pregnant. She kept this secret from her married friend for three weeks, finally confiding in her.

Margaret Hall knew what to do. Having seen the newspaper ads, or perhaps the gaudy sign on Market Street, she took Jennie to 39½ Market Street and the second-floor rooms of Mrs. Dr. Alice Guilford.

They waited half an hour until Nancy was free. Then Margaret stayed in the reception area while Jennie was directed to the back room. She was left there alone while Nancy engaged Margaret in a lengthy conversation, presumably to find out who Jennie was, her source of revenue, and whether she had "folks" who might "make trouble." Satisfied with the answers, Nancy went to attend her patient.

Jennie asked for "medicine," presumably abortifacients, to end the pregnancy. Nancy brusquely informed her patient that medicine "would do no good." A long conversation ensued. At the time, Jennie said, she had no idea that abortions could be brought about by instruments. Nancy confirmed the pregnancy with a speculum exam and scheduled Jennie for an abortion, telling her to bring the $25 fee.

Eager to get things rolling, Jennie assured her new doctor that she'd return in less than a week, on the following Thursday. Nancy replied, "Come when you have the money."

Jennie returned as promised, but with only $10. Nancy agreed to allow her to owe the rest. The prior week's chat with Mrs. Hall had established Jennie as a housemaid. Often in need of extra hands, Nancy could find ways for Jennie to make up the balance. In fact, Nancy's longtime and loyal housekeeper, Mary McLean, had been asking about taking a vacation. Sometime in the next few weeks, Nancy might need a temp, or *second girl*, to fill in.

Before starting the procedure, Nancy asked her patient not to "give her away" to the authorities. Hardly an ironclad agreement, this gesture may have been an appeal to her patients' consciences. Or perhaps it was meant to remind them of their complicity.

Nancy had a set of professional instruments, similar to ones used by midwives. The one she used for this procedure was probably a sound—a slender, slightly curved piece of metal notched with measurements. Designed for determining the length and position of the uterus, it could also puncture the gestational sac and induce labor. Nancy found the sound so useful that she wouldn't travel far without one.

Before leaving the office, Jennie asked when she could expect to feel "sick." She was told there was no definite way to know. Within a week, she was back, still owing $15 and still pregnant. She reported "feeling no better," meaning that she hadn't experienced bleeding or any hoped-for signs of change. Again using a sound, Nancy made another try, muttering, "All creation wouldn't bring some people along." Like the previous procedure, it was over in a matter of minutes.

The second attempt had been no more effective than the first. In late September, Jennie saw Nancy again, still owing $15 and still pregnant. Margaret Hall again accompanied her. By now, six weeks had elapsed since Jennie discovered her condition, most likely after missing at least two periods.

Nancy again deplored the difficulty of "bringing some people around." Including Margaret in the conversation, she explained that the "first style of operating was not enough to secure the desired result" in cases like Jennie's. She said she'd need to turn to a "different style" of surgery, and that this could only be done at her house on Lewis Street, where Jennie would stay overnight. At least obliquely, Nancy was informing her listeners that abortion became more difficult as pregnancy advanced. The increasing chances of complications were not mentioned.

Margaret Hall asked if it couldn't be done at her own house instead. Nancy declared that this was out of the question. "Everyone knows who I am and what my business is," said Nancy, explaining that an operation at Lewis Street could remain confidential while a house call could not. But that wasn't true: visitors seen entering and exiting the Guilford house could also be connected to her business. Nancy didn't share all her reasons to confining her activities to spaces she could control. For one thing, there would be no Mr. Hall around, nor any unexpected callers.

But first, Jennie would need to do some work to defray the balance of her bill. According to Nancy, three weekends of dusting and mopping should set things right. Jennie agreed. Nancy's trusted housekeeper—"my Mary," as she called her—got her promised vacation. Jennie declined Nancy's offer to occupy Mary's room, preferring to stay with the Halls.

By mid-October, Nancy was paid up, and Jennie was three weeks further into her pregnancy. She packed some clothes for her next visit to Lewis Street, where she would occupy a bed in the house she'd cleaned. According to her recollection, Nancy took her to a bathroom there, opened a drawer, and again reached for a sound. However, Jennie's memory could have been fogged. The Guilfords were known to have used sedatives on their inpatients, sometimes for prolonged periods.

Nancy had said she'd use a different approach to this hard case, and that is probable. By this time, a range of methods were used to end pregnancies, and the medical literature described them. Some journal articles described procedures performed in countries where abortion was legal. In the United States, too, some physicians had no apparent qualms about discussing the latest methods. The procedure could be legal—generally when at least one medical doctor determined that the life of the mother or child was in danger. Indeed, many of Lynn's wealthier women would never need Nancy's services.

Endangerment of the "life of the mother" could be interpreted as quality of life. In an era when physicians believed that many women suffered from hysteria, a doctor might abort a valued patient to relieve her of that imagined affliction.

Writing in the *Journal of the American Medical Association* some years later, a Chicago physician described, without the slightest whiff of apology, an abortion he'd provided to a suffering woman. Like Jennie, his patient had previously undergone two unsuccessful procedures, with a crochet hook and then a sound. At least one of those attempts had produced a septic abscess in the uterus, causing intolerable pain as the pregnancy progressed.

Without bothering to discuss points of law, the author wrote of his "breaking down of the gestational sac," after which the patient was revived from sedation, and contractions began. Thirty-six hours later, he wrote, "a four and half months' macerated fetus was expelled without much pain, the patient having been given codeine." The mention of maceration, a sign of fetal death, clarifies the result of breaking down the sac. In a few hours, foul-smelling fluids from the abscess were also expelled.

Relief was immediate, wrote the physician, regretting only that he'd induced labor instead of "emptying the uterus," presumably by dilation and curettage. If faced with another "extreme case," he wrote, he would probably choose the latter. His patient fully recovered, but it took her many months.

With Jennie Peters in her bathroom, Nancy might have done something along those lines to induce premature labor. First, however, there were unintended consequences. Becoming seriously ill, Jennie remained bedridden, likely with fevers, rigors, and severe abdominal, pelvic, and back pain. The first two tries may have been in vain, but this one threatened to be fatal.

Booked up with cases at the house and on Market Street, Nancy was forced to hire a private-duty nurse for this one patient, practically a charity case. Returned to domestic service, Iva Marsh lived out of town. However, she must have kept in touch with Nancy, who hired her to care for "a very sick woman."

If Henry hadn't taken notice of Iva during her earlier rotation at Ocean Cottage, this time he would. Known in Brockton as quite the ladies' man, he also took note of the ladies at his residence in Lynn. Iva began living in.

As Iva did what she could for Jennie, the two women formed a bond. A week or two after her nurse's arrival, Jennie went into contractions. Iva Marsh helped her patient void the contents of her uterus, described by Iva as a "small body" or a "baby," but not a living one. Henry was also at the bedside. The nurse wrapped it in cloth and walked out of the room with it, passing it to Nancy, who said she'd "take care of it."

But, unlike the case in the medical journal, this did not end the patient's distress. A few weeks before, Jennie had been hearty enough to dust and scour. Now she continued as an invalid.

Nancy wanted to keep Iva on but not for one patient, and a charity case at that. She may have worked out her abortion fee, but as Nancy told her patients, that covered one month of treatment. Jennie had passed her expiration date. Her failure to recuperate also presented a legal risk. Despite the neighbors' frequent complaints about the unloved lying-in hospital, the police so far had left them alone. A death under the Guilfords' roof would change all that. So, with no home to go to, Jennie was evicted from her bed.

Still seriously debilitated, Jennie turned to the Halls for help. Charles expressed outrage at Nancy for turning "a sick girl out on the street." However, he wasn't eager to house her either. Even Margaret could do nothing for a thirty-year-old unmarried woman unfit for work. After a few days with the Halls, Jennie understood she'd have to leave. She decided to go to Boston, the place she knew best of the many she'd known. Margaret Hall could do nothing more than give her $1.50 for the streetcar ride.

Lynn wouldn't miss Jennie. She was one of legions of "floaters," as longtime Lynners called their transient neighbors. The city's churning population, a boon to dance halls and saloons, inspired a folk rhyme still known in the Boston area. It begins, "Lynn, Lynn, city of sin. You never come out the way you go in."

That was certainly true of Jennie Peters. According to Margaret, she left the city "in very bad condition" and "could not eat or walk hardly." Margaret's husband took note of this. Although his heart didn't bleed for others, Charles Hall dimly recognized this as injustice—with possibly something in it for him. Knowing the Guilfords to be wealthy and vulnerable to exposure, he squirreled his knowledge away.

Meanwhile, with Jennie gone, life on Lewis Street resumed its usual rhythms. The business of the house downstairs was generally walled off from upstairs family life. However, one day, raised voices brought Nancy to a staircase landing. Without the benefit of a telephone, sound was traveling clearly between the floors. To Nancy's amazement, her nurse was arguing loudly with the master of the house. Summoned upstairs for an explanation, Iva Marsh declared that Henry had been forcing sex on her, not just once but repeatedly.

Nancy received this news by unleashing her fury on the victim. It might have come as no real surprise; Jennie Peters had probably said much the same thing. However, it wouldn't be quite so easy to push Iva Marsh out the door. By now, the young nurse knew the signs: she was pregnant.

Wanting an abortion, Iva had to seek it from the wife of her tormentor. As usual, Nancy used a sound. Outrageously, she charged a fee for a pregnancy caused by her rapist husband. The amount paid is unclear, but Nancy's usual fee was $25, worth more than $800 today. For Iva, this would have been a staggering sum—she was earning $3.25 a week at the Guilford home. She came up with it somehow, by working several weeks without pay or borrowing from relatives.

Moreover, Nancy drove Iva out of the house, refusing her a reference when another nursing opportunity arose. The refusal must have been a harsh blow to a young person trying to improve her lot. Iva had so far managed to avoid the shoemaking jobs that had robbed her older siblings of a childhood. She eventually found a family to hire her as a servant, reverting to the status she'd had when Nancy found her.

The psychological fee for this abortion long remained unsettled, although Iva would find a way to move forward. As for Jennie, Nancy had suffered some jitters about her last dealings with her ex-charwoman. She was relieved to learn that Jennie had gone to Boston, perhaps to die. Those two troublesome wretches were no match for the doctress. But now the Guilfords' fraying marriage was turned to rot. Joined to a gambler and philanderer, Nancy threw herself into work. She and Henry shared few interests besides the children.

Although practicing almost openly, Nancy could scarcely take part in the Lynn community. She had her hands full, running an office, a private hospital, and a household with three children. Then, too, there was the isolating nature of her activities. Maybe the Lynn police force and their supervising officer, the city marshal, could be persuaded to look the other way. The fee for Iva Marsh's abortion exceeded one month of a patrolman's pay.

But when not marketing her services, Nancy had to keep a low profile. Despite her personal sympathies for the temperance movement, she could scarcely testify about the evils of drink before the city's police committee. That honor went to "Dr." Martha Flanders, widely respected by the local medical community despite her lack of formal training. Nor could Nancy sing in duets at women's club meetings like Mary E. Newcomb, who eventually earned a medical degree after years of practicing in Lynn without one. Not for Nancy were patients like the Spragues of Swampscott and others on the local social register. They preferred Dr. Stella Manning Perkins, a graduate of the Boston University School of Medicine.

Nancy was a farmer's daughter. She lacked the advantages enjoyed by Newcomb, born to a box manufacturer. She was no Stella Manning Perkins with a surgeon for a father. Still, if she didn't move in the same circles as her sister practitioners, she almost certainly shared some of their patients. Unwanted pregnancies observed no social boundaries, and the time would come for Nancy to boast of her ties to high society.

Outcomes like Jennie's, and worse, were widely known. Newspapers reveled in stories about deaths caused by abortion, as they'd done for decades. That didn't stop the married and single women of Lynn from seeking Nancy's services. Curtains twitched as neighbors surreptitiously watched the parade at no. 70 on Lewis Street, where picket fences marked property boundaries. Other types of boundaries—like appropriate behavior for women—weren't as easily defined. But those who transgressed the limits drew censure and mockery.

Witches were no longer executed in Salem, where Henry continued to maintain an office, and stocks no longer stood in Lynn's common. Still, the *Daily Evening Item* effected a similar public humiliation by printing a front-page story about the suicide attempt of a local woman. One warm night, a bar owner's wife, Annie J. Dyer, went on a loud, drunken tour of Lynn's Ward Three, climbing on a cart to speak to a crowd, falling off, and attempting to jump from a railroad bridge until stopped by a passerby. While observers notified the police, she waded fully clothed into the city's Goldfish Pond, then screamed for help and was rescued by a young man from Lewis Street.

The newspaper account found rich humor in Dyer's determination "to try her luck at self-destruction," noting that when the police arrived at the pond, "they found the woman not much the worse for her midnight bath, but it had considerably sobered her." The report said Dyer was taken to her father's house, slightly closer to the pond than the residence she shared with her husband and young daughter over the saloon. "She vows she will try it again," the piece concluded, as if promising readers another amusing installment.

The readers didn't have to wait long. A headline on the next day's front page read, MRS. DYER AGAIN. Below it, the paper gleefully wrote that the woman "evidently did not get completely sober after her first bath, or else she got filled up again." Rising at dawn after her failed attempts, she'd again tried suicide, the paper reported. Published in a city with a half-dozen temperance organizations, many of which linked alcoholism with immigration, the paper again mocked Dyer's attempt to "end her earthly troubles."

In fact, she seemed to have been deadly serious, walking before 6:00 AM toward Red Rock on the Atlantic Shore. A coachman named Robert Williams—likely related to Dyer—was also out early and happened to see her. When told of her intentions, he pursued her. She broke into a run and plunged into the sea. He followed, first telling some bystanders to call the police. After a struggle in the water, Dyer was persuaded to walk home with her rescuer. An ambulance left emptyhanded, but the *Daily Evening Item* got its story.

Dyer had started her sad trek toward the ocean by walking down Lewis Street, although she turned right on Atlantic before reaching the Guilfords' address. Later, she and Nancy would have a fateful meeting. At this point, they undoubtedly shared mutual acquaintances: people involved with the police or the police court. It was later said that the Lynn police were fully aware of the "peculiar cases" nursed at the Lewis Street infirmary. As for Annie Dyer, she was about to leave a lasting impression on several patrolmen.

The trouble began at her husband's saloon, where Annie Dyer had been arguing with an employee. Taking a fire poker to assault the man, or perhaps defend herself, she cut his arm. When the police came to arrest her, she resisted. Her younger brother, John, was present at the time and slugged a policeman. With considerable difficulty, three officers managed to take the woman and her brother to the police station, where "Mrs. Dyer continued to show fight and break chairs and everything else she could lay her hands on."

Dyer appeared before a judge who fined her twenty dollars plus about six dollars to cover damages. The alternative was six months in jail. Fines settled most arrests made in Lynn, which totaled 1,431 in 1880. But while Dyer's brother paid his fee and went free, Dyer appealed her sentence and was held on a bond of one hundred dollars. Presumably, Dyer's saloonkeeper husband came to bail her out. In the meantime, she stayed on at the police station, where "lodgers" got only crackers and coffee, and the place stank. The police-wagon driver, who stayed there overnight, complained of its poor ventilation.

The *Daily Evening Item* ran a front-page account of these events, although in briefer form than the suicide attempts. Barroom brawls were hardly unusual in Lynn, where the leading causes of arrest were inebriation, assault, and larceny. But Dyer was a woman, and that made her slugging and chair-breaking newsworthy. In the newspaper's report of how she continued to fight at the station, one can practically hear the guffaws.

Dyer had good reason for her anger and despair, as the paper could have easily discovered, had it bothered to speak to her or anyone who knew her. Her three-year-old son had died of meningitis just months before these humiliating articles appeared in the paper. Even before the strain of that tragedy, Annie Williams Dyer and her relatives had not been models of self-restraint. One of Dyer's brothers had served a six-month sentence for assaulting her. On another occasion, Dyer and an aunt had exchanged blows with fists and a lager bottle—a "lively and interesting" battle, according to the *Daily Evening Item*, which had delightedly followed the family's mishaps but ignored the child's death.

Life for the Dyers had once seemed full of possibilities. Annie's entrepreneurial husband, George, had opened his saloon at age twenty-three. The year was 1879, the city's 250th anniversary, memorialized in a collection of photographs. Labor unrest was temporarily forgotten as salesclerks and shoe stitchers gathered outside shops and factories to pose with their bosses. In one striking image, George stands before the door of his saloon. Boyishly thin,

George Dyer (left) with an unidentified employee in front of his bar in Lynn. *Photograph courtesy of the Lynn Museum & Historical Society*

with a derby hat cocked over his beardless face, he grips the jacket lapels of his three-piece suit. He's trying to project confidence but looking as if he's playing dress-up. Beside him stands a bartender in shirtsleeves and cuff protectors, hoisting a beer in bold salute. Signs on the wooden building note the saloon's special distinction: in addition to serving fine lager, it housed Lynn Exchange No. 2, an early outpost of the town's nascent telephone service. With its young owner and cocky barkeep, the new saloon seems to radiate optimism and forward thinking.

Six years after that photo was taken, Annie Dyer discovered that she was pregnant again. Her son's death had left the Dyers with one child. Lizzie, baptized in the Catholic Church as Anne Elizabeth, was about to turn seven. Even as many members of Annie's generation sought to downsize their families, an only child was somewhat unusual. That, of course, hadn't been the Dyers' plan: Lizzie had lost her little brother to illness. The new pregnancy was unwanted, and Annie was determined not to go through with it.

Her reasons weren't likely financial. Dozens more Lynn saloons had opened since George launched his, but he had a prime location on busy Union Street. The saloon's phone exchange—presumably equipped with an operator and charging for calls—undoubtedly had turned profitable. Few Lynn homes had phones, but a growing number of businesses did, and a newspaper editorial urged the high schools to get on board. George Dyer's early embrace of the technology suggested business savvy. Now twenty-nine, he was probably earning more than Annie's shoemaker father ever did.

Yet Annie had sought solace from her father, not her husband, on the night of her suicidal drunken binge. Following her thwarted suicide attempts at the bridge and the pond, she'd slept at the home of her father, David Williams, slipping out early to try to drown herself in the ocean. The decision to return to her childhood home on that tortured night doesn't necessarily indicate marital problems. Soaking wet in Victorian clothing, she might have gone to her father because he lived closer to Goldfish Pond. Moreover, to enter her home over the saloon, she would have had to endure the stares and jeers of her husband's customers. Still, the question remains of why George didn't retrieve her from the old shoemaker's residence on Fayette Court. With or without a telephone, he surely would have heard about her movements. Instead, he left her to court death again at dawn, perhaps dressed in clothes barely dry from her previous attempt.

Now, there was no father to turn to. David Williams, widowed long before, died shortly before Dyer set out to end her pregnancy. There's no way to know if this latest loss affected her decision or if her previous bouts of anguish had persisted. But like other Lynn women who didn't wish to bear a child, Annie Dyer found her way to Nancy's door.

Mrs. Dyer's reputation, if Nancy knew of it, wouldn't have diminished her appeal as a new patient. A saloonkeeper's wife, presumably with access to cash, would have received a warm welcome, particularly at that time. Nancy's financial pressures were mounting.

Henry's father had died suddenly, leaving his mother more dependent on Nancy than ever. Rev. H. P. Guilford's business dealings hadn't made him rich, but they'd brought in something. Now the old evangelist had preached his last sermon, written his last insurance policy, and opened his last health-lift gym. Henry's mother, living just west of Lynn in Cliftondale, was on her own. Her firstborn, Henry, felt an obligation, but he was laying low and dodging creditors. Nancy would have to shoulder the burden.

Always glad for new business, Nancy added Annie Dyer to her roster. By now, Nancy's reputation had spread far beyond Lynn's borders, and she drew customers from Boston and other points near and far. It wasn't her policy to ask questions about the cause of pregnancy, but she did want to know where her patients were from. In the unlikely event that Dyer mentioned her husband's saloon, Nancy wouldn't likely have known of it. Although just a short distance from her Market Street office, the bar was on Union Street, Lynn's "other" downtown. Such an establishment wouldn't have interested teetotaling Nancy.

On the other hand, Nancy did learn the address of one of Dyer's sisters, who may have accompanied Dyer to the appointment. The sister became Dyer's emergency contact, suggesting that George Dyer either knew nothing of his wife's visit or opposed it. If the latter were true, that could explain why Dyer ended up in a bed at the Lewis Street infirmary. The sister may have told George a story to explain his wife's absence.

It's also possible that Annie Dyer went home but fell too ill to stay there. It can be said with certainty that her procedure didn't go well. Like Jennie Peters a year before, she fell gravely ill.

On August 10, 1885, the *Daily Evening Item* had something new to report about Annie J. Dyer. She had died "very suddenly" two days before at 11:30 PM. The piece continued: "The police have investigated the matter, but as far as we can learn, her death came from natural causes. An inquest is being held at City Hall today."

For once, there were no snide allusions to Dyer's drinking or her expressions of misery. The paper reported that Dyer had died at her residence. More likely, her body was moved there from Lewis Street. Later reports said that Nancy had been present at the time of death, along with a nurse named Elizabeth Tyler. Death occurred late on a Saturday. Even if Nancy had been called to the Dyer home, she wouldn't have brought a nurse with her. Besides, as later events showed, she preferred to treat patients suffering from complications at her infirmary, although her remedies were useless. Once dead, their remains became evidence, and she wanted them out of the house.

George Dyer was not among the first people informed of his wife's death. He might have known nothing about the abortion. Instead, Nancy summoned the dead woman's sister. She also tracked down Henry, who wasn't at home. He could have been on one of his prolonged stays at a Brockton hotel as Dr. Gill, Dr. Ford, or any name besides that of the heavily indebted Dr. Henry M. Guilford. For all of Henry's shortcomings as a husband, he was soon at Nancy's side. This was a crisis for both of them.

The Monday morning inquest was private, but Tuesday's issue of the *Daily Evening Item* reported that Dyer had died "under circumstances which at the present appear rather suspicious." The paper learned that several witnesses had appeared, including four unnamed doctors. The article continued:

> Nothing can be learned today regarding the facts in the case, but it is understood that Mrs. Dr. Alice Guilford, the attending physician, and the nurse, Mrs. Elizabeth Tyler, have been or will be summoned to appear at the next hearing. Both of the above-mentioned parties were present when the woman died.

None of Henry's various names appeared, but the piece said that Dr. Guilford's husband had been "spoken of in connection with the affair." It ended, "Further developments are looked for and promised."

But the newspaper never made good on its promise. It found nothing more to report beyond a brief description of the "numerous" wreaths and bouquets at Dyer's funeral, held two days after her death and just hours after the inquest. The location was the former home of Dyer's parents, now occupied by a brother. George Dyer had left the arrangements to his in-laws. He appeared to be close with his wife's family, having none of his own in America. He'd immigrated from England at age eleven, one of seven children raised in a farmer's cottage. If any members of his family had accompanied him, they'd since returned home.

Annie Dyer was quickly buried, and so was the investigation into Nancy's practice. The City of Lynn recorded dozens of deaths in the first weeks of August, attributing several to old age, cancer, dysentery, and heart disease. Next to Dyer's name, the cause listed is "abortion." However, no one was ever prosecuted. There wasn't enough evidence to tie it to Nancy, and Tyler, her assistant, must have stood by her. If George Dyer and his sister-in-law appeared at the inquest, they didn't volunteer anything that could be taken to a grand jury.

Months later, a police court judge closed the investigation into Dyer's death from peritonitis caused by abortion. Bundling it into his conclusions about a half-dozen other deaths—of men struck by trains or horsecars—he found that "in each case that no one is to blame but the parties themselves, and that death resulted from no act or carelessness of any other person." In other words, nothing could be proven.

Nancy didn't even wait for that judgment. Within weeks of Dyer's death, she was placing ads in the *Daily Evening Item* again, the same ads she'd run for years, noticed mainly by people in need of her services. One of the city's most prominent businessmen would soon find himself drawn to them.

4 | LETHARGY

AS NANCY'S ADS REPEATEDLY WARNED, "Ladies wishing to employ the doctress must see her in person and not by proxy. Gentlemen not advised with." They were, however, negotiated with. That certainly was the case with Charles E. Ames, who made small beer in a large factory. Wagon teams hauling his brews and carbonated concoctions were a familiar sight on Lynn's Western Avenue.

Wagons lumbering toward "wet" destinations like Marblehead might be stopped in "dry" ones like Swampscott, where the local constabulary once raided a mixed beverage shipment, questioning the driver and confiscating the wares until satisfied that only "soft stuff" had been dropped off inside their jurisdiction. Charles Ames bottled beer and ale while also aerating a vast array of syrupy solutions for the temperance crowd.

Floods of phosphates, tonics, and mineral water gushed from his factory, equipped with the latest in siphons, filters, pestles, meters and percolators. Kettles rattled, steam pipes hissed, and acid-feeding generators produced plum and peppermint pop, orange blossom phosphates, and other innocent delights, while wood captured beer in another corner.

Ads for Ames's business featured Belfast ginger ale in bold letters. Beer, ale, and lager were listed below, as if in afterthought. But accompanying the text is a sly illustration. Two winged creatures, naked from the waist up, occupy an aisle between shelves of bottles and a line of barrels. The smaller and more cherubic of the figures totes baskets of bottles, apparently filled with soft drinks. The other, larger and older, with horns half-hidden by his hair curls, prepares to tap a keg.

Charles Ames, too, had a dual nature: street angel and house devil. As he sought out Nancy in Lynn, he was a prominent young manufacturer of beer

49

and aerated waters, married and the father of a five-year-old son. At home, he was an unfaithful husband to his wife, carrying on a yearslong affair with another woman to whom he was passionately devoted.

It was his devilish side that brought him to the door of another of Lynn's loyal newspaper advertisers. Despite her professed refusal to deal with men, announced in costly extra lines of type, Nancy didn't shove Charles Ames away. A footwear stitcher named Susie Taylor was pregnant by him, and he wished to arrange an abortion.

Without a doubt, he was good for the fee. Customers like Ames kept Henry and Nancy in the fine clothing they wore, which made a fine impression and gave them an aura of legitimacy. Dressed tastefully but quietly—Nancy's lavish jewelry tempered by her choice of dark fabrics—they could move in the best society.

Although not a member of the beachfront set, Ames was listed in a directory of the leading manufacturers and merchants of Lynn and its neighboring towns. A history of his bottling company, liberally sprinkled with descriptors like "large," "prominent," and "important," traced its founder's meteoric rise.

And how did Charles Ames, a twenty-one-year-old former farm laborer, find overnight success? He'd had a partner for a while, an elderly man who quickly retired, leaving Charles as the sole proprietor. But behind it all was Charles's father-in-law, Stephen C. Heald, himself a former bottler. Concerned that his only daughter had been approaching age thirty with no wedding on the horizon, Heald had bought her a husband.

It was a bad deal for Mary Ellen Heald Ames. Once a working woman by choice, she'd worked as a shoe fitter in a Lynn factory, after first trying a career in photography. As Mrs. Ames, she led a life of humiliation. Presumably, she and Charles lived with their child in one of her father's properties. However, friends seeking Charles knew to look elsewhere. For years, he'd been in love with another woman, persuading her to move from the countryside to a Lynn rooming house. There, with the knowledge of the landlady and almost certainly of Mary Ellen, the pair conducted an intimate affair. Ames's frequent visits to 35 Summer Street, not far from his house, became a "matter of general comment," a paper later said.

Nonetheless, the affair continued unimpeded until Susan Ella Taylor discovered that she was pregnant. Soon Charles was on Nancy Guilford's doorstep, wanting to turn back the clock, and with ample cash to do so.

One thing he couldn't change is that Susie was on to him. Whatever promises he'd made to lure her to Lynn would have sounded hollow by now. Divorce was possible, but he'd taken no steps toward it. He'd been lying since meeting her three years before at a country dance in her native village of Burlington. Though less than twenty miles from Lynn, it was in a quieter corner of Massachusetts. There, Charles had been passing as an unmarried man.

The relationship began with all the trappings of propriety. Charles had likely been drumming up beverage orders in Woburn, the nearest town of any size. He and his wagon became a familiar sight to local businessmen. One, a florist, spotted Charles at the dance, and introduced him to a "beautiful, pre-possessing blond" named Susie. Married to one of Susie's sisters, the florist was probably glad to free himself of escorting duties. If his sister-in-law took a liking to an unattached manufacturer, there was no harm in that.

Ames had maintained the bachelor ruse for quite a while, driving his buggy to visit Susie at the florist's home and even her father's farm. Now, with eyes wide open, she told Charles of her pregnancy, listing the options available to her. Once her condition became visible, she could no longer stay under the roof of her landlady, whose tolerance had a limit. Nor could Susie continue to work in the shoe factory that employed her as a stitcher. As she told Charles, she had one of three choices. First, she could go home to Burlington. Second, she could go to a hospital. Third, she could go to Charles's house.

The third choice was a threat, and the first was unthinkable. With one of his nine surviving children still at home, Susie's father was about to marry a widow with children of her own. That left the hospital, by which she meant the kind of facility run by the Guilfords at their home on Lewis Street.

Since Annie Dyer's death five months before, the cops supposedly were keeping a close watch on the house. However, there was still no way to know if women were pregnant when they entered but not when they left. One death had not deterred business. Having survived the Dyer inquest without tremendous legal expense, the Guilfords still had the means to buy silence, although often that wasn't even necessary. Shame about sex kept some from testifying. For others—like George Dyer, already burned by the press—it was a simple desire for privacy.

Moreover, as one former Lynn cop observed, there was a "lethargy" among the officers concerning the criminal activities on Lewis Street, with which they could have been personally familiar. Unlike Susie Taylor's father, a rural man of an earlier generation, not many Lynn cops had ten children.

Charles may have been anxious to avoid detection by one particular police officer. His wife's brother, Otis Heald, had long ago left the family bottling business to become a patrolman. However, despite the notoriety of the Dyer case, Charles deposited Susie on Lewis Street, undisturbed by Otis or any other law enforcer.

Whether or not Susie Taylor had undergone a previous procedure, there was no reason to anticipate complications with this one. She was twenty-four, eight years Charles's junior and fifteen years younger than the older woman he'd married. And, unlike the grieving Annie Dyer, she didn't spend her evenings stewed in alcohol. With Christmas two full weeks away, Susie might recover in time for the holiday and soon be back at the factory table.

But something went wrong with the procedure, and Charles was summoned to a meeting with Nancy. Vomiting frequently and suffering intense pain and fever, Susie was exhibiting the symptoms of peritonitis. An instrument had perforated her uterus, and sepsis had set in. Nancy would have known the likely outcome, although there was some chance that the young woman could throw off the infection. Hadn't that penniless girl, Jennie Peters, survived the worst of it, occupying a bed in Nancy's house until she was finally turned out? This one had a man who could pay for the nursing.

But Susie's agony continued over the next two weeks. As Charles visited from time to time, Nancy made a show of medical care, ordering a nurse to apply hot water bottles and mustard seed poultice, which could only have served as annoyances to a patient racked with pain. Powders and liquid medicine did no good either. As Christmas of 1885 approached, Susie Taylor endured agonies in the home of strangers who tended her, plotting to get rid of her body as soon as she left it behind.

Charles had long reserved the sabbath for his family, but he was at Susie's side on Christmas Day. After he returned home, she took a turn for the worse, vomiting any food or medicine given to her. On the morning of December 26, Charles went back to Lewis Street. Either before he arrived or soon after, Susie Taylor drew her last breath.

A thorough sentimentalist, Charles had to hold back his tears. He had just become an accessory to murder, and he needed to concentrate. That was made very clear to him.

For a change, Henry was home. So often away in Brockton or in parts unknown, he was acutely aware of Susie Taylor's condition and ready with a plan. Although Nancy was the person most vulnerable to criminal charges, Henry's plot made minimal use of her. She would have to leave this to the men: Henry, Charles, and Susie Taylor's father, whom Charles would need to notify.

There is no doubt that Charles had felt deeply about Susie. But she was gone, and he had to save himself. Even without a conviction, the scandal could cost him everything he had—his family, social status, and bottling plant.

Hence, Charles abandoned his post at his dead sweetheart's bedside. He owned a buggy, which he drove from Lynn to Burlington. At a public stable in Woburn, he changed horses, perhaps because he didn't want to take his own over the rough roads to the Taylor farmhouse. Arriving after a journey of several hours, he found John Taylor, Susie's father.

The two men had met before. In the early days of Ames's pursuit of Susie, the putative bachelor had visited the farm. Since his daughter's move to Lynn, however, John had seen her only once. Obviously, Susie's "suitor" had never become her husband.

By the time Ames arrived, around noon, the farmhouse would have been buzzing with activity. Most of Taylor's children were married, but a daughter and son still lived with him and his second wife, the former Elizabeth Williams Ivester. Ames, their surprise visitor, apparently managed to pull Taylor aside. Whatever words were exchanged, they left the others with the impression that Susie was gravely ill and wanted to see her father. Ames offered to drive Taylor to the nearest train depot in Woburn. Given the rough roads in icy condition, that could have been the quickest way to Lynn.

Arriving around midnight, Taylor found his daughter's body laid out in all the finery Charles had bought her over the course of her relationship. She was fully dressed, as if "she had just returned from an evening call," someone said, although slightly overaccessorized for that. Diamond-drop earrings hung from her lobes, and a gold ring engraved with the initials "S. E. T." adorned a finger. A gold watch, chain, and bracelet completed the look, an unusual one outside the confines of a casket.

It must have been a surprising sight for Taylor, who had seen this daughter once since she'd moved to Lynn. Top wages for female workers in Susie's line of work were under $400 annually, and her jewelry was worth at least that much. But there was no time for Farmer Taylor to either marvel or sob over his daughter's corpse.

One of the Guilfords took a book down from a shelf to read to him the city ordinances regarding the removal of a body from a private house. A fee was involved, but that would have been no obstacle for Ames, the benefactor of all his beloved's jewelry. The father was made to understand what the lover knew already: the death couldn't be said to have occurred here, or there would be another inquest. The daughter's shame, as the father saw it, would be known far and wide. An old-fashioned farmer with a large family and limited resources, he had no desire for encounters with the law.

So, when the Guilfords gave John Taylor a script to follow, he followed it to the letter. It had enough of Victorian sentimentality to appeal to him, although with touches of a genre that would soon become popular—Grand Guignol. The ruse even employed a theatrical prop—an improvised "bed" on which the corpse would lay. They would transport the dead woman to Burlington, saying she had wanted to die in her childhood home but didn't survive the trip.

In their house, the Guilfords produced a pine board which was sawed to the desired length. A three-quarter-length mattress was placed on this. Over this they laid the cadaver—bejeweled and fully dressed. They would say that, knowing she was dying, she chose this attire for her burial.

That one detail about the choice of grave clothes was the only truthful part of their story. In her short life, Susan Ella Taylor had been loved enough to be covered in diamonds, and death would end the secrecy about that.

A passageway led to the Guilfords' stable, so close to their house as to resemble an L-shaped addition. The bier was carried to the couple's carriage, a four-seater pulled by a single horse. With the front bench either turned up or removed, the planked cadaver fit lengthwise along the bottom of the interior, with room on the rear bench for one living passenger. The father took that seat, at least for part of the journey. If stopped, he could say that he'd been there to comfort his daughter, holding her hand until she expired.

Henry took the reins of the carriage, letting Ames start first in his buggy to lead the way. The two vehicles made a grisly procession, moving slowly on treacherous roads. Any surveillance of the house triggered by the Dyer case must have been porous; no one halted their departure from Lynn. Beyond the city limits, every mile was to their advantage. If anyone questioned them, they could convincingly say that an ailing woman failed to survive the frigid night.

Arriving at the farmhouse at 4:00 AM, the players soon had a sizeable audience. Besides Taylor's new wife, Elizabeth, several of his children and step-children were staying at the farmhouse. They awakened to find Susie Taylor's body lying in a room, plank removed.

Explaining events to his family, Taylor probably skipped the embellishments. However, he wasn't truthful either. At least while Henry was there, he stuck to their story about the time and place of death. And at least to the younger generation, he made no mention of pregnancy or abortion. However, they were growing up in a different America when family size was shrinking. Moreover, Charles was still in the house, raising questions.

Always convincing as a physician, Henry said that Susie had died of a bowel inflammation. Perhaps going off book, never a wise idea in these cases, he added an additional flourish. His wife had treated Susie for the same condition two years earlier, he said. That small detail stuck in the mind of one hearer. Eddie Taylor, two years younger than Susie, might have wondered why he never heard of these stomach ailments.

Another member of the household was both curious and prying. Nineteen-year-old Mary Ivester, a daughter of Eddie's new stepmother, had never met Susie while she was living. But she was awake as "Father Taylor," as she called him, brought the body into the house. Weeping, the father absented himself from the Lynn visitors. Undoubtedly hungry from their exertions, Henry and Charles followed some of Susie's siblings into the kitchen. Uninvited, Mary stood at the door and eavesdropped on their conversations.

Eddie must have raised questions about the stomach ailments. Aware that the old deceits would not work with a young man, Henry told him of the pregnancy, at least in code language. He talked of Susie's awareness that she had three choices, two of them not viable, so she had chosen the Guilfords' lying-in infirmary.

Now that the nocturnal machinations were concluded, Charles was crying his eyes out and telling all. The recipient of his confession was Susie's youngest sibling, Lucy Taylor. At fourteen, "Lulu," as she was called, might have been mystified by some of it. But Mary, standing near the door, caught the meaning of every word.

Charles told Lulu that she mustn't blame Susie for what happened, that it was all his fault, not hers. If in need of a short course in sex education, Lulu got one that morning in the kitchen. Charles told her that Susie, announcing her condition a month before, had listed her options, including going to a hospital. Ruling out the possibility that she could have gone to his house, Charles also made his marital status plain. Undermining his own statement, that Susie was not at fault, he warned his lover's little sister "to be careful with whom she went, and to find out who a man was before she went with him." In other words, Lulu should steer clear of men like him.

And, despite his tears and self-recriminations, Charles assured the girl that "he had done all he could for Susie before she died, and he would do all he could for her after." Or so Mary Ivester heard, straining to listen.

Mary had undoubtedly gotten that last part right. Charles would pay the funeral expenses. That was made clear to the undertaker who was called to the Taylor house. The man, Benjamin A. Tripp, later said he wasn't pleased to discover that no physician had filed a *return*, or official statement regarding the death. Asking about this, he was told that Susie had consulted with doctor after doctor only to abandon them because nobody could help her. Tripp also said he was unhappy to see that the body remained clothed.

However, Tripp's discomfort didn't prevent him from agreeing on a fee, which he believed would be paid jointly by Taylor and Ames. At any rate, he knew he would be away the next day, leaving undertaking duties to a substitute. A local farmer, Leonard Allen, had been the area undertaker until the previous year, when he relinquished these duties to Tripp. Allen could fill in at Tripp's funeral home in Woburn, but only if he chose to.

The father and the lover couldn't have been happy about this turn of events. Wanting the evidence underground as soon as possible, they asked Allen to arrange a Tuesday funeral, two days hence. For John Taylor, a fellow farmer, Allen agreed to resume his undertaking duties, promising to treat the case as if it were his own.

On Monday, Susie Taylor's body was moved once again, this time to the Tripp undertaking rooms in Woburn. Ames and Taylor arrived early to meet with the substitute undertaker, now familiar with their account of the journey from Lynn. Only a year removed from his old job, Leonard Allen remembered the requirements of Massachusetts law. Again, the two men were asked if a physician had filed any paperwork. When they replied in the negative, he produced a blank form and asked for the place of death. Told that it was "near enough" to Burlington to be called that, he inquired how long the decedent had been ill and whether a physician had attended her.

Changing the story slightly from what was told to Tripp, Ames said there had been no doctor, only a spiritualist, and that the illness had lasted just a few days. Allen dutifully completed the form and submitted it to the town clerk, who later said he had misgivings about the missing physician's signature. Nevertheless, the clerk accepted it.

The next task was casket selection. For the benefit of his fellow small farmer, Allen began with the cheap ones, but the family friend from Lynn insisted on a luxury model lined in white velvet. Flowers were ordered in profusion, undoubtedly from the brother-in-law who had introduced Charles to Susie. Donald K. Colgate's floral shop and greenhouse were in the Cummingsville section of Woburn.

A night's rest had done nothing to strengthen Charles's self-control. Perhaps feeling shielded by his wealth, he spoke openly of his relationship with Susie, as he had in his kitchen confessional. However, here his audience was not just an awestruck adolescent girl. Three other sisters had come to the funeral home in the company of their husbands. Remarkably, Charles unburdened himself to these village men and women, telling them of his devotion to Susie.

The eldest of these sisters, Mary Lizzie Colgate, was married to the florist who had introduced the lovers. She noted that Charles was very particular about the arrangement of the flowers, wanting some in the lace around her late sister's neck. He also took charge of the placement of the jewelry, with which the body was to be buried.

Despite the sudden death and the haste of the preparations, a large crowd of mourners attended the Tuesday funeral. John Taylor might insist on his story, made perfect with practice, that his daughter died of a gastrointestinal ailment. But, feeling the entitlement of his checkbook, Charles made no attempt to conceal his relationship to the decedent. Letting his tears flow, he bent over the casket to kiss his beloved, multiple times. It also became known that he had commissioned a poem to accompany a death notice in the *Woburn Advertiser*, ordering dozens of copies for delivery at his address.

Susie Taylor was buried in Burlington's new cemetery, where Charles was said to have "staggered" to the gravesite. The same minister who had officiated the recent Taylor weddings consigned her body to the earth, while a man married to another woman made an ass of himself.

Charles already had supplied Woburn and the villages nearby with a year's worth of gossip. Things might have stopped there, had Charles not indulged in one final bit of poor judgment. The jewelry, including the diamonds, was buried with the body. Of all the things they'd witnessed that day, the mourners and gravediggers found this the most remarkable. They couldn't stop talking about it.

The news reached the ears of the Woburn police chief, Wilmont D. Nelson. Although Burlington was outside of his jurisdiction, Chief Nelson immediately took an active interest in the case. He had come to his position from Lynn, where he'd been a mere policeman. Learning of the body's strange trip home, and of the presence of a Lynn doctor at the Taylor farmhouse, Nelson put two and two together. He was convinced of a connection with the Guilfords' Lewis Street house.

Chief Nelson applied himself to the matter with gusto, collaborating with one of his own detectives, Inspector John Tidd. He paid a visit to the Taylor farm. Although standing by his story, and declining to be cooperative, John Taylor would at least have confirmed the identity and address of the Lynn doctors. Interviewing other members, Nelson worked up enough of a case to present to the Lynn authorities. Telephone lines linked the two police departments, and a call was made.

Hearing of the father's recalcitrance, the Lynn district attorney might have worried whether this case, like Annie Dyer's, would fall apart for lack of evidence. But he also sensed that the public might support his prosecution of a case like this. This time the victim was an innocent-seeming young girl, not a drunken brawler like Annie Dyer.

Still, the Lynn prosecutor wanted something more solid than testimony from witnesses who could change their stories or fail to appear. New Year's Day would be a busy one for Chief Nelson. He'd spend the morning in Lynn, collaborating with his former colleagues on a joint action. Then he'd head back to the countryside around Woburn for a special assignment.

On that first day of 1886, police surrounded the Guilford house in the early morning. Armed with a search warrant, detectives inspected the rooms, finding one patient in a bed and unable to be moved from it. If the three children of the family were home, as they likely were, arrangements were made for their care. The parents were taken to the police station housed at city hall, and the press soon got wind of it. The local *Daily Evening Item*, long fascinated with the Guilfords, had to jostle with reporters from Boston and other parts of Massachusetts.

The Lewis Street house fell under the control of the city physician Joseph G. Pinkham, who, aided by a nurse from the city hospital, stayed to tend the bedridden patient. The police also took an interest in this young woman. Told she was expected to recover, they extracted from her a promise that she'd testify against the Guilfords. They also had her sign a statement to that effect, knowing that promises of this sort were often broken.

In an unconscious nod to the Guilfords' professionalism, Dr. Pinkham didn't suggest moving their patient elsewhere. Apparently, he found neither cleanliness nor equipment wanting in their self-styled infirmary.

Before noon, the police station cells had two unusual guests. One out-of-town journalist described them as "a fine appearing and exceedingly well-dressed gentleman and lady," who "had not the appearance of criminals." They gave their names as Dr. Henry M. Guilford and Mrs. Dr. Alice Guilford, but the more skeptical members of the press corps framed those titles in quotation marks.

They were being held for the charge of criminal malpractice that led to the death of Susie E. Taylor. This time, things were serious. Bail was set at the staggering sum of $5,000.

Henry was searched and locked in a cell, from which he sent for a lawyer. For Nancy, however, there was one more taste of freedom. Lacking a search warrant for the Market Street office, not involved in the Taylor death, the police asked Nancy to take them there. Four men escorted her on the short walk to her downtown office. She likely pointed out her set of surgical instruments. They were commonplace ones, used by many physicians and midwives. Taking these with them, two detectives brought Nancy back to the police station. The city marshal and a police lieutenant stayed on at her office, examining her medical books and medicines. When a reporter for the *Boston Herald* found the men there, they said that nothing of a suspicious nature had been found. Similar instruments had been found at Lewis Street, but they were ones in common use, as a medical expert would testify.

Nevertheless, the *Herald* would report a finding of "an extensive lot of the more approved instruments known to be used by abortionists." Some papers of the era shied away from the word, but others did not.

The Lynn police station hosted about four lodgers per day, mostly charged with drunkenness, assault, or larceny. On the day after New Year's celebrations, the Guilfords likely had some company. Most of the drunks and petty thieves left quickly, after friends or family paid their fine. Nancy and Henry, however, had to settle in for the night.

However, one cellmate that day matched them in social status. Indeed, he was a gentleman of their acquaintance. The police also arrested Charles Ames on the charge of procuring abortion.

Friends of Charles said he must have "lost his head" to have displayed his involvement so openly. By now, he would have received his order of the *Woburn Advertiser*, with the notice of Susie's death embellished by the poem he'd had written. It's hard to imagine why he wanted fifty copies, if not to distribute them.

The poem began,

> Mournfully, tenderly, we have laid her away,
> Where the spring flowers bloom many a day
> How often we shall miss her day after day,
> And how sadly we felt as we laid her away.

But there were no spring flowers at the Burlington cemetery when Chief Nelson arrived there after his busy morning in Lynn. The gravediggers must have been at work already, because he arrived in time for the casket to be dragged from the earth and opened.

Susie hadn't been laid away for long. Three days after her funeral, the body was exhumed. Dr. Frederick Winsor, a medical examiner who was present, saw few signs of decomposition, thanks to the cold weather. In fact, the body was lightly frozen, but this did not prevent Winsor and another physician from performing an autopsy in a small building near the cemetery.

The medical examiner found no signs of illness except in the womb, where he found evidence of peritonitis, which he cited as the cause of death. Noting what he called thickening of the uterus, he determined there had been a "miscarriage" seven to ten days earlier. The Lynn prosecutors now had more to go on than in the Dyer case.

The body was reburied, this time without its jewelry. Nelson put the gold and diamonds aside for the young woman's father. But neither he nor the Burlington town clerk, also at the cemetery, took immediate steps to notify the family.

The next day, waiting for a train from Woburn to Boston, John Taylor bought a copy of the *Boston Globe* and learned of his daughter's exhumation.

His first impulse was to find out on whose authority this had been done. But, while retaining a lawyer, he made no move to protest the disinterment. Charged with a crime, Charles Ames might reveal the father's role in the cover-up. After retaining a lawyer, Taylor made himself elusive. He was of no further help to the police.

The first newspaper accounts portrayed the father as a sympathetic figure. Racing to his ailing daughter's side, he had tried his best to fulfill her last request to die in her native village. In these early reports, printed in Boston and Lynn, the pine board tied to the corpse became a "bed" prepared for his poor child's comfort. Instead of mounting Charles's buggy, the father somehow squeezed into the back of Henry's carriage with the plank, mattress, and daughter, who "leaned heavily" on the "heart-broken father," sinking quickly and "dying in her father's arms."

Even before the autopsy results were known, the press was quick to dismiss the father's claim that his daughter had died of a stomach ailment. However, they swallowed this hogwash, only noting with some surprise that the transport of an invalid had been undertaken on a night that "was one of the most disagreeable of the year."

It couldn't have been easy to catch sleep in the cells at City Hall. In expectation of the arraignment of the doctors and the lover, people had queued up outside the building. As soon as the doors opened, they swarmed into the police courtroom. With all seats taken, the crowd swelled into the hallways. Latecomers gathered outside, where young boys perched on the basement windows. There was no school on this day, Saturday, but the youth of the city were getting an education.

Only Henry and Nancy seemed uninterested. Brought in around 10:00 AM, they were seated behind a desk. Henry looked through a newspaper while their lawyer waived the reading of the charges and entered their pleas of not guilty. Appearing for them was attorney Henry P. Moulton, who two years before had run for Lynn district attorney, narrowly losing to the man who was now seeking to punish his clients.

Their bail was set at a staggering sum of $5,000 apiece. For Charles Ames, also pleading not guilty, it was $3,000. To the spectators' disappointment, the entire affair consumed all of ten minutes. The spectators dispersed.

But while the Guilfords remained in police custody, Charles left the courtroom on his own, having made bail. His wife's father was now his bondsman. Stephen Heald had made a bad bargain in selecting a husband for his daughter. Nonetheless, the father-in-law was protecting his investment. Charles Ames would return home that night to little Charlie and Mary Ellen, and his bottling company, made famous by reports linking it to him, could continue to operate.

Sprung from jail, Charles nonetheless was not a free man. There would be questions, legal expenses, and perhaps an indictment and trial. There would be motive and opportunity for Charles to flee, but Heald would keep a close watch on him. In this, Heald could count on the support of at least one Lynn patrolman. Otis Heald, son of Stephen and brother of Mary Ellen, still wore the blue uniform and brass buttons of the Lynn Police Department.

Henry and Nancy spent the rest of the day trying to raise bail. The marshal brought them someplace where they made entreaties. They were also allowed to receive several visitors in the courthouse. Failing to produce the required amount, they were put on the 4:30 PM train to Salem and taken to the county courthouse, better equipped for long-term guests than the Lynn lockup.

The Guilfords already had a Salem address, as the press quickly discovered. Boston and local papers wrote of the "alleged medical firm" Brown & Co., located in a Salem office building, where creditors could never seem to find anyone. Also revealed was Henry's nomadic existence in Brockton. One enterprising reporter interviewed the woman who'd cleaned his rooms and lent her life savings to him, never to see that money again. A list of his pseudonyms consumed a column inch of print.

After first describing Henry as a physician "of the old school," the Globe, as well as the smalltown papers, quickly grew skeptical about his background and medical training. The Guilfords were said to have "unenviable reputations" and to be "of doubtful character." Still, no one denied they had established thriving practices. Criticisms of Nancy's "extravagant" clothes and diamonds had undertones of admiration.

The most sympathetic figure at the beginning, John Taylor was soon branded in print as a liar. Within days of the arrests and autopsy, the press started suspecting that his daughter was already dead when he came to Lynn. The Globe reconsidered the farmer's version under the headline CONFLICTING OPINIONS AS TO WHERE AND WHEN SUSIE TAYLOR DIED. A Lowell paper bluntly stated that previous reports about death on the road were "not correct." As the police gathered witnesses for an inquest, the papers revised their description of the grim procession that left Lynn that fateful night, moving the father to Charles's buggy while leaving the daughter inside of Henry's carriage, dead and attached to a board.

The press owed this correction to Mary Ivester, the stepsister Susie had never met. After eavesdropping on Charles in the farmhouse, she apparently continued to investigate. Awakened by Charles's midnight visit, Mary's mother would have known the true circumstances surrounding the death. Whether told the facts directly or having ferreted them out, Mary chose to share her findings with the police. John Taylor was reportedly "incensed with her" for doing so. As the prosecutors struggled to prove their case against the Guilfords, the father was a key witness. But he stood by his story, even as his stepdaughter contradicted him.

If Mary was less than loyal to the newly merged Ivester-Taylor family, she also had less connection to it than others. Born in England, like her mother and sister, she had recently followed them to America, sailing from Liverpool to Boston in steerage. All three found jobs in domestic service around Burlington. But her relatives soon abandoned that to wed Taylor men—the sister marrying Susie's brother William a month after their parents' nuptials. A year after immigrating, Mary was essentially alone again. Her conferences with the police may have offered the attention she craved. Or, consciously or not, she may have wanted to pay the Taylors back for leaving her out.

Mary Ivester was one of many witnesses summoned to an inquest in Lynn in early January. This time, the police doors were firmly closed to the public. The prosecution had gathered more than a dozen witnesses, many of them related to the Taylors by blood or marriage. Ushered into a room, each was interviewed separately. The board and saw used to construct the plank for the cadaver were examined. They'd been found in the Lewis Street house.

Lewis Street had also produced another witness, here under duress. This was Mary McLean, the nurse who had cared for Susie Taylor as she suffered from the infection that turned fatal. McLean had temporarily gone missing after the defendants' arrest. The prosecution had located her and served a subpoena, which the nurse had defied. Now she was being held in the city hall lockup under a bond of one hundred dollars.

Nancy and Henry, brought from Salem during a snowstorm, spotted their loyal former nurse, also under police escort. The three prisoners enjoyed a brief reunion in the city hall corridor leading to the jail cells. The women exchanged smiles. The press described that informal "reception," but, excluded from the inquest, it could only print the names of the witnesses.

Chief Nelson of Woburn and his right-hand man, Inspector Tidd, appeared in these lists. However, Nelson complained to the *Globe* days later that neither he nor the inspector had been asked to testify. According to the *Globe*, the chief was unhappy with the handling of the case, believing that certain "important witnesses" in Burlington could have furnished essential testimony, had they been asked to.

Others in Burlington shared the chief's sentiments, wrote the *Globe* under the headline SUSIE TAYLOR'S FRIENDS DISSATISFIED. In the village, "there is a strong feeling that the father should tell of the matter, all he knows," the Boston paper wrote, as well as "a slight feeling of dissatisfaction at the lethargy of the Lynn officers." That latter sentiment clearly came from Nelson. Speaking of the chief, the piece concluded, "All he had to say was that he could not spend Woburn money any further on the case, it being a Lynn affair."

Lethargic or not, the Lynn police had to beat back overflow crowds at a preliminary hearing on the Susie Taylor case held over the next two weeks. On each of three days, Henry and Nancy arrived by train from Salem. The *Globe* wrote approvingly of the "ladylike" elegance of "Mrs. Dr. Alice M. Guilford," finding "nothing of the criminal about her," as she made her entrance in heavy furs over a gown of dark watered silk.

However, Nancy's jewelry was not mentioned. As legal expenses mounted—husband and wife had separate attorneys—the diamonds might have gone toward legal fees. There was also the matter of child support for Herbert, the son Henry had brought to the marriage, and the children born to the couple, Eudora and Harry. The three were scattered among relatives in the Boston area and upstate New York. Nancy, for whom the children were a constant worry, looked careworn beneath her velvet bonnet, while Henry "seemed unconcerned."

The Guilfords sat in the courtroom dock while Charles Ames, arriving from his West Lynn home, was positioned a short distance from them, just inside the rail. He was represented by two attorneys, one local and the other from Boston. Keeping close watch over Ames was Stephen Heald, his kinsman and bondsman.

Expected to attend the first day of the hearing, Mary Ivester vomited instead. The detective assigned to her took her to his own home to give her medicine. Pleading illness, Mary returned to the home in Lynn where she was employed as a domestic. Probably not coincidentally, her stepfather was one of the chief witnesses in that first session.

Hewing closely to his now-familiar version of events, John Taylor added a few embellishments. He said he arrived to find Mrs. Guilford working over his daughter with hot bottles and washcloths. In this telling, there was no talk of stomach trouble. Instead, remarkably incurious, the father realized that his young daughter was dying, yet never asked about the nature of her illness. Hitting all the familiar notes, he spoke of fulfilling her last request by fixing a wooden bed for her and taking her home. This time, he said she had died around Wakefield, farther from Chief Nelson's jurisdiction than in his previous accounts.

Nancy came off as a ministering angel. "My daughter said that Mrs. Guilford had done everything for her that she could, and that her mother could not have done any better," said John Taylor. The villagers of Burlington could wag their tongues as much as they pleased. He had no interest in seeing the Guilfords and Charles Ames punished if that meant openly acknowledging his daughter's condition.

That task was left to the medical examiner, Frederick Winsor, who also took the stand that day. Describing his autopsy of Susie Taylor's body, he spoke of signs of a previous "miscarriage" and his findings of peritonitis. He said the infection could have been caused by inflammation, although he found no indication of that, or by "external violence."

Perhaps because Chief Nelson was less knowledgeable about women's anatomy than police procedure, the medical examiner said he had not examined the body to see if "an instrument had been used." He said he certainly would have noticed any indication of that, but that it was possible for instruments to be used without leaving a visible mark.

Cross-examined by Nancy's attorney, Henry P. Moulton of Salem, Winsor was shown an array of scalpels, probes, and other paraphernalia, then asked about their purpose. Winsor identified them as instruments of "common use," although not found in every physician's office. The search warrant for the Lewis Street house and the extended tour of the Market Street office had turned up nothing uniquely demonic.

The district attorney then asked the witness if the dead woman's peritonitis was caused by abortion. However, Nancy's attorney objected to the question, and the judge sustained the objection.

The hearing was continued to the following week. It had been a bad start for the prosecution. There might be enough evidence to persuade a grand jury to indict the three defendants. But would there be enough proof for convictions, still notoriously difficult in abortion cases? The lethargy surrounding the case in Lynn extended beyond the police. District Attorney Henry F. Hurlburt had barely squeaked out an election victory against Nancy's lawyer. A courtroom victory over this formidable opponent could be more difficult.

If only Hurlburt could feel sure that public interest in the case indicated a thirst for conviction. Instead, the people of Lynn vied to catch glimpses of Nancy as if she were a celebrity. As the hearing resumed, women and girls in "ribbons, feathers and furbelows" occupied the front seats with "a small army of men" behind them, and the windows darkened with faces pressed to the glass.

The district attorney had again marshaled his own army of witnesses, brought from the Woburn and Burlington area. By now, they had grown familiar with the Lynn streetcar line, sometimes glimpsing Charles Ames in another seat on their courtroom commutes. District Attorney Hurlburt was mounting an expensive prosecution—the public would eventually pay for those streetcar fares and other expenses.

But, needing the testimony of John Taylor's stepdaughter and perhaps desperate for more time, Hurlburt asked for another continuance. The defense objected, pointing out that the government had gathered a large roster of witnesses and called only a few of them, failing to prove its case.

A Taylor relative said that Mary Ivester was on the mend and could be in court Saturday. Remarking that a "case of this magnitude" should not be cut off, the judge granted the continuance. The prosecution would have exactly three hours to present all evidence.

Again, the crowds converged, and the defendants took their places in the dock. Mary Ivester, looking pale but "ready for business," took her place among three stepsisters and their husbands, all prepared to testify. However, the first person called to the stand was unknown to them. Mary McLean, the Guilfords' former nurse, had been brought from a jail cell, still held as a material witness.

However, the nurse's testimony didn't do the prosecution many favors beyond establishing Charles Ames's close relationship with the decedent. A housekeeper for the Guilfords before taking on nursing duties, she had slept in their house. She described Susie's illness as it progressed for more than a week. Nancy took charge, laying hot water bottles over the patient's "bowels," administering powders and other medicines orally and internally. The nurse described her own duties as limited to tasks like boiling water and preparing poultices. When Susie took a turn for the worse one afternoon, Nurse McLean fetched Nancy from her Market Street office and was relieved to turn things over to her.

The nurse also cataloged Charles Ames's visits to the sick woman, noting that he had spent considerable time in her room or pacing in the hallway outside it. McLean said that Susie Taylor hadn't lifted her head after her first bout of abdominal pain and couldn't keep down food or medicine for a week afterward. But she also said that the patient had been "bright" on what proved to be the last day of her life.

Stating that Mrs. Guilford had told her Susie had inflammation of the bowels, McLean offered no new information about the time and place of death. She placed John Taylor in the house early on Susie's last day there, adding that Charles seemed to have read the patient a newspaper in the final hours of her agony. Adding another gruesome detail, the nurse said she she'd aired Susie's clothes and warmed them on the register for the cold ride.

Indeed, that might have been necessary. If the bedroom in which the body lay had been left unheated to delay decomposition, the clothes selected for the journey could have been in a wardrobe, damp and frozen.

The nurse claimed to know nothing further about the events of that night. She'd retired an hour before the others left the house. From her upstairs room, she heard carriages come and go, and no one in the house asked for bedclothes. According to the nurse, none of these strange breaks in nocturnal routine had prompted her to descend the stairs or look out a window.

The prosecution returned Nurse McLean to her cell, convinced that she was withholding information. But today, the clock was ticking. The case had to be wrapped up by noon.

Mary Ivester's long-awaited testimony came next. The Taylor stepdaughter gave a full report of what she had heard from the kitchen doorway. She told how Charles Ames had taken the blame for Susie's death, warning his sweetheart's youngest sister to be careful of the men she went with. She also recounted Henry's conversation with Eddie Taylor about the limited choices open to Susie in her situation.

Eddie Taylor was not available to confirm or deny his stepsister's testimony. Another reluctant witness for the prosecution, he had ignored a subpoena that wasn't correctly filled out. However, three of Susie's sisters were present, along with their spouses. In the remaining time, all six rotated through the witness stand. Most of their testimony centered on Charles Ames's peculiar behavior at the funeral parlor and burial, as well as his assurances that he had spent most of the prior week at Susie's side. Donald Colgate, the florist, recalled introducing Charles to Susie, his sister-in-law.

The defense called no witnesses. The judge brought his gavel down at 11:40 AM. The government had beat its deadline by twenty minutes. The next step would rest with the grand jury.

The sisters and spouses had been useful in involving Charles, who could turn government's witness at trial. For the purposes of the hearing, the court had ruled all their conversations admissible. But was there enough to establish that an abortion had taken place? Apparently unimpressed by the other testimony, the papers plucked their next headline from the florist: THEY MET AT A DANCE.

Anticipating problems from the beginning, Lynn authorities had told the press on the day of the arrests that "if this affair can't be proven, there's another that can." That statement was supported by vague reports of a woman encountered at the Lewis Street house who said she'd been operated on several times. It was never clear if the woman had occupied a bed there, happened to come by during the house search, or perhaps contacted the police. It was said that the police persuaded her to sign a statement in case she reconsidered later, as often happened. However, nothing more was heard about the mystery woman during the inquest or hearing, and there was no more news of this case for several months.

On May 10 the Superior Criminal Court of Essex County opened a new term in Newburyport, announcing that a grand jury had indicted Henry and Nancy for abortion upon Susie Taylor of Burlington in Lynn. Charles Ames had been indicted as an accessory. Two days later, the proceedings moved to Lynn, where defense attorneys raised several questions about irregularities in the selection and conduct of the grand jury. The Guilfords declined to enter a plea, which was recorded as not guilty.

The bail for the three defendants was set the same as previously, with one exception: Nancy alone was indicted for an abortion on a second woman, Jennie Peters, and her bail was doubled to $6,000.

Jennie Peters, who had washed floors to pay for her abortion, had risen from the dead. Nearly two years had passed since Nancy had shoved her out the door—homeless and barely able to board a Boston-bound streetcar. Now she was back in Lynn, well enough to stand and swear on a Bible.

5 | THE SALEM TRIALS

THE TRIAL OF DR. ALICE GUILFORD for attempting abortion upon Jennie Peters wasn't an audience favorite. No crowds beat down the door, scrambled for seats, or filled the hallways. The crime was abortion, not murder, and the alleged victim was no lovely Susie Taylor of the countryside. Jennie Peters was a lying tramp who'd been around, or so Nancy's lawyers would paint her and any other woman brazen enough to back her up.

Fresh from the grand jury, Jennie was prepared to discuss her abortion in open court. Her former nurse, Iva Marsh, would corroborate, adding some flourishes of her own. Unlike the witnesses in the Susie Taylor case, which would be tried after this one, neither woman faked an illness or dodged a subpoena. They were willing to tell their stories.

The trial began on May 17, 1886, in Superior Court in Salem. The trial for the death of Susie Taylor wouldn't begin until the verdict for this charge came in. This was a sideshow—a dull one, with no diamonds, no sobbing, and no poems.

The government was buying time, trying to look tough while scrambling around for more evidence in the Taylor death. The Woburn police chief's charges of "lethargy" in Lynn still stung. The shoemaking capital had awakened and was putting in the man-hours, however belatedly.

In this interim trial, District Attorney Hurlburt would again face Moulton, his former election opponent, who had represented Nancy at the Lynn hearing. Another familiar member of the defense bar was present—George Searle of Boston, previously Henry's lawyer but this time here for the wife. The city lawyer and Salem-based Moulton would collaborate on Nancy's defense.

71

Around 9:30 AM, Henry was brought into court with another male prisoner. Although not charged with any crime in the Jennie Peters case, he nonetheless was still a guest of the county. Thus, he was seated in the dock alongside men whose cases would be heard that morning. There was no sign of Nancy yet.

The jurors were already at work, listening to testimony about a man charged with selling liquor illegally and creating a nuisance. After retiring briefly, they delivered a guilty verdict, and the defendant was fined. Two other defendants pleaded guilty to liquor-related crimes, also paying fines.

Nancy made her entrance at 10:40 AM. With fewer journalists present here than in Lynn, no one described her outfit nor noted her jailhouse pallor. Certainly, prison life must have taken a toll on her. Two of the Guilford children, Herbert and Henry, were in upstate New York with Nancy's relatives. Just weeks before this trial, Nancy's father, Horace Brown, had died at age seventy, leaving her mother alone with the children. Eudora, the pet of the family, was not so far away. Living with one of Henry's sisters in Somerville, just west of Boston, she had likely visited her parents in prison. Still, her devoted mother would have yearned for her and wondered about her care in the hands of in-laws.

Even if no one was counting Nancy's facial wrinkles, the press had been busy. Indeed, Moulton began by asserting that an article in the previous day's *Boston Sunday Herald* surely had prejudiced the jury, making a fair trial impossible. The judge observed that if trials covered by the press had to be voided, there would be no trials at all.

The jury that Nancy faced was basically the same one that had tried that morning's liquor-sales case. After the verdict was delivered, a few changes of jurors were made. The judge instructed members of the reassembled panel to step down if they'd already made up their mind about the Guilford case, or if they'd read anything that influenced them about it. Nobody budged.

However, there was some playing of musical chairs. Moulton planned to take the risky step of putting Nancy on the stand to defend herself, confident that she would outshine her slatternly accuser. Given the late start, she might not testify until the following day. Still, as a protective step, Moulton asked that all government witnesses leave the courtroom. Granting that request but broadening it, the judge ordered that all witnesses leave until called.

With that, Henry was returned to his jail cell, never to return during this trial. It would be nearly an all-woman affair, with the arguments framed by men. The defense attorneys planned to pit Mrs. Dr. Guilford—a genteel physician who had nothing to do with abortion—against a penniless slut. As Moulton would tell the jury, "I don't think any twelve men can be made to believe the story of the Peters woman."

Certainly, Jennie Peters was not the sympathetic figure District Attorney Hurlburt might have wished for. Because of the wording of the indictment, he needed to give the jury a neat summary of the witness's discovery of her "trouble," the two abortion attempts at the Market Street office, and the third procedure at Nancy's home. No matter how straightforward his presentation, it must have shocked its listeners to the core.

Sworn in, Jennie Peters unblinkingly answered the prosecutor's questions, detailing her visits to the back room of Nancy's office, the two procedures that had failed, and the bathroom abortion that had left her so disabled she could no longer work. Answering queries comprehensively and clearly, she moved the focus from her sexual habits to the shady nature of Nancy's enterprise.

Recalling conversations with apparent precision, Jennie provided fodder for the press and prosecutorial ammunition. In each recalled dialogue, Nancy played the part of the villain, exacting promises that "you won't give me away," withholding treatment until "you have the money," and essentially blaming the patient for the failure of the first two abortion attempts by saying, "All creation won't bring some people around."

With the scene shifted to Lewis Street, the mood darkened. Jennie recounted the work she'd done there and the little she remembered of the bathroom procedure. After that came her agony, her delivery, and her premature discharge. In Boston, she'd sought and found medical care at Massachusetts General Hospital, staying for weeks until her transfer to a shelter for homeless women, where she was still staying, partially recovered but unable to work again.

A lifetime of being kicked around had somehow left Jennie with an air of authority. She described the Market Street office, down to the number of windows in the back room. Claiming that she'd never known abortions could be brought about by surgery, she was far less credible. At age thirty, did she believe that Mrs. Dr. Guilford had some magical pills that worked when others didn't? And if she expected to get a prescription or gulp some medicine, why bring Margaret Hall along for the visit?

Moulton was aware of this as he rose to address the jury. But more than just challenging Jennie Peters's innocence, he promised to destroy her credibility completely. Indeed, he intended to show that the criminal in this case was Jennie Peters, a lying conspirator who had joined with Margaret and Charles Hall to blackmail his client, a legitimate physician prepared to testify in her own defense.

Moulton began his cross-examination of Jennie with gloves off: "Who was the cause of your trouble?" he asked. An objection was made and sustained.

Asked about her personal history, Peters detailed a poor and rootless life of housecleaning, boot-making, and providing table service at two Boston eateries. Viewing waitressing jobs as particularly disreputable, Moulton stored up that tidbit for later. His present focus was on Jennie's last job as a domestic for a Lynn family.

"Was any man in the habit of making visits on you at the time?" he asked. Predictably, the court upheld an objection.

Having done his best to demean the witness, Moulton set out to prove that this was a blackmail case from the start, that Jennie was up to her ears in it with this fabricated story of abortion and was testifying only to avoid indictment for conspiring to extort money.

No, she said, she wasn't aware that Charles Hall had attempted to force the Guilfords out of money, or that he'd gone to the Lynn police to try to obtain a warrant on this matter. She also denied that her conversations with the Lynn police had anything to do with Charles Hall's machinations, of which she'd known nothing.

A barbed question followed. No, said Jennie, "Charles E. Hall was not the cause of my trouble." With one stroke, Moulton had suggested she was both conspirator and whore. Adding to her humiliation, Charles Hall was present to hear these words spoken.

Margaret was not. Following the court's instructions, she took the stand as Jennie exited. Furious notes were taken at the defense table, as Margaret spoke about learning of her friend's pregnancy, the visits to Market Street, conversations had, and payments made. There was one minor discrepancy about where a payment was made, whether in the front room of the office or the rear. The defense would seize on that, grilling Margaret about it, and shaking it before the jury like a dead rabbit.

The cross-examination also inquired into how someone like Jennie happened to have ten dollars to pay the doctor. Jennie had testified that the Halls, owing her exactly that amount, had paid it to settle their debt.

Margaret, however, said she thought her own son, Oscar McDonald, had given Jennie that sum. Seated in the dock and listening closely, Nancy took note of that point.

Married to Charles E. Hall for fourteen years, Margaret had a grown son with a different surname. Presumably, she had remarried after divorce or widowhood. According to her testimony, she and her second husband didn't always confide in one another. She recalled that a young man from Salem named Mr. Averell called on Charles some months after Jennie's departure and that the two went to "Mrs. Guilford's" together, although for what reason, the witness could not say.

If Hall had willingly accompanied the mysterious Mr. Averell, he must have trusted the stranger, thus compounding his errors. As Margaret might not have known then, but surely learned afterward, her husband had written to Nancy threatening to expose her. Feigning outrage that Mrs. Guilford had pushed a sick girl out the door, Hall had tried to exploit the situation. Almost certainly, he felt that he deserved some payment for the scraps his wife's friend had eaten at his table.

Therefore, Charles Hall had taken up a pen to write Nancy some lines of a threatening nature, or so said attorney Searle, relieving Moulton for the moment by cross-examining Margaret Hall. Not actually producing such a letter but seeming prepared to do so, the lawyer showed Margaret a sample of handwriting and asked if it was her husband's. Here, some wind went out of the defense's sails. The wife wasn't able to say, having never learned to write.

The undaunted Searle continued, calling the prosecution's integrity into question. Somehow Hall had threatened Nancy with exposure, he said. The Guilfords referred the matter to the lawyers, who engaged this Mr. Averell to pay a call to Hall in the guise of a helpful mediator. Escorted by his new "friend" to speak to Nancy in her office, Hall instead found Henry and was kicked into the street. Unashamed of his part in this, Hall lodged an official complaint, "for which he"—meaning the district attorney—"had never seen fit to prosecute," declared Searle. "The next heard of it was this indictment. Is this a prosecution or an appendix to the letter?"

Searle's clear implication was that a desperate prosecutor, unable to mount a convincing prosecution in the Taylor case, had railroaded Nancy. One thing was true enough. After Charles Hall lodged his complaint, Margaret had been summoned to police headquarters. She added that Jennie had been there, too, brought from Boston by a Lynn detective. If so, Margaret must have revealed her sick friend's whereabouts.

On that day, the police spoke to them separately. According to Margaret, Jennie had resolved not to talk of her abortion. Because of that, or due to the Lynn "lethargy" noted by the Woburn police chief, nothing had come of those talks until now.

Searle may have stretched credulity with his efforts to cast the prosecutor as a coconspirator in a blackmail plot. However, if Margaret's account was true, why had Jennie been closemouthed then, yet so forthcoming now? She'd said that no one had forced her to testify through the threat of legal consequences. But sick, poor, and dependent on charity, she was vulnerable to subtler forms of coercion.

With dinnertime near, court adjourned. Jennie left, presumably for the shelter in Boston, while Margaret returned to the home she shared with an aspiring blackmailer. As the defense had worked hard to establish, the only well-bred lady here was the one returned to her jail cell. Tomorrow, Nancy would have a chance to speak for herself.

However, the government wasn't finished presenting its case. As on the previous day, witnesses waited outside the courtroom until called. The Tuesday session opened at 9:30 AM, with Nancy in the dock and Henry nowhere in sight. He'd been left in the Salem prison.

Iva Marsh—the young woman abused sexually, emotionally, and verbally at the Guilfords' home—was first to testify. Subpoenaed the week before by a Lynn police officer, she was here to talk about Jennie Peters's abortion, not her own mistreatment. Despite knowing that, and despite Henry's absence, Iva was a jangle of nerves as she took the stand.

Guided by the district attorney's questions, she spoke of "relieving" Jennie of "the child," wrapping it in a napkin and handing it over to Nancy. Despite her couched language, there could be no doubt about what she was describing. Asked what Jennie Peters's ailment was, she replied, "Miscarriage." Shown an instrument, she said it had been kept in a commode drawer at Lewis Street.

She said she'd been surprised to be asked to testify only one week before the trial. A Lynn policeman had found her in South Abington, about thirty miles south of Lynn, in domestic service for a woman she declined to name. Like Jennie, Iva reeled off a sad litany of other service jobs she'd filled in a half-dozen towns, none lasting more than a few months. Being six years younger than Jennie, only twenty-four, Iva had a shorter work history. She had so far avoided factory and restaurant work, remaining "purer" in that sense than her former patient.

But she was none too pure in the defense's eyes. Moulton began his cross-examination with a sneak attack. Obviously aware of Iva's abortion—Nancy would have told her lawyers of it, even if withholding details—he began by telegraphing his knowledge. Pointedly, he asked Iva if she was in good health.

Yes, she answered, except for some "nervous trouble in Lynn." She could use the telegraph, too: roughly a century before rape victims openly discussed their trauma, this was a reference to hers.

Asked why she had left employment with Nancy, she moved farther behind the curtain. There was "a little dispute," she said. Quizzed about her salary, she answered, making clear that the matter had not been related to wages.

Up to this point, only a few people in the room fully understood the discussion. But now Moulton had finished circling his nervous prey. He came in for the kill. Had Iva ever threatened Nancy? No, Iva said emphatically. But the next question took her off guard.

"Do you feel you were insulted by any person?" asked Moulton.

Not a natural liar, Iva searched the room for the district attorney, hoping for a signal.

The counsel for the defense followed her eyes. "You needn't look to anybody to know whether to answer or not," he said.

District Attorney Hurlburt strenuously objected to such "cheap utterances," and Iva, taking her oath seriously, was spared the need to answer.

But the prosecutor had a few more questions for Iva. Her little "dispute" with Nancy still hung in the air. With Moulton doing his best to taint all government witnesses with Hall's blackmail attempt, Hurlburt didn't want the jury to think Iva was here for vengeance.

He asked his witness when she'd first met Charles Hall. She answered that she'd never set eyes on him until the first day of the trial. That ruled her out as a coconspirator—provided that the jury believed her.

Putting a coda on this, Hurlburt asked what was likely meant as a rhetorical question: "Have you any unkind feeling against Mrs. Guilford?"

The defense raised an objection, but before it could be heard, a "Yes" rang out in the courtroom. Iva was telling the truth, as she had sworn to do.

Next to testify was the only male witness in this trial. Dr. Frederick W. Johnson of Boston had seen Jennie over the course of six months, first at Massachusetts General Hospital, where she initially sought help. Later she was moved to the Free Hospital for Women on Springfield Street, where Dr. Johnson was a surgeon for the outpatient department.

Jennie had already testified that the doctor had told her she'd been badly "cut up" by Nancy. Dr. Johnson's testimony presented much the same information in more technical terms.

Leaving the physician's medical testimony alone, the defense seized a question of his patient's identity. The doctor said he had registered her as Jennie Peterson, not Peters. She'd already answered questions about this disparity in her own testimony, stating that she'd been born Jennie Peters in Danvers, Massachusetts, with no middle name.

It should have been obvious that a postabortion patient, particularly an unwed one, might want to use an alias. Nonetheless, the defense seized on this tidbit, implying that use of a false name was a sure sign of criminality.

Now it was time for the defense to call its only witness. As Nancy prepared to testify, Moulton yielded to his cocounsel. After a morning of attacks on the prosecution witnesses, Moulton left the questioning of their client to George Searle of Boston.

Moulton's acid tongue wasn't needed here. "His brother Searle," as the press called him, tossed gentle questions to Mrs. Nancy Guilford—essentially prompts for her work of fiction.

Uncharacteristically, the press made no comments about Nancy's attire. Her attorney noted the hardship she'd suffered, having to prepare her defense behind bars on short notice. The same conditions applied to her toilette. This time there was no gown of watered silk. But her words and confident manner distinguished her from Jennie, the sickly charity case, and Iva of the furtive glances. Mrs. Dr. Guilford was an employer, not a servant. Above all, she was a married woman.

She didn't dispute that Jennie Peters had been her patient. She spoke of seeing Jennie five times at her Market Street office, examining her with a speculum, and treating her with a tonic and a sulphate of zinc. But, according to Nancy's account, this had nothing to do with pregnancy or abortion.

As for Jennie's time at Lewis Street, Nancy said that was strictly for cleaning. Hearing that the Halls, as employers, rode her patient too hard, Nancy had kindly offered Jennie some light weekend work. But, except for a headache, Jennie had never been sick at the Guilfords' house, and there was no operation. According to Nancy, the last time she'd seen Jennie she had a duster in her hand. Then came letters from Charles Hall with demands for money—letters that Nancy couldn't get her hands on anymore.

However, she could counter Dr. Johnson's testimony. Examining Jennie at Massachusetts General, he would have found indications of an abortion. Indeed, Nancy told the courtroom, Jennie had discussed this during her initial visit to Market Street. She said she'd terminated a pregnancy previously, and that the father of the child was the Halls' son.

It's possible that Nancy and her lawyers had hurriedly added that flourish, after hearing Margaret Hall say that her son might have helped Jennie with money. With one stroke, Nancy had absolved herself and cast shame on her accuser.

With no more questions, Searle let that zinger penetrate the jury. Now the prosecutor had the defendant all to himself. Rapier in hand, Hurlburt made the best of the opportunity.

First, he asked about those missing blackmail letters. Nancy said she'd turned them over for safekeeping to a woman named Morgan on Sea Street. Only the woman no longer lived there, nor was she named Morgan anymore—she'd married and moved, without telling Nancy her new name and address.

However, others could attest to the content of the letters, Nancy said. Her husband, brother, and Mr. Moulton had read them, as well as Mr. Averell, the man who had lured Charles Hall to the encounter with Henry. Waving these assurances away, the district attorney declared that he doubted the letters' existence.

Moulton interrupted at this point. Addressing the court at length, he indicated that Jennie Peters and the Halls were linked in a conspiracy to force money from the Guilfords. The judge pointed out to him that Jennie had already testified that she knew nothing of attempts to force the Guilfords to pay, and that she hadn't gone to the police to expose them.

The judge decided this had gone far enough. Nancy and the jurors were asked to leave the courtroom for a ten-minute recess while the lawyers continued their conference with the court.

Moulton was allowed to recite the gist of the letters. The district attorney observed how strange it was that so many letters should be missing. More important to the judge was the lack of evidence showing that Jennie Peters or Margaret Hall had any knowledge of letters written by Mr. Hall, or that they knew anything about any conspiracy against the Guilfords.

As the jury and the defendant returned, Moulton knew he had to leave the matter alone, at least for the moment. The cross-examination continued. Nancy's medical credentials came under fire, as Hurlburt grilled her on her experience and education. When she mentioned her years in Worcester, the district attorney asked if she'd departed under cover of darkness. Pretending to miss his meaning, the witness said she'd left separately from her husband but did not recall the time of day.

Regarding formal education, Nancy said she'd studied for a few months under a Dr. Scott at New York's Bellevue Hospital. She graced herself with some additional months of study at Brown Street University in Philadelphia, overseen by one Dr. Buchanan. That latter claim likely had a grain of truth. Five years earlier, a federal court had indicted John Buchanan for selling bogus medical diplomas. A former porter for a Philadelphia oilcloth store, Buchanan had issued thousands of fraudulent sheepskins, many supposedly from institutions in that city.

It took some hubris for Nancy to utter Buchanan's name in her testimony. The Philadelphian had captured national headlines, popularizing the term "diploma mill," until he committed suicide rather than face trial. In designating Brown Street University as her alma mater, Nancy may have added her own creative touch: Brown was her maiden name. There was a Brown Street in Philadelphia, but a namesake university, if it ever existed, didn't commonly appear on Buchanan's sheepskins. The fraudster typically purchased the charters of schools once real but now defunct to use for his purposes.

The prosecutor had done his best to raise doubts about Nancy's competence, but what had he really accomplished? There was no denying that she had conducted a thriving practice in Lynn for the past five years, drawing flocks of female patients. Moreover, she didn't claim to have graduated from Brown Street University or anywhere else. In the absence of state licensing requirements, she hadn't needed to claim a degree. The courses of study she named were brief enough to be believable.

Hurlburt next took aim at Nancy's domestic arrangements, asking if it was true that Henry had ever lived in Brockton under the name Dr. Ford. Proving herself worthy of her lawyers' confidence, Nancy said only that her husband lived in Lynn. As the district attorney would soon discover, any doubts she had about her marriage would not be aired in court.

Returning to medical matters, Hurlburt produced one of Nancy's newspaper ads, by now a staple in the local Lynn papers. After asking the witness to approve their authenticity, Hurlburt read the copy aloud, focusing on the phrase "diseases peculiar to women." The double meaning of "peculiar"—which could mean unique or strange—seemed to fascinate the district attorney, who would later return to it. Others less nimble with words might not have been similarly impressed: the Free Hospital for Women, where Jennie Peters was treated, used similar wording in its mission statement. Squeamishness about women's bodies reduced language to vagueness.

With fastidiousness came ignorance. Many decades would pass before feminists encouraged women to take control of their bodies by learning about them. The prevailing prudery worked to Nancy's advantage as Hurlburt produced a cash book discovered in her downtown office. Page after page listed the same diagnosis, he said accusatorially: ulceration of the womb.

Unrattled, Nancy agreed that a great many of her patients "were troubled with that." Some patients came to her for confinement, she said, others for "misplacement"—perhaps a reference to fetuses in breech position.

In tag team style, Moulton had taken over from Searle once the blackmail defense was scuttled. So confident in Nancy that he'd let her take the stand, Moulton remained quiet through most of the cross-examination. Then came the question of whether her patients were married or not. Moulton raised an objection. After his strenuous exertions to demean and vilify two single women, Jennie and Iva, he upbraided the prosecutor for "slinging mud."

The question was allowed. "Both married and single," said Nancy. She could have added, as her Market Street receptionist had already told the police, that most were married.

Converting Hurlburt's revelation into her own moment, she added, "Many babies have been born in my house, but [there was] never a miscarriage." That, of course, was the crux of the matter.

But the district attorney wasn't through with her yet. Hoping to leave the jurors imagining Satan on Lewis Street, he peppered Nancy with questions to which she gave calm answers. No, she knew nothing of infants yowling for hours on shelves in her house. Yes, she sometimes arranged to have a woman in Brighton care for babies; their mothers, of course, paid for the boarding. But she had no idea that the woman ran an establishment for foundlings.

With not a hair out of place, Nancy endured this barrage of implications, often deflecting gunfire back on its source. She was a well-spoken, middle-class woman, and the persistent questions seemed like bullying. But Hurlburt had saved his best bit for last. He asked her about her hiring and dismissal of Iva Marsh.

If she'd seemed fragile before, Nancy now took on an air of disdainful hauteur. Yes, Iva Marsh might have been at her house when Jennie Peters was there, but "I dismissed her when she accused my husband of making an indecent attack on her." Out of the courtroom when the blackmail narrative was scuttled, Nancy seemed unaware of the shift as she added, "She said she would try to injure my husband and me when she had a chance."

But Nancy told contradictory versions of Iva's departure. After stating that the girl had left swearing vengeance, she added that "first, she took back what she said about my husband." She ended by speaking of Iva's "audacity" in returning several weeks later to ask for a recommendation.

Nancy left the stand at 12:15 PM, but lunch today would be late. The government called on Iva Marsh again for a rebuttal.

And quite a rebuttal it was. Iva told the court about the heated argument between her and Henry that had prompted Nancy to summon her upstairs. She spoke of telling Nancy, despite Henry's repeated warnings, that he "had forced me to have connection with him," ultimately bringing her "into trouble." She said she'd had to seek an abortion from Nancy, who charged Iva $25 to end a pregnancy caused by Henry's assault.

A century before feminists began sharing their experiences of sexual assault, laying the groundwork for the #MeToo movement, Iva Marsh spoke these words in open court. The Boston papers that had been covering the trial, the *Globe* and the *Herald*, made no mention of this testimony, apparently finding it unsuitable to print. The only coverage that has survived was in the *Daily Evening Item*. The Lynn paper may have compelled Nancy to encrypt ads for her services, but it reported Iva's testimony in straightforward language that wouldn't be out of place today, neither ignoring nor sensationalizing it.

With the testimony concluded, the closing arguments began. Searle spoke first. Obliquely reviving the blackmail defense, he presented Jennie Peters as a moral accomplice in this case, whose testimony could not be relied on for conviction. After those brief remarks, Moulton took over.

Acknowledging the power of Iva Marsh's revelations, the lead defense lawyer tackled them first. Accusing the prosecution of trying to "blacken" his client by "displaying her husband's exploits," he didn't deny that rape had occurred but only that it didn't prove the case. It had been unfair, he continued, to force the defendant to prepare on short notice while confined to prison.

Questioning why this matter had even been brought before the jury, Moulton portrayed Nancy as the innocent victim of the district attorney's political game. Nobody had cared about Jennie Peters a year before when she first spoke to the city marshal. Then suddenly, he said, the Lynn police were put to work on this flimsy affair with the goal of "working up a feeling against the defendant" to "help out" with an unrelated complaint involving Susie Taylor. That last point, certainly a convincing one, launched Moulton into a tirade against the government's witnesses.

"No respectable persons have given testimony in this case excepting Dr. Johnson," said Moulton, pointedly singling out the only man who had been heard.

Taking misogynistic aim at the female witnesses in turn, Moulton began with "the Peters girl," doubting that in September 1884 she didn't know what was meant by an 'operation.'" As proof, he offered her resume, saying, "Certainly she could not have been so pure as she represents, for she has been traveling through the country for some five or six years working in straw shops at Framingham, shoe factories at Brockton, as a waiter [sic] in Boston restaurants, and as a domestic in many places."

Moulton went somewhat easier on Margaret Hall, respectfully calling her "Mrs. Hall" while implicating her in blackmail, conspiracy, and falsehoods. He was reserving his most potent venom for Iva Marsh. He demanded to know, "What kind of a woman must this Marsh woman be to take the stand and talk about abortions and operations as if they were everyday occurrences with her? If the county of Essex should be hunted over one could not find a person who can come and tell more deliberate falsehoods than she."

Not even deigning to return to the question of Henry's "exploits," he concluded by saying, "The Marsh woman is one of the same kind as the Peters woman and Mrs. Hall, tarred with the same brush, and how much weight can be placed on her testimony?" Having applied the finishing touches with his own tar-laden brush, he rested his case.

It was late afternoon, twenty minutes to three, when District Attorney Hurlburt began his summation. He congratulated Moulton and Searle on having managed to call all the prosecution witnesses except Dr. Johnson "blackened characters and liars, while the defendant, Mrs. Dr. Alice N. Guilford, is held up as a person of great morality, and that personified." Complimenting his counterparts on using "all the sharpness that both their brains can muster," he noted that they still hadn't "blotted out the fact that this most remarkable doctor had performed an abortion on the Peters woman."

Next, Nancy's credentials came under attack. Pretending to marvel at the "seventeen whole months of study" she'd laid claim to, he mockingly admired how she "knows all" after her purported brief stay in Philadelphia and a few months in New York. He ridiculed "the talented Dr. Guilford" for claiming she had studied at Brown Street University. "Who can say if there ever was such a college?" he asked.

Hurlburt's barbed words might have missed their target. In the wide-open world of nineteenth-century medicine, he couldn't say that Nancy had broken any laws by establishing a practice without a specific course of training. The gentlemen of the jury likely took little interest in the practitioners who attended their wives and daughters. If anything, there was a general sense that women doctors, however trained, were preferred by female patients. As patent-medicine ads aimed at women said, "It is revolting to relate your private troubles to a man."

Taking on the blackmail theory, the prosecutor walked on shaky ground. Trying to dismiss all possibility of mercenary motives, he asked, "Would this Peters woman take the stand and say she ever had an abortion performed on her if she never had such an operation performed? Would she submit to being pointed at by her acquaintances and the parading of the whole matter in the daily newspapers all over this state simply for the purpose of entering into a conspiracy?" Hurlburt's answer to his own questions: "Certainly not."

The jury may not have been so sure. Hovering over this argument was the matter of prostitution. Sex work, in the eyes of many, proved that some people would do anything for money. Moreover, the government's reference to its key witness as "the Peters woman" was a constant reminder of her social class.

Attacking the defense's portrait of Nancy as a legitimate businesswoman, Hurlburt hit his stride. Drawing heavily on one witness's testimony, he placed the Lewis Street house in one of hell's innermost circles. "What a sorrowful tale was that told by Miss Marsh, when she tells of bodies of children dead and alive, thrown about the house, one day in a commode drawer, and another alive on a shelf in a closet, and crying at that," he told the jury.

As he continued, the *Daily Evening Item* quoted him at length, apparently unaware that, despite its boldness in reporting Iva Marsh's words, it had omitted some of her most damning allegations. Perhaps inadvertently, the Lynn paper revealed them as it quoted Hurlburt's question to the jury: "What kind of a place must this house of an abortionist be, where her husband goes about committing rape on the unfortunate, and almost homeless patients in the house who have gone there for treatment by Mrs. Guilford?"

The husband's "exploits" had victimized patients as well as their nurse. But Henry wasn't on trial in the Jennie Peters case, and the prosecutor, despite his expressions of shock, expressed no desire to pursue the matter further. The husband's multiple assaults of vulnerable women merely provided color for the case against the wife.

Ignoring Nancy's many years of clinical experience, he implied that she'd "butchered" Jennie Peters for lack of a diploma. In a preview of coming attractions, he thundered, "More than this I may say she has not only taken money after abortions, but she has taken human lives at times." Never mind that the grand jury had made no such charge in this case. The Susie Taylor trial was set for the following week, and the press was listening, except when it stuffed up its ears to accounts of rape.

Charging the jurors, the judge told them to convict only if convinced beyond a reasonable doubt that "an instrument was used by the defendant on the person of the Peters woman with the intent of procuring a miscarriage." He also instructed them to focus only on the third such attempt and not the previous unsuccessful ones.

In plainer language, the judge said the jurors must satisfy themselves that Jennie Peters had been pregnant and had gone "to Mrs. Guilford to rid herself of the shame which must have followed." With this sentence, the judge swept the shelves of the infants, living and dead, that the prosecutor had conjured. There was no question of whether babies had been gotten rid of, as well as shame. The defendant was to be convicted for one felonious operation or not at all.

Having stanched Nancy's blackmail defense without eliminating it entirely, the judge addressed the question of the credibility of the prosecution's female witnesses. Either sharing the prevailing biases against working-class women or simply acknowledging that these prejudices existed, the judge began, "It must be said that the government cannot always have witnesses of the very highest respectability." But, he continued, referring to the slight disparities in the testimony given by Jennie and her married friend, "It is for you to determine whether the different stories told by Mrs. Hall and Jennie Peters are material or not." Nor did he dismiss Iva Marsh as a foul-mouthed harlot. Instead, he urged the jury to "consider the story told by the Marsh woman as to whether in the main it has been fairly and truthfully stated."

The blackmail theory was flattened beneath the bench as the judge continued, "and strictly speaking the Hall, Peters, and Marsh women are not accomplices in the same offense with Mrs. Guilford and could not be indicted," adding, for the sake of form, "but this is left for your decision."

Shortly before four o'clock, the judge sent the panel to the jury room, telling them to stay there until midnight unless a verdict was reached before then. Four hours later, with the jury still deliberating, a late edition of the *Boston Herald* ran a short item headed CONVICTION IMPROBABLE. Relying on an apparent leak from the jury room, the *Herald* reported that at 8:00 PM, the jurors stood eight to four in favor of acquittal. If the headline left any doubt, the report itself didn't, ending by declaring, "There was no hope of conviction."

Word of this spread quickly, undoubtedly reaching Nancy and her defense team. On the following morning, she sat in the dock. As the jurors filed in and took their seats, her face flushed as if the anticipation of acquittal had rouged her cheeks.

But either this report was wrong in the first place, or its premature release somehow triggered a reversal. However it came about, the jury delivered a verdict of guilty the next day. "The result is a surprise to the community," wrote the *Item* of Lynn, suggesting that the previous day's reporting was widely known and credited. Asked for an explanation, or simply volunteering one, the foreman denied that the jury at any point had leaned toward acquittal. He said the first few ballots had indeed been eight to four—but for conviction, not acquittal—with two more jurors later switching to the majority. Agreement was reached twenty minutes before midnight.

For the defendant, the face-reddening excitement was over. Nancy "took it very coolly," the *Item* wrote. Sentencing would be delayed until a higher court reviewed the many exceptions taken by her lawyers to the rulings on evidence, including questions about the instrument and Jennie's legal surname.

In Denver, a paper found these distant events worth a brief mention on its front page. It copied the Lynn paper's report verbatim, adding a coda: "The woman is notorious as a practitioner and has operated extensively in the cities and town of Eastern Massachusetts." Someone, at least, believed Nancy's puffed-up resume.

Nancy was taken back to her cell, which would have been her destination even if found not guilty. Reporting the verdict accurately this time, all the papers were mistaken about one thing. They said that the main event—the Guilford-Ames-Taylor trial, as the *Item* called it, would begin in about a week. That was not to be.

Certainly, all the parties involved thought the Susie Taylor trial was imminent. After nearly five months of imprisonment, Henry was looking forward to freedom. As he'd told the police during his arrest, he could no more be held as an accessory after the fact than could Susie's father. Perhaps for that reason, he was said to be bearing the strain of prison remarkably well.

Now, a few days after the Jennie Peters trial, another Lynn gentleman joined Henry in the Salem prison. The manufacturer Charles Ames, with whom Henry had passed a memorable day and night, was locked up in a neighboring cell. Unlike Henry, Charles had easily raised thousands of dollars to post bail. Free since New Year's Day, when both men had been arrested, Charles apparently had used that time to cultivate a new hobby.

Having consulted spirits through a Boston medium, Charles had concluded that his best course was to jump bail and flee Massachusetts. Or so said the *Item* in a report that was later partially amended. At any rate, his behavior was so erratic that his bondsman withdrew his $3,000 guaranty for Charles's appearance at the Susie Taylor trial.

That bondsman, of course, was Stephen Heald, father of Charles's wife. Another of the Heald children, Otis, was still on the Lynn police force and could have played a role in this. Charles was shadowed for some hours by a sheriff before his arrest, which was explained to him. Raising no objections, Charles went along to Salem and prison.

That was on a Saturday night. By Sunday, Charles had managed to communicate with Heald. Apparently granted special prisoner status, he may have been allowed to use the telephone. According to the *Item*'s first report on this subject, Charles had some property that he signed over to Heald, who, thus assured, posted bond again. But the father-in-law, having read that account, contacted the paper to set the story straight. He said Charles had simply clarified that it had always been his intention to appear at the trial.

It was a busy Sabbath for the jailkeepers. A court official was summoned to sign release papers. Bail was set the same as before, with the father-in-law again furnishing sureties. Charles was free again, and one of his lawyers assured the *Item* that "his client has not been mixing up with spirits."

However, Ames was communicating with the prosecutors through two mediums, William B. Gale, Esq. of Boston, and J. H. Sisk, Esq. of Lynn. It was generally understood in Lynn that Ames would turn government's witness to avoid prosecution. But there still was the question of whether his testimony would persuade a jury. He knew of his lover's pregnancy, her desperate situation, and her illness. However, if an operation had been performed, he hadn't been present to see it.

In the Jennie Peters case, the judge had cautioned the jurors that they must find that an operation had been performed beyond a reasonable doubt, depending on the evidence submitted because "human evidence is not absolutely certain." In that case, a Boston physician had examined the victim's organs and found lacerations. In contrast, the autopsy of Susie Taylor's body had revealed no signs of the use of an instrument.

As for nurse Mary McLean, she'd been put on the rack in Salem but, unlike the witch-trial victims of centuries past, she survived her ordeal. Tightening the screws hadn't loosened her tongue. District Attorney Hurlburt couldn't get anything out of her even as her bail was raised from $500 to $1,000 to $3,000.

At the Lynn hearing, Nancy had brightened at the appearance of "my Mary." In the women's quarters of the Salem prison, they might have seen more of each other. McLean was imprisoned for more than a month as a key witness until finally released. Out of loyalty, or—as subsequent events suggest—in hope of future employment, the nurse offered little to bolster the hopes of the prosecution.

Setbacks like these postponed the Susie Taylor trial to the following year. Finally, in a new session of court, the prosecution's great gaggle of witnesses reconvened, brought to Salem from Lynn, Woburn, and Burlington. Nearly nine months had passed since Nancy's conviction in the Jennie Peters case. Moulton and Searle would again face District Attorney Hurlburt. This time,

THE SALEM TRIALS | 89

Searle represented Henry, still held as an accessory despite his protests, while Moulton appeared for Nancy.

The trial was set to begin March 1, 1887. By now, Henry and Nancy had spent more than a year in prison. As Salem had become more acquainted with them, the press wasn't so sure of Henry's surname. Henry had once had an extensive practice in Salem, where, courtesy of his cooperative brother-in-law, he went by "Dr. Brown." As he languished in a Salem cell, the city's inhabitants recognized him by his former identity. The press took to calling him "Dr. Henry Guilford, known in Salem as Dr. Brown" or "Dr. Henry Guilford-Brown." The *Boston Globe* settled on "'Dr.' Guilford," bracketing the title in scare quotes.

These were the last days that Henry and his family would be known collectively as the Guilfords. The couple's delayed wedding had authenticated their lies of marriage, but only complicity and their children bound them together now. Hearing Iva Marsh's charges against Henry in private, Nancy had unleashed her rage on the victim. Now all the world knew, or at least the part of the world that believed and cared about servant girls.

And that world seemed to be expanding. If a jury could credit the likes of Iva Marsh and Jennie Peters, how much easier to believe the florists and farm families of Woburn and Burlington! There would be no more postponements of the Susie Taylor trial; a score or so of witnesses were ready to descend on Salem. And no spirits would charm Charles Ames away. It was known he'd turned government witness to secure his freedom.

On March 1, 1877—fourteen months after Susie Taylor's death—the trial was set to begin with the usual crowd of witnesses assembled. But they and the spectators saw nothing of Henry and Nancy until a few minutes past noon. Separately, husband and wife conferred with their lawyers in private rooms of the courthouse, an Italianate brick-and-brownstone structure. The law library fireplace burned beneath a magnificent Romanesque arch. But if one spouse was treated to these elegant surroundings, the other was taken elsewhere. Having decided not to risk a trial, they were to work out separate plea deals.

Although meeting privately with their clients, the defense attorneys compared notes from time to time. Even after an agreement was reached with the district attorney, the spouses and their counsels continued discussions. The government was satisfied, but something remained unsettled.

Shortly before noon, the prisoners entered the courtroom. Henry took his place in the dock, while Nancy was escorted to a small enclosure surrounding the sheriff's desk. Ames was seated slightly outside it.

After some murmured negotiations, Henry was permitted to sit closer to Nancy. There were some whispered exchanges between the two. Then Nancy was called on and pleaded guilty.

Next, the stunned spectators and witnesses learned that Henry would be freed on his own recognizance, posting a surety of $500 to ensure his appearance if ever required. Otherwise, he was to leave the Commonwealth of Massachusetts and never return. Ames, as expected, would also go free, having furnished the government with evidence.

As Nancy wept and sighed, District Attorney Hurlburt summarized the Jennie Peters and Susie Taylor cases in preparation for the judge's sentence. With every eye fixed on Nancy, the prosecutor explained that the details of the case prevented him from bearing down on her husband.

The district attorney gave no lectures on the evils, or even dangers, of abortion. The Lynn *Item* reported that Hurlburt "did what was plainly his duty," speaking briefly with "much feeling and apparent sympathy for the defendant."

Henry's attorney, Searle, spoke next. By now, it was clear that the government had made a proposition to place a portion of Nancy's liability on Henry, thus shortening her prison sentence by distributing some of it to him. According to Searle, Nancy had rejected the offer, preferring to have Henry free so he could care for the children.

As Nancy sobbed loudly behind him, Henry's lawyer told the courtroom that she'd consented to her plea "believing it to be the only remaining service she can do for the sake of her three small, homeless, houseless, and penniless children." For that, Searle said, the mother had shouldered "the whole burden and the whole punishment that now remains in connection with the Guilfords."

All around the courtroom, handkerchiefs were put to use. Even Henry was in tears, according to the *Item*. Searle concluded by recommending mercy.

Next up was Nancy's lawyer, Moulton, who reminded the court that she'd already been imprisoned for more than a year. The same attorney who'd dismissed rape as "the husband's exploits" described the spouse as a "faithful wife, a devoted mother and the sole support of her parents for several years past." Ignoring the jarring accounts of the goings-on at Lewis Street, Moulton spoke of the "reputation" that Nancy had already sacrificed.

Nancy was called to the stand to give details about her children, "scattered around the country," according to the *Item*. In fact, Eudora was still in nearby Somerville with Henry's sister, while the boys were with Nancy's family in western New York. Nancy told of her financial responsibilities toward her parents without adding that her father had recently died. She also described a heart problem, probably fictitious, from which she suffered. All this was an obvious bid for less prison time.

The judge pronounced sentence. For the Jennie Peters case, Nancy Guilford was to pay a $500 fine and serve one year in the women's reformatory at Sherborn. At the expiration of that sentence, she would serve five and one-half years more for the Susie Taylor case.

The *Item* reported that although it was "thought by some" that Nancy had wanted Henry to walk out free, actually Henry had refused the government's offer to split the sentence. The Lynn paper concluded its sentimental report on the day's proceedings with this terse remark: "No sympathy was expressed for Mr. Guilford."

Hurlburt pronounced Massachusetts satisfied. "To rid the state of such a man as Dr. Henry Guilford-Brown was considered quite a service to the community," the prosecutor said. But five states border Massachusetts, and Henry was free to roam there and beyond.

6

NEW HAVEN, HOTBED OF ABORTION

LYNN HAD CHANGED SINCE Henry and Nancy's arrest. The city's first electric streetcar was rolling down Market Street, past the site of Nancy's office. Progress was in the air, but Nancy was traveling back in time. On the same day her sentence was pronounced, she was transferred to the Massachusetts Reformatory for Women in Sherborn. Although widely praised as a forward-thinking institution, Sherborn had its deficiencies. For one thing, it was still awaiting electrification.

Prison superintendent Ellen C. Johnson placed the blame squarely on a foot-dragging contractor, who surely suffered her wrath. "Sherborn is run by Mrs. Johnson, and don't you forget it!" wrote the *Boston Globe*, bemused by an institution headed entirely by women. The prison's physician and chaplain were also female, as were the "matrons" or jail keepers.

In itself, the wiring delay was unremarkable. Sherborn kept cows and chickens to train its inmates for jobs, and other farms made do without electricity. Still, Johnson was frustrated. Maintaining control through an elaborate system of credits and demerits, she'd planned to reward model prisoners with electric lamps in their cells.

That treat would be reserved only for the most obedient prisoners, those whose credits (and lack of penalties) had ranked them at the highest of four levels. The rest were plunged into darkness after their return from evening chapel. Everyone started at Level Two—differences in the checks or plaids of the prison uniforms distinguished the levels—so they could rise or fall according to the rules.

This incentive system, introduced by one of Johnson's predecessors, was already entrenched at Sherborn when she became superintendent. But

93

her relentless promotion of the system's effectiveness linked it to her name, enshrining her as its creator while shielding her from its shortcomings.

More than nightlights were at stake. Compliant prisoners could accrue points that would shave off months from their sentences. That was particularly important for Nancy. Older and more educated than most of her 224 cellmates, she was among the small number convicted of serious felonies. Most were in for offenses against "chastity" or public order—mainly drunkenness and prostitution. Each was sentenced to at least a year, the minimum time demanded by Johnson for reforming a prisoner. But only Nancy and a handful of others faced terms exceeding five years.

Visitors to Sherborn found it a marvel of efficiency, order, and humane discipline. Cell windows in the Gothic-style buildings were covered with heavy wire mesh rather than bars. Many offered views of the cow barn, stables, and fields where, in summer, inmates learned the rudiments of dairying and farming. In all weather, they rose early to scrub the kitchen and floors under strict supervision. Evening chapel sessions and Sunday church services were compulsory. The idea was to shape alcoholics and "common nightwalkers," as rap sheets described them, into docile servants or farm maids.

Nancy, formerly a business proprietor with a house full of nurses and servants, had more in common with the prison superintendent than the other inmates. Both thrived on work. For Ellen Johnson, Sherborn filled a void left by her husband's death. Nancy had maintained a hectic schedule at least partly to crowd out thoughts of Henry's sexual abuse of other women. Both had known wealth. Nancy had worn diamonds to the police court in Lynn. Johnson was a "lady of independent means."

But these similarities apparently meant little as Nancy began her six-and-a-half-year sentence as Alice Guilford, Prisoner 3490, classified as "temperate"—unusual in an institution where many had been drinking hard since childhood. If her education and bearing earned her special privileges—and there's no way to know if they did—that was not enough to ease her misery and desperation. In her first year at Sherborn she lost so much weight and, apparently, strength that she was diagnosed with a fatal illness.

Appointed separately by the governor, the prison's superintendent and physician frequently clashed, but on one issue they were in perfect agreement. Both supported Nancy's petition for a pardon, which she submitted before completing a year of her sentence. After taking to her bed some months earlier, Nancy had persuaded the prison authorities that she was barely able to hold up her head. According to Dr. Anna Wilkin, the prison physician, death could come at any moment.

Watching this development closely, the *Daily Item* sympathetically reported that Nancy had slimmed down considerably since her transfer to Sherborn, at one point weighing only 111 pounds. That was 50 pounds less than at arrival. She was now decidedly thin.

According to the *Item*, the governor and commissioners were initially inclined to approve the petition. It wasn't unusual for a few Sherborn prisoners to win a reprieve. In the same year, a Lynn woman convicted of larceny was released early. However, her petition had the support of some of Lynn's leading citizens.

Nancy couldn't say the same. All signs pointed to her rapid release until "certain people in this city" gave "false" information about public opinion in Lynn concerning the petitioner, and the case was indefinitely suspended. Or so said the *Item*, clearly partial toward a woman who'd nurtured the newspaper for years, first with ad dollars and then sensational news items.

As her chances for pardon receded, Nancy showed some signs of recovery, which Johnson credited to her charge's "strong will and great desire to live." If Nancy's illness was an act, as is likely, she'd made a fool of the superintendent, who prided herself on hard-nosed practicality. The prisoners "come to have the nonsense taken out of them," Johnson told an overseas visitor. "To be reformed is to be made over."

Beneath its veneer of feminine domesticity—cut flowers in vases, silk-culture lessons with donated worms—Sherborn was not vastly different from other correctional institutions. A professed believer in the healing powers of nature and outdoor activity, Johnson also relied on an area of punishment rooms, known as the dungeon. Newcomers were effectively muzzled for their first four months at the institution. Although allowed to leave their cells to work, they could speak to supervisors but not to other prisoners.

Showing off the bucolic surroundings in her guided tours, Johnson omitted one point of information. She was certain that the prisoners as a whole respected her authority. Nonetheless, shortly after Nancy came to Sherborn, reports of inmate unrest appeared in the local papers. Downplaying these incidents in an annual report, Johnson blamed a small group of hardened criminals who managed to "drag others down to their own degraded level," persuading them to become unruly while avoiding detection and punishment themselves.

In fact, discipline was breaking down completely at Sherborn, resulting in a full-blown riot, said to involve every prisoner except one "woman who for three weeks has hardly been expected to live," the *Globe* reported. Given the timing—the uprising began around the time of her pardon application—that sole exception was Nancy, keeping to her bed as chaos swirled around her.

It was a good time to stay beneath a blanket. One day in February 1888, a conflict arose in the factory-like sewing room. There, unpaid prisoners produced garments for the Leominster Shirt Company. The work had to meet the high standards of matrons, who frequently rejected pieces. On this particular Friday, an uprising broke out, resulting in screams, shouts, and the hurling of furniture and objects.

Unable to regain control, the matrons sought help from the small number of men who worked part-time on the grounds. Attempting to intervene, a carpenter was surrounded by a group of women and thrown on a table, breaking two ribs and suffering other injuries. With the situation rapidly deteriorating, prison commissioners summoned from Boston asked the South Framingham authorities to step in.

Still, the fighting raged on. Frustrated in her efforts to identify the leaders of the uprising, Johnson transferred six prisoners out one day and another six the next. But, if these were the leaders, others arose in their place like Hydra heads. Led out of Sherborn, one prisoner warned that the worst was yet to come. Sure enough, the rebellion continued through a second day and part of a third until finally quelled by the state police.

The February riot ended with 175 panes of glass broken and chairs and window sashes smashed. Fifty women were put into solitary confinement. But Johnson remained in her position, still the highly visible face of the prison-reform movement.

As for the deathly sick woman—who stayed in bed while others stamped and pounded on her ceiling—she'd made it through another month without demerits. Inmates who rose to the highest level got bigger rooms, more privileges, and—more important to Nancy—the chance for early release. Exemplary prisoners could be freed to their families on a "ticket-of-leave," a forerunner of the parole system. Miserable over her separation from her children, Nancy had no reason to buck Johnson's authority. With a pardon impossible and death not imminent after all, her only recourse was to maintain the superintendent's sympathy.

That, apparently, was the route she took. It couldn't have been easy to be the warden's pet. Two more outbursts rocked Sherborn that year. A minor disruption in June was followed by a Labor Day insurrection. As the prisoners defied the female staff, perhaps shorthanded on the holiday, sounds of destruction summoned men from their outdoor tasks. Order was restored within an hour or two, but Johnson's electrical system, finally installed, suffered some damage. Wires were strewn about, along with bed clothing.

Still, neither the prison commissioners nor staff wished to see Johnson replaced. Ever eager to point out failures in the woman-run reformatory, the *Globe* was frustrated by the employees' loyalty to their female boss. Two weeks elapsed before the Boston paper even learned of the Labor Day rebellion. Getting the details was hard labor for its reporter. Nearly everyone claimed to know nothing about it.

The prison commissioners gave Johnson a vote of confidence in their annual report. Obviously referring to the three days of mayhem in February, they wrote, "The year has been marked by an outbreak at the prison, the first of the kind there. The participants in the trouble replied to all questions put them by the Commissioners and by the prison committee of the Legislature, that they had nothing to complain of, and only did it 'for fun.'"

The commissioners followed that incredible claim by stating that some "ringleaders" were sent to other prisons only because of Sherborn's limited number of solitary-imprisonment rooms. They concluded by saying, "There has been no change in the administration of the prison in any respect in consequence of this outbreak."

If there were any further rebellions during Nancy's stay at Sherborn, they must have been small. None were mentioned by the commissioners or the press. Twenty-five miles from Harvard, Sherborn was in its own way a selective institution, and Johnson could have grown more adept at ridding herself of troublemakers by transferring them to other jails.

While writing off or shipping out the Level One prisoners who rebuffed her incentives, Johnson upped the rewards for those meeting her moral standards. A proponent of temperance herself, she spent the year after the riots promoting the movement within the prison walls. Temperate inmates on Levels Three and Four were encouraged to organize self-governed temperance clubs.

By now, Nancy was on her feet, presumably restored to her usual physical proportions. A member of the temperate minority—only one-third of Sherborn's population identified as such—she might have joined in their weekly recitations and singing. After years of living on the margins of society, Nancy could have finally been a clubwoman.

She may have also had a chance to use her medical skills. Despite all the talk of progressivism and enlightenment, prison labor provided half of Sherborn's income. Most inmates toiled in the factory-like laundry and sewing rooms. However, the best behaved were placed in homes as indentured servants, trusted with a large measure of freedom. Earning this coveted status, Nancy was indentured to the superintendent herself.

Prison logs record Nancy's indenture without details of her servitude. Clearly, Dr. Wilkin could have used assistance. At least a dozen babies were born at Sherborn annually, and in some years, Wilkin included abortion among the medical complaints treated. A rare female physician for a state institution, Wilkin found her reports scrutinized—the press ridiculed her for listing "cranks" as an illness. But no one asked questions about the abortions she recorded in the same column. If not begun before incarceration, they must have been self-induced or performed by a cellmate.

Fulfilling the terms of her indenture, Nancy survived Johnson's successful campaign to have Wilkin replaced. (THEY FIGHT LIKE MEN was the bemused *Globe*'s headline.) Assisting the new doctor or otherwise helping Johnson, Nancy made steady progress toward a ticket-of-leave.

In the meantime, Henry had kept at least part of his promise to support the children in her absence. He had little to do with their everyday care and upbringing. His Somerville sister and brother-in-law remained in charge of Eudora, busy with school and piano lessons. Harry was in western New York with Nancy's brother Stephen. There, sailing was not convenient, but he may have discovered bicycling.

Herbert, Henry's older son, didn't aspire to these middle-class niceties. Like many of his Lynn forebears, but not his father or paternal grandfather, he got a job in a Massachusetts shoe factory and stuck with it.

However well cared for, the children needed money. Pleading guilty, Nancy had wept for her children, saying they were homeless and houseless. That wasn't literally true: they were with relatives as she and Henry spent fourteen months in pretrial detention. But unable to post bail and facing staggering legal fees, the couple may have contributed little to their off-spring's support.

Now, though, Nancy had taken the fall so that Henry could take care of Eudora and Harry. Others could listen to their troubles and wipe their noses, but Henry had to send cash.

That he did. Exiled from Massachusetts, Henry almost immediately found his footing in a neighboring state. His past dissolved with a simple name change. The years of experimentation with aliases came to an end. Henry M. Guilford was no more. For the rest of his life, he'd be Dr. Henry Ford Gill. (The similarly named automaker was not yet famous.)

Soon after expulsion from Salem, Dr. Gill, "the medical clairvoyant," established the Waterbury Medical Institute in one of Connecticut's major cities. In this burgeoning center of brass manufacturing and watchmaking, Henry claimed exclusive rights to something called the Combination Treatment, guaranteed to cure chronic diseases. It required the services of an electrician. For this, Henry hired a self-styled healer named Elijah A. Bond.

Like Henry's health-lift partnership, and like his marriage, this union didn't go smoothly. But it seems to have been profitable. By some estimates, two-thirds of Waterbury's adult inhabitants were factory operatives, eager to try new medical technology even if they didn't understand it. Within a year or two, Henry sold his lease to Bond and established a sole proprietorship on Waterbury's South Main Street. The partnership was dissolved.

That didn't prevent Bond from continuing to promote the so-called institute as though nothing had changed beyond the addition of hot tubs and massages. Incensed, Henry ran an open letter in a newspaper. He informed the public that, as he'd been the only physician and surgeon associated with the Waterbury Medical Institute, it couldn't exist without him. That was true, he added, even if "Bond pleases to call himself an 'Institute.'" Including his new address and hours, he signed it, "Henry Ford Gill, M.D., Graduate '67." No medical school name was given.

The former partner countered with his own announcement, confirming that the "medical clairvoyant" had only briefly assisted with clerical work. Clearly, there was no honor among Connecticut quacks, still allowed to practice freely there, as in Massachusetts. However, there was cause for Henry's defensive posture and the flaunting of his bogus degree. In many parts of the nation, opinion was moving in favor of medical licensing.

For the moment, though, Henry could offer miracle cures for all kinds of ailments. Free of his partner, he began running the cluttered ads that had launched his career in Worcester. Nearly buried under the other claims was a promise not made when he'd been working with his electrician partner: "Board and nurse for patients when required; cottage hospital system. Night calls in midwifery promptly answered."

No one needed to be clairvoyant to understand what was on offer: Henry had arranged for the nursing of patients after their abortions. "Married and single ladies can consult the Doctor in the strictest confidence," said a man who had raped an employee and patients.

A Waterbury paper introduced its new advertiser to the public, confirming the twenty-one years of experience and "first-class reputation" of Dr. Gill— never mind that no such person had existed until recently. Eventually, Bond would stop irking Henry with ads for his so-called institute. However, his copycat behavior didn't end there. Henry's former electrician also provided abortions, growing wealthy enough to buy property and carriages.

With enough business to accommodate multiple abortion providers, Connecticut was about to receive another. In May 1892 Nancy was released from prison, having served five years and two months of her six-and-one-half-year sentence. The discharge on a ticket-of-leave was supposedly conditional. For most prisoners, the leave meant that their families would take charge of the prisoner and oversee her behavior. Johnson, the Sherborn superintendent, claimed that she wasn't interested in what had brought her inmates to prison. That statement was particularly incredible in the case of Nancy, whose sensational conviction was followed by Johnson's support of her pardon. Yet, for the remaining portion of her sentence, Nancy was to be supervised by the husband banished from his native state.

Sherborn's agent for discharged prisoners usually sent them off with donated clothing and a referral to a service position, preferably in a rural area. "We are ever mindful that self-supporting work away from the city is their best protection," wrote one such agent, noting the dangers of recidivism. As Henry's wife, Nancy needed no reminders of the value of self-support. Heading straight for Connecticut, she seems to have set up shop again almost immediately.

If she ever joined Henry in Waterbury, her stay would have been brief. Shortly after Nancy's release, he interrupted his almost daily newspaper ads, resuming them several months later with a notice of address change. Before long, they stopped completely. The *Waterbury Democrat*, for years a beneficiary of his advertising largesse, later wrote that a local man, formerly living in Massachusetts, had rattled Henry by greeting him on the street as "Guilford." The man told the *Democrat* his story, but the paper decided there wasn't enough evidence to justify running it. The paper said it had looked further into Henry's credentials, learning he'd told people that his diploma, from a medical school no longer in existence, had burned in a fire.

Also learning that authorities were preparing to arrest Henry but then backed off when a former patient refused to testify, the *Democrat* ceased accepting his advertising. According to this self-aggrandizing account, printed years later in the paper, that's why Henry left Waterbury. However, after a brief quiet period, he resurfaced in nearby cities, where other papers were glad to take his money.

Meanwhile, he and Nancy were legitimized as medical practitioners, grandfathered into a state registry, notwithstanding his burned diploma. Like many other states, Connecticut instituted licensing requirements for physicians, surgeons, and midwives. As of October 1, 1893, candidates for registration had to pass exams and present proof of graduation from a recognized medical school. However, those who beat the deadline could be registered by filling out a form and paying two dollars.

Henceforth, Nancy and Henry could legitimately use the title *Dr.* and call themselves physicians—something Henry had done for years without attracting suspicion. Nancy, despite the new law, would continue to be "Mrs. Dr." or "Mrs."

Filling out their applications some months after Nancy's release, Henry gave his address in Meriden, close to Waterbury with a slightly smaller population, where he saw patients a few days a week. Nancy had tapped into a new and potentially lucrative market. She established a base in Bridgeport, a busy port and rail hub, where word of her services spread quickly. Opening an office on Broad Street, amid handsome brick homes and turreted churches, she may have also lived at that address for a time.

Nancy reunited with her son and daughter. Age sixteen when her mother left prison, Eudora attracted at least one male admirer in Bridgeport. She also attended Bible classes at the South Congregational Church. Henry, two years older, may have refreshed his sailing skills along Bridgeport's shoreline. For cycling, there were miles of city streets, some paved with cobblestones, and an expansive drive with ocean views at Seaside Park.

Sherborn's gingham uniforms and thick white stockings receded into the past. Rapidly building a robust practice, Nancy restored her wardrobe to its former glory. Her jewelry chest was replenished, and she and Eudora were beautifully gowned.

Meanwhile, Henry made a grand entrance into the hotly competitive New Haven market. His office at 548 Chapel Street was on elegant Wooster Square, a short walk from the ivy-covered Georgian buildings of Yale. Beyond the bucolic campus were a busy harbor; a rail terminal; the L. Candee and Company Rubber Works; Winchester Repeating Arms Company; and other industries employing hundreds. With nearly ninety thousand inhabitants, New Haven was the largest city in the state.

It was also a "hotbed of abortion," according to a member of the board of health. He used the phrase to describe a house on 45 Stevens Street where young women "three months or so along" regularly slipped from sight for several days, reappearing in pale and weak condition before leaving.

The Stevens Street house, formally Vaughan's Maternity Hospital, was roughly equivalent to Henry and Nancy's former lying-in hospital. However, the proprietor, Gertrude Vaughan, made no claims to being a doctor or nurse. As the ads for the Stevens Street house assured, patients could bring their own physicians. No longer living with Nancy, Henry was one of three men dependent on Vaughan for postabortion care. Another was his old nemesis from Waterbury, Dr. Elijah A. Bond.

Since his days of electromagnetic cures, the sandy-haired Bond had done well for himself. Like Henry, he had an office in the heart of New Haven. Bond's was on Orange Street, a less picturesque setting than Henry's Wooster Square location, but closer to Yale. And like Henry, as well as Nancy, Bond beat the cut-off date for medical licensing and was grandfathered in. Abortion might remain illegal, but at least three who practiced it were now bona fide doctors.

Gertrude Vaughan had something equally valuable: a city license to operate a maternity hospital. Eventually, Vaughan would open a new facility near Yale—indeed, in the backyard of one of its secret societies—and her license would ignite moral outrage and dominate the headlines. But that was several years off, after police-corruption scandals had rocked New Haven and forced the firing of top officials in law enforcement. At the time Henry opened his Chapel

Street doors, the neighbors on Stevens Street constantly complained about the havoc at Mrs. Vaughan's place at no. 45. However, it was a less-than-fashionable area southwest of Yale and the New Haven Green, and the police—soon to be exposed for willful inefficiency—did nothing.

Henry and Nancy had withstood similar hostility in Lynn, but the charges against Gertrude Vaughan went even further. She was operating a brothel. Neighbors were regularly awakened at night by drunken men looking for her premises. Well-known among New Haven businessmen as a house of prostitution, it also drew customers from distant points.

Vaughan was said to have initiated women into sex work after their abortions. In Massachusetts, Marsh had accused Henry of rape and Nancy of complicity and cruelty. Jennie Peters spoke of working out her abortion fee by housecleaning. If Lewis Street had doubled as a brothel, no one mentioned that.

Like Nancy, Vaughan was said to be connected with infant-kidnapping operations, or baby farms. The neighbors even suspected her of infanticide, saying she'd left her house carrying an infant in a basket, returning emptyhanded shortly before the body of a dead baby was found at a nearby beach. Vaughan was also rumored to have buried an infant in the Stevens Street backyard.

However, while in its off-the-beaten-track location, the hospital-cum-brothel was mostly left alone. That remained true even as New Haven's deputy coroner, Walter Pond, resigned after "strong evidence" indicated he'd been "intimate with Mrs. Gertrude Vaughan." New Haven's Law and Order League, a vigilante group led by a prominent minister, forced some corrupt officials from office—including police commissioners engaged in protection rackets—but it didn't sweep clean. The city was divided on moral issues. Not everyone agreed with the league's president, Rev. Dr. Newman Smyth, that gambling, Sunday drinking, and extramarital sex were pathways to hell.

As for abortion, New Haven's pragmatic view of the procedure had been obvious for a decade. Dr. Ernest LeRoy Thomson, a physician with a medical degree from Yale, was tried for performing an abortion on a woman who ultimately didn't testify against him. Although not convicted, Thomson was expelled from the New Haven Medical Association because of words said in his defense. In a statement reported in papers across the country, Thomson's lawyer said,

> There is scarcely a father in Connecticut whose moral sense is so strong, whose rectitude is so invulnerable, that if his daughter, a

daughter well connected in society, were to fall as the unfortunate girl in this case fell—there is scarcely a father, I repeat, who would not apply to a physician to help her out of her difficulty and save her from lifelong shame.

Unfazed, Ernest Thomson was still at his craft when Henry set up shop in New Haven. There seemed to be enough business for three abortion providers. However, Henry began suspecting Bond of poaching his customers—stealing away patients who had sought out Henry, perhaps for an initial consultation. And who might be abetting this but Mrs. Vaughan?

Henry needed a female spy to confirm his suspicions. The assignment fell to one of the nurses, or "attendants," he employed. Pretending to be a few months into a pregnancy she wanted to terminate, the employee called on Gertrude Vaughan, seeking a referral. She said she was told not to have "anything to do with Dr. Gill; he is no good," while Dr. Thomson was "too high-priced," but Dr. Bond is "all right."

There is no way to know if the warnings against Henry were related to his history of sexually assaulting patients. On at least one occasion, Vaughan had called the police about aggressive male customers. For whatever reason, she and Bond had a harmonious working relationship that survived the law-enforcement shakeups of 1894. Two years after the reformers claimed victory, New Haven still held its title as "a focal center for the crime of abortion."

Although based in Bridgeport, where the children lived, Nancy also had a bite of this apple. Two years after her release, she was summoned to New Haven on a house call. Only twenty miles separated the two cities, and Nancy's house was within walking distance of the Bridgeport train station. By now commonplace, electric streetcars could take her to her final destination.

On this occasion, she was headed to 23 Whiting Street in what was then a northern portion of New Haven, now part of Hamden. The house was a modest frame affair, but its occupant could cover Nancy's fee. A porter for a downtown store, James H. Egan was a middle-aged widower who'd gotten his housekeeper pregnant.

As was often the case, "housekeeper" didn't capture the scope of the relationship between Egan and Annie Reynolds, about twenty years his junior. He'd employed her in that role a year earlier after the death of his wife. Judging by the need for Nancy's services, an affair soon ensued. For Reynolds, the relationship had the element of romance, or at least the promise of financial security.

Although disappointed that Egan insisted on the abortion, Reynolds went through with it. There were complications: a sister said she had rushed from Hartford to Reynolds's bedside, having been told the situation was grave. Months later, Reynolds went to Bridgeport to see Nancy at her office there. But these sufferings didn't end Reynolds's life or any hopes she had of being the second Mrs. Egan.

That dream ended suddenly one winter day as Egan kicked his ex-lover onto the street. Turning to friends for support and solace, she recounted the story of the abortion. They encouraged her to explore legal ways to teach Egan a lesson.

Taking that advice, Reynolds brought her tale of woe to the office of city attorney Charles B. Matthewman, who proved an enthusiastic audience. Her only aim was to settle scores with Egan. But in 1896 New Haven, where the Law and Order League was still on alert, the prosecutor had bigger fish to fry. Although based in Bridgeport, Nancy A. Guilford had performed an illegal operation in New Haven, and that's where the case would be heard.

Neither law enforcers nor the public were yet aware that the Bridgeport midwife was married to Dr. Henry Gill of Chapel Street, who for years had been targeting "ladies suffering from any difficulty" in ads in the *New Haven Evening Leader*, offering "board and care if desired"—that is, if Gertrude Vaughan didn't steer them away.

The arrest came as a complete surprise to Nancy. In early March 1896, a New Haven police detective visited Nancy's Bridgeport residence in the evening when the children would have been home. The New Haven police superintendent, wanting her in his jurisdiction, had prohibited her from posting bail until morning. However, she was allowed to consult with her lawyer, Jacob Klein, before the detective took her away.

Arriving at New Haven police headquarters at ten o'clock in the evening, she was divested of her jewelry. Four diamond rings, a pearl ring, a watch, and a pocketbook were entrusted to the desk sergeant. Asked the usual question about her property, Nancy assessed its value as $1,000. This startling figure, about $30,000 today, was entered on the police record. A matron took charge of Nancy, and she spent the night in the lockup.

Egan was arrested at his workplace early the next morning. Instantly notified of Nancy's arrest, probably by the children, Henry had sprung into action.

Egan, a humble working man, found himself in good legal hands. Isaac Wolfe, a prominent New Haven lawyer, represented the porter in city court. Attorney Klein, up from Bridgeport, appeared for Nancy.

The day was off to a busy start. Hearing of the arrest, the publisher of the *Waterbury Globe* placed a lien on Nancy's jewelry, saying that she owed him forty dollars for unpaid ads. Her lawyer challenged the legality of the move but ultimately advised her just to pay the bill.

She would have had no difficulty settling her account. Harry had arrived at the lockup with $1,500 in cash to bail her out. But Henry, without revealing that he and Nancy were married, had already secured her release by pledging his surety. Free on bond, Nancy pocketed the cash brought by her son.

Appearing in city court that morning, both Nancy and Egan were charged with committing an unlawful practice. Klein asked for a continuance of a week, arguing that the arrest came as a complete surprise to his client, who denied knowing Miss Reynolds. Nancy, he said, was "well and favorably known in Bridgeport," where she had a large practice and "moves in the best society." He added, "She is a regular licensed practitioner, being a graduate of the Woman's Medical College of Philadelphia." In Massachusetts, Nancy dared only to say she'd had a "course of study" at a med school. Connecticut had emboldened her. Klein had doubtlessly consulted her application for the state registry. His client had been less than totally forthcoming with her lawyer.

Henry, too, grew bold—indeed, reckless. Reporters were curious to know why Dr. Gill of New Haven had posted bond for Bridgeport's woman doctor. Pretending to be nothing more than a supportive colleague, Henry practically invited further investigation.

"I have known Dr. Guilford by reputation for several years," said Henry, adding that she had a "large practice in Bridgeport among the most respectable people there. She is a lady, and not an impostor, in any sense of the term, and is justly entitled to fair treatment and any courtesy that would be given a regular practitioner in the case."

With those unnecessary words—no one was accusing Nancy of being an impostor—Henry was sending her a valentine or, at very least, an olive branch. Perhaps fed up with Mrs. Vaughan's professional sabotage, he was ready to join forces with Nancy again.

Egan left the courtroom a free man. Bail was posted for him, as well. People of means wanted this workingman on their side.

Henry's paean to Nancy was, as intended, widely distributed through the press. In Massachusetts, it reached one very interested reader. This was Wilmont D. Nelson, the former Woburn police chief who had doggedly involved himself in the Guilford-Taylor case, ordering an exhumation. After lamenting the "lethargy" in Lynn, Nelson had returned there to become its deputy marshal.

Still, he was not too busy to travel to New Haven. There, he told the authorities that Dr. Nancy Alice Guilford was the wife of "Dr. Gill." His job done, Nelson returned to Lynn. Nancy had to post bail again, this time using a professional bondsman. Even her lawyer, Klein, hadn't known the two were married.

While another continuance pushed the case off, the *Waterbury Democrat* chortled over the revelations. A report headed DR. GILL'S SECRET OUT informed readers that the *Democrat* had long been wise to Henry's marriage to Nancy Alice Guilford, as well as his assumed name, his questionable credentials, and the charges made against him in Massachusetts.

The case against Nancy was nearly forgotten as the county health officer took a close look at Henry's state registration. When registering, he'd signed his name as Henry F. Gill and attested to his 1867 graduation from Geneva Medical College, which by then had merged into Syracuse University. The health officer told the press that he'd investigate whether Henry had violated the state registration statute. Later, it was reported that a graduation record had been found for Henry under his original name, Henry Guilford. Most likely, the county health officer thought it best to drop the matter.

In the end, Henry benefited from the scrutiny. Thanks to his gender and his talent for duplicity, he was generally believed to hold a medical degree. From this point on, the state of Connecticut and respected medical journals would accept him as a physician. Henry had come a long way since posing as a doctor at his father's health-lift gyms.

While the press pursued the diploma flap, the case against Nancy quietly evaporated. Facing the prospect of mounting the witness stand, Annie Reynolds grew hesitant. Housed in a women's shelter run by a charity, she was a "mental and physical wreck," friends supposedly said, although newspapers often described women that way. Threats or bribes could have changed her mind. A New Haven man, Frank P. Carr, was arrested for witness tampering, having allegedly encouraged Reynolds not to testify. Carr might have known Egan, her former lover and employer. Both men worked as porters.

Having lost control of her quest for simple justice, Reynolds failed to appear in court. His key witness gone, the city attorney dropped charges against Egan and Carr for lack of evidence. With the social reformers watching, disposal of the charge against Nancy wasn't so simple. Washing his hands of the case, the city attorney bound it over to superior court, where nothing more was heard of it. The lethargy in New Haven, as he might call it, disappointed Massachusetts law enforcer Wilmont Nelson—a real-life version of Victor Hugo's obsessed Inspector Javert.

Their marriage now out in the open, Nancy and Henry reunited. Henry bought a three-story Italianate home at 9 Wooster Place. With its slate mansard roof and wrought-iron balconies, it is still a showplace. Riding high, quite literally, the couple kept carriages and horses. Joined by Eudora and Harry, when he wasn't crewing on yachts, the couple shared the prestige address. Feeling no need to lay low, Henry festooned the house with banners promoting William McKinley's presidential campaign, earning compliments from a newspaper.

The lying-in hospital at 9 Wooster Place, New Haven, Connecticut, as it appears today. *Marcia Biederman*

This spacious, high-ceilinged structure was Nancy's new lying-in hospital. But Henry didn't give up his office in the nearby Chapel Street building, which he also owned. Now he could refer patients to Nancy's facility without fear they'd be steered to some other doctor. The spouses had again forged a partnership, albeit with escape routes: Henry didn't cut his ties to Mrs. Vaughan and perhaps other boardinghouse proprietors.

Their uneasy alliance didn't suffer from too much togetherness. Nancy may have moved from Bridgeport, but she kept up her robust practice there. Renting first-floor space in a residential building at 51 Gilbert Street, she converted it into a medical office. There she saw her Bridgeport patients on Mondays, Wednesdays, and Fridays. She spent the other two weekdays and Saturdays in New Haven, when Henry was at his branch office in Meriden. Covering New Haven in rotation, while also serving other markets, each maintained some independence.

Henry might be listed as the owner, but people called the stately brick home at 9 Wooster Place "Nancy Guilford's house"—she was no longer Alice—and its purpose was no secret. Newspapers in New Haven and elsewhere regularly ran her ads. Fathers and lovers of women who'd gone missing knew where to look for them.

Indeed, just a year after her New Haven arrest, Nancy's name was back in the papers. A Meriden man told police he believed his girlfriend was inside the Wooster Place house. He claimed that she'd spoken of her intention to seek Dr. Guilford's services. Nancy denied knowing anything about it, and the matter fizzled out.

If the neighbors didn't like it, they didn't voice their concerns loudly enough to be heard by the Law and Order League. Temperate and unassociated with prostitution, Nancy became part of the city's social fabric. The bulletin of the New Haven Public Library ran her ad next to one for the May B. Lyon School of Stenography. Addressing herself to "ladies suffering from any difficulty," Nancy promised them the "most skillful and scientific treatment known to modern surgery and medicine."

She could not, however, guarantee her patients bodily safety. Unlike Gertrude Vaughan, she didn't have men knocking on her door all night or caressing women in her yard. But Henry was on the premises, and if she hadn't believed what Iva Marsh had said of him, she was about to learn through experience.

Not long after the couple had resumed their partnership, Nancy felt a desperate need for advice about Henry. In late afternoon on a Saturday in July, when Nancy worked until noon in New Haven, she sent Eudora on a fantastic errand.

Although it was the weekend, Charles S. Hamilton was still at his office in the Yale building on Chapel near State Street, not far from Wooster Place. There, a woman called on him, a total stranger "young, beautiful and handsomely gowned," as he told police later. She said her mother needed to see him at their home on an urgent matter.

Ushered into the house, he was introduced to Nancy, who spoke to him "of her troubles." The two were deep in conversation, when Henry suddenly appeared at the door, flushed with rage. As told by a Hartford paper, the "aged" Dr. Gill—Henry was fifty-seven—began demanding that the lawyer leave his house immediately, and "as the physician's anger grew his language became more forcible."

Accordingly, Mr. Hamilton left the premises. However, he was joined on the sidewalk by Nancy and Eudora. The three were engaged in dialogue when a shout raised their eyes to a second-story window. Henry had a double-barreled shotgun trained on the lawyer and "with wild words, he threatened to shoot Mr. Hamilton if the latter did not instantly take to his heels."

Not doubting Henry, Hamilton ran to the nearest police station to report the incident. Seeing the lawyer's extreme agitation, police thought that Henry might still pose a danger to others. A patrol wagon was dispatched immediately, only to find things all quiet at 9 Wooster Place. No arrests were made.

Reported as a "serious row" or "domestic quarrel," the event quickly receded from the headlines. More than two decades would pass before women had the vote. Husbands had the right to control their wives. Because no shots were fired, one newspaper concluded that Henry's "prudence" was stronger than his temper. The business in which the couple was engaged didn't rate a mention. Henry's use of an alias was forgotten: Nancy was said to "practice medicine under her maiden name, Guilford," when she'd been born Nancy Brown.

To the press, it was a domestic dispute like any other except for the fashionable setting and the lovely daughter in an expensive gown. The image of a shotgun appearing at a window of this gracious home was almost comical.

In the couple's history, however, this was an emblematic moment, underscoring Henry's need to isolate Nancy from the mainstream. Like other criminal families, they were amply staffed with lawyers. Since leaving Massachusetts, they'd more than tripled their fees for abortions, partly because of inflation but also to pay attorneys like Klein and Wolfe. But in reaching beyond the defense bar to consult Hamilton on a personal matter, Nancy had broken the rules.

Well-known in New Haven, Hamilton was an experienced seaman and the owner of several yachts. Nancy's son, Harry, could have met him at the New Haven Yacht Club, where the lawyer was an active member. Because Hamilton's criminal practice was not extensive, it can be assumed that Nancy wished to consult him about a divorce.

As always in such cases, Eudora and Harry found themselves in an uncomfortable situation. Forced to form an alliance, the children seem to have sided with their mother—with Harry, perhaps, referring Nancy to the lawyer, while Eudora agreed to bear the secret message. More physically attractive than Harry, Eudora experienced both the costs and benefits of beauty. Stuck at home with warring parents, she increasingly attracted public attention.

Always busy with work, Nancy often packed Eudora off to western New York for extended stays with relatives. After the long absence caused by her imprisonment, this may have seemed neglectful, but it was also protective. There were no familial comforts at 9 Wooster Place, just a flourishing business. At any rate, even if Nancy wasn't much of a mother—as people said then, and still say, of women with careers—she had the deep devotion of her children.

Eudora Guilford. *Bridgeport Herald*

Another child would come into Henry's life—a sixteen-year-old patient named Emma Taylor. Like Susie Taylor of Massachusetts, for whose death Nancy went to prison, this Taylor was the daughter of a farmer. But twelve years had passed, and times had changed. Connecticut's farmer Taylor decided not to help cover up his daughter's abortion. Instead, he raised hell about it.

William Henry Taylor sensed something wrong when his daughter Emma avoided him during one of her visits. Employed as a domestic in Cheshire, not far from home, the teenager soon gave her parents more cause for worry, skipping one of her biweekly visits entirely. Conferring with Emma's employer, the father deduced that his daughter was pregnant. Although he initially suspected her boss of being responsible, he soon realized his mistake.

Teaming up as amateur detectives, the father and employer immediately assumed that Emma had gone to get an abortion. The procedure was so commonplace that any reasonable adult or adolescent would have reached that conclusion. The only mystery was the location. Taylor solved this by riffling through the *Meriden Daily Journal,* where Henry regularly advertised himself as the "Old Reliable Specialist" providing "board and care" in complete confidence for "ladies suffering from any difficulty."

The ad listed the hours of Henry's Meriden branch office, also giving his office address in New Haven with detailed directions on how to get there by streetcar from the train station. Evidently, William Taylor heeded that advice, soon arriving at Henry's office on Chapel Street.

Henry told the anxious father that Emma was being cared for at his home. By this, he meant the house on Wooster Place, a short walk from Henry's office. Nancy admitted Taylor to the house and allowed him to see Emma for fifteen minutes. He returned the next day with his wife, finding no improvement. Henry appeared and took the father aside.

Still using the same playbook as a decade ago, Henry advised Taylor to take his sick daughter away. She might never recover, he said, and, for the sake of privacy, it would be best to take her home. The father had learned that a Cheshire youth named Clifford Johnson had impregnated Emma and was paying her medical bills. Henry advised keeping Johnson "out of the way."

However, Emma wasn't dead yet. Moreover, something didn't smell right. The father feared he could be charged as an accessory to a crime. Returning to the area around his home, north of New Haven, the father sought the advice of a local judge. Alarm bells sounded. Before visiting his daughter again the next day, the farmer had a conversation with the New Haven coroner, Eli Mix, who listened intently. Then, as instructed, the Taylor parents went to Wooster Place as if willing to take their daughter away.

After a brief visit with Emma, they were asked to wait in Nancy's parlor. Details of the move had to be worked out. Henry was willing to lend a carriage and team to the farmer, who had none, but there was also talk of a livery rental. In the meantime, Coroner Mix arrived, with the city medical examiner and another physician.

A survivor of New Haven's police scandals, Mix was untouched by bribery and corruption. He would remain at his post for decades, famed for his detective skills. He'd had his reasons for asking the Taylors to play along with Henry's ruse. When Henry told Mix there was no sick young lady in the house, Mix beckoned to the parents seated in the parlor. Henry pantomimed a "keep quiet" gesture in William Taylor's direction, which the father ignored. As the parents led the way to their daughter's room, Henry told Mix he'd been guarding his patient's privacy.

Emma was examined. The city officials had brought in Dr. Francis Bacon, a Yale-educated surgeon and member of a distinguished New Haven family. Bacon would later testify at a public hearing that private lying-in hospitals were unnecessary. According to Bacon, the area's city hospitals regularly offered maternity care to unmarried women, whether using their real names or not. He added that there "was no refusal to accept cases where abortion had been committed." But, he neglected to add, those cases would be reported to the police.

The officials left, and an ambulance was sent to take Emma to New Haven Hospital. Twice, Henry sent it back to the hospital empty. Finally, Mix reappeared, and the patient was transported. Henry said he'd only been concerned with her welfare; in fact, he could have been vamping for time, hoping she'd die in the interim.

Soon after, both Nancy and Henry were arrested and charged with criminal malpractice. Police had also arrested the man in the case, Clifford Johnson of Cheshire, Connecticut, charging him with procuring a criminal operation. It would have been difficult for Johnson to deny having had a sexual relationship with Emma. Improving daily at New Haven Hospital, she was expected to testify.

The warring spouses, Nancy and Henry, were released on bail. Scheduled to be tried separately before the same jury, both were in it up to their necks. Henry had twice met jointly with Johnson and Emma, once in Meriden and subsequently in New Haven, to arrange the payment. Then Nancy had provided the bed and performed the surgery.

Henry's trial came first. His usual defense lawyers, Klein and Wolfe, were working in tandem. But there was little they could do for him. Johnson, Emma's nineteen-year-old former lover, testified first. As had been widely predicted, he turned state's witness in exchange for having his charges dropped. Amazingly, the two teens had managed to come up with the amount required: $100, almost $3,600 today. Like his sexual partner, Johnson had been born to a farming family. He would spend much of his life working in factories.

Even that staggering bill wouldn't have changed his life as much as marrying or becoming a parent against his will. Whether he now thought of Henry as a devil or a savior, the youth was forced to testify against him.

Next up was Emma Taylor. Recovered but still pale, she accepted the judge's offer to sit in a morris chair. Her story was of an unwanted pregnancy that advanced far into the second trimester, making abortion more dangerous, because she couldn't end it earlier. Discovering she was "in trouble" months earlier, she'd taken pills to no avail before finding Henry and arranging her stay in New Haven. She spoke of occupying a bed at Wooster Place for two days while under sedation (likely because laminaria or other material had been inserted into her cervix to dilate it, easing access to the uterus). Then, she said, Nancy operated.

Although this was Henry's trial, Nancy was put on the stand. Whether she had a choice in the matter is unclear. It was a strange turn of events, particularly with the same jury set to hear her case afterward. After answering a few gentle questions in the direct examination, Nancy underwent intense grilling from the state's attorney.

At the defense's request, the judge reminded Nancy that she didn't need to answer anything that would "incriminate or disgrace her." That did little to deter State's Attorney William H. Williams, an aggressive prosecutor known as the "terror of evil doers." Having grilled her about her conduct in the Emma Taylor case, he asked about her Massachusetts conviction. When Nancy refused to answer, the prosecutor produced records of her imprisonment and was allowed to present them to the jury.

As the barrage continued with probing medical questions, Nancy resorted to sabotage. She cried loudly and exhibited other signs of an emotional breakdown until the questions ended.

The jury returned a guilty verdict, and Henry was sentenced to three years and three months at the state prison in Wethersfield. The sentence was stiff, considering that Dr. Elijah Bond, Henry's old partner, had just started serving a similar prison term, even though he had been convicted for an abortion that led to death. As Henry waited to be transported to the state penitentiary, Isaac Wolfe, his lawyer, sued him for unpaid legal fees.

The *Waterbury Democrat* crowed that Henry, long their faithful advertiser, had finally "met his Waterloo." No longer claiming sole credit for having driven Henry out of Waterbury, the paper now attributed the victory to ministers in its city, whom it never before had mentioned. The spirit of reform sweeping Connecticut cities had a religious bent.

In New Haven, Rev. Smyth of Center Church was shaking up the city again. Still president of the Law and Order League, he'd found new allies among the Yale faculty. Gertrude Vaughan had moved her operations to stylish Prospect Hill, neighboring three Yale professors, some former judges, and the headquarters of an elite Yale secret society.

Homeowners petitioned the Board of Health to investigate her license. In the summer following Henry's trial, New Haven would be transfixed by a day of hearings on the matter. Physicians would testify about their suspicions of abortion amid the resurrection of old complaints about caressing and nudity at the facility's former Stevens Street location.

Portraying herself as a legitimate hospital administrator, Vaughan was among those testifying. Needling the good Reverend Smyth, both she and her lawyer studiously mispronounced his surname as "Smith," ignoring his more aristocratic use of the long-*I* vowel sound. It was also revealed that Vaughan had named two illegitimate children born under her roof for the clergyman, writing "Newman Smyth" as their first and middle names on birth documents. Her lawyer compared Smyth to the Puritan clergyman Cotton Mather, declaring that Gertrude Vaughan's "persecution" was "the most outrageous and dastardly since the burning of the witches."

In this atmosphere, Nancy's trial was set to begin. Williams, the prosecutor who'd driven her to tears, had a long line of witnesses ready to appear. However, when the defendant was called, no one responded. Isaac Wolfe informed the court that his client was missing and believed to be in New York State.

Her bond of $1,500 was forfeited. NANCY GUILFORD SKIPPED, announced the excited *Waterbury Democrat*. The reaction in New Haven was more pragmatic:

Williams, the state's attorney, attached the property of Conrad Weis, who had posted bond for her. Presumably a professional at these matters, Weis's next step could have been to bring Nancy back, hiring a bounty hunter if necessary.

Instead, she followed the advice of her lawyers and paid the bondsman the full amount. Coming on the heels of Wolfe's lawsuit, this was a devastating blow to the family finances. However, the attorneys apparently believed that the state's attorney might quietly drop the case once the bond was settled. Nancy even hoped that some portion of the bond might be returned to her. But no refund came, and Henry was convinced that the lawyers had purposely lied to her.

In an antisemitic screed penned on prison letterhead, Henry lumped together Wolfe and Klein, who maintained separate practices in different cities. Using their first names, he wrote of "these dreadful Jews—Isaac and Jacob," calling them "arch traitors" for raising Nancy's expectations. There had been no such promises from the state, Henry asserted, and she'd been deceived in an attempt to "draw more money."

Between his spates of hatred, Henry was full of solicitude for Nancy. Addressing his letter to Eudora and instructing her to share it with her fugitive mother, Henry claimed that his one comfort was that Nancy was still free. He wrote, "Your poor, broken-down mother could not stand the discipline and accommodations of this place a month, and nothing would kill me quicker than to learn that such a calamity had befallen her."

No one acquainted with the author of those lines would have imagined him brandishing a shotgun before his wife and daughter. The two seemed to have reconciled, although Henry's sincerity is hard to assess. All prison mail was reviewed by the authorities—criticizing Williams, the state's attorney, Henry cautiously wrote his name as "W—s." A prisoner with a stable marriage might qualify more easily for early release. Also, the letter would be read by his "Dodie," who would want to think that her parents loved each other.

In an unmistakably affectionate tone, he advised his daughter to sell every-thing in the house "that your mother does not wish to keep," not neglecting the back rooms and stable. Recommending a New Haven auctioneer, he wrote, "There is nothing too small or insignificant but will bring something. . . . Some-one must see to this with energy, for your mother cannot."

But Nancy, it should be remembered, had survived more than five years of prison. Although financially pinched and claiming to feel ill, she had a busy summer. Henry's condemnation of "W—s" for the "heartless zeal" of his "prosecution, now become persecution" turned out to be unfounded. By paying the full bond, she'd bought her freedom. As she stayed with relatives in western New York, no one went after her.

Eudora and Harry closed up the New Haven house, storing what would not be sold. In early August their mother returned to Onset Bay in Massachusetts. Her two adult children likely joined her there, as the three shared a deep love for the Cape Cod area. They had a special guest that summer, as Nancy and Eudora took charge of eight-year-old Willie Guilford, a child of Henry's son Herbert. Over the years, Nancy had maintained a close relationship with her stepson and his family.

By the middle of August, Nancy no longer considered herself a fugitive. All rugs and furniture still in New Haven were moved to Bridgeport. She'd rented all the rooms above her medical office at 51 Gilbert Street, a capacious brownstone building.

Nancy could resume her busy practice, no longer confined to three ground-floor rooms. This would be her third lying-in hospital. Patients could stay upstairs. As long as she stayed away from New Haven, nobody cared.

7 | ROAD TRIP

EMMA GILL—HER REAL SURNAME, not an alias like Henry's—had known Harry Oxley her entire life. They'd both grown up in Southington, where everyone knew Oxley's variety store on Center Street, founded by the father of its young manager. In addition to selling candy and notions, it was the town's principal newsstand, stationer, and ice cream parlor. And the handsome young man who ran it became the source of Emma's troubles.

They might have met each other in primary school, but from there their paths diverged. Managing his parents' store since adolescence, Oxley had been groomed for entrepreneurship. His brother Alfred, a pharmacist, would eventually become a prominent local businessman. Once, their British-born father had been a factory worker. Now Harry had spending money and impressive friends, including the son of a former Connecticut state legislator. He was also a bit of a rake, never without a magnolia in his buttonhole and often cultivating friendships with bartenders.

Like Harry's parents, Emma's mother and father had emigrated from England. However, they hadn't enjoyed the Oxleys' good fortune. Her father was one of hundreds employed by the Southington Cutlery Company, and her mother was unwell. Emma was one of eight siblings, born somewhere in the middle. She had older sisters who also worked in the cutlery plant and little brothers who affectionately teased her about the mole on her neck and her prominent nose. The family was close, but several members lived elsewhere for work. Emma, in service for a Southington household, didn't travel in Harry Oxley's social circles.

However, she was close friends with Lillian Katzung, who cleaned for the Oxleys. Calling on Lillian, Emma became a frequent visitor to the house

119

near the Oxley store, where Harry, twenty-six, lived with his parents and a sister. The young master of the house, it was generally agreed, was remarkably good-looking. Dark-haired and of medium height and slender build, he was clean-shaven or, as some put it, beardless.

Emma and Oxley had known each other since childhood, at least by sight. Now, however, there were opportunities to be alone, and they quickly grew intimate. Between February and June 1898, they had sex eight or ten times, though where these encounters occurred is unclear. Young boys were employed to run messages between the couple. It's possible that the encounters happened at the Oxley home when the rest of the family was out. No one would have questioned Emma's visits to the house; she was best friends with Lillian.

Judging from his later behavior, Oxley didn't view this as a lasting relationship. Nor did Emma. Sex aside, she didn't tell family members about a new romance. Nor did she break off with another man who thought she planned to marry him. Walter C. Foster of Hartford had been seeing Emma for more than a year. He considered himself engaged to her, and her family had the same impression. A sales agent for Fleischmann & Company, makers of yeast, Foster was often on the road, but Emma continued to write him and see him throughout her involvement with Oxley.

There is no way of knowing what the secret affair meant to Emma or if she willingly participated in the sex. It could have been from pressure but just as possibly for pleasure. Foster, her professed fiancé, was dependable but twelve years her senior. His parents were both deaf—"deaf-mutes," as they were called. When younger, they'd been institutionalized in the Hartford Asylum, eventually becoming self-supporting and raising hearing children. One daughter, indeed, had done well for herself, marrying into the industrial aristocracy of Connecticut's Tolland County. In similar up-from-poverty spirit, Walt Foster had stuck to his sales route for over a year, never taking a day of vacation. That couldn't have been much fun for Emma.

Oxley said he knew nothing of this fiancé when he began his affair with Emma. However, he was soon enlightened. In late June 1898, Emma told Oxley that she thought she might be pregnant, and if so, only by him. Oxley claimed to have learned of her engagement at this time, but he didn't seem to question that he, not Foster, was responsible. Racing against the clock, he and Emma embarked on a joint project.

The young couple sought confirmation—and a solution, if necessary—from someone unknown to their families. The timing was unfortunate. Southington was just a few miles from Meriden, where Dr. Henry F. Gill's branch office was an established fixture in the healthcare underground. But the *Meriden Daily Journal* no longer carried his ads declaring FEMALE COMPLAINTS A SPECIALTY. Henry was behind bars in Wethersfield State Prison.

Instead, they went to a Dr. Callaghan of Waterbury. This was doubtlessly P. J. Callaghan, who would later face charges for practicing medicine without a license. Callaghan did seem to have a degree from an Alabama medical school, but he failed the Connecticut licensing exam when given an extra chance to take it. In turn, he sued the state licensing board for making the test unfairly difficult.

When the young couple consulted him, Callaghan's troubles with the health authorities had not yet begun. He later said he'd met with Oxley twice, and Emma once, charging four dollars for a consultation that had nothing to do with abortion. Whether or not that was true, the trip to Waterbury cost plenty in money and time.

They arrived separately, Oxley in a carriage, and Emma later by train. Oxley put her up in a hotel while he spoke to Callaghan about the situation. Leaving things in the doctor's hands, he went back to Southington, where his absence at the store would have been noted. Returning to Waterbury, Oxley was surprised to learn that the doctor had conducted his examination of Emma in her hotel room. Apparently, they left with only a referral and a bill. Charged each time he met with the doctor, Oxley undoubtedly paid more than four dollars.

There were also unforeseen expenses. In Waterbury, Oxley offered Emma a carriage ride back to Southington. But, perhaps wanting to take some control of the situation, she insisted on extending her hotel stay by several days.

Waterbury's commercial center, Exchange Place, boasted shops and a coffeehouse that Southington couldn't match. Living out, Emma was no longer expected at home. Perhaps because it was summer, her employer didn't demand her constant presence. Her boss, James Pratt, had the vague impression that their servant took some days off. He let his wife deal with that.

Oxley, who had a tighter work schedule, had a companion on one of his trips to Waterbury. He had taken a close friend, Howard Guernsey, into his confidence. The son of Sherman Guernsey—a businessman and former state assemblyman—Howard was Oxley's age but already a husband and father. He advised his friend to marry Emma.

That suggestion was flatly rejected. Emma wanted to marry Walt Foster, her longtime beau. Or so Oxley told Guernsey and others, obviously to cast himself in the best possible light. If Emma Gill wrote about her feelings on the matter, those writings haven't survived. But the self-serving statement is hard to credit. Marriage to Oxley would have elevated Emma's social status. What's more, it would have eliminated the need to hunt for an abortion.

Believing his friend, or choosing to believe him, Howard Guernsey ceased persuading him to marry. Instead, young Guernsey—a pharmacist, like his father—continued to aid Oxley as events unfolded.

The action shifted to New Haven, abandoned by Henry and Nancy. Prospect Hill and the Law and Order League were smug with victory. Gertrude Vaughan's license to operate a maternity hospital had been revoked. It was now early August. Emma and Oxley checked into the Globe Hotel, near the New Haven train station. It was not a romantic setting for what might have been their first full night together. In the era before air conditioning, the room must have been stifling. It was a basic travelers' hotel, briefly famous when a guest died by suicide in one of its rooms.

As their cash reserves drained and Emma's pregnancy progressed, she moved to a boardinghouse at New Haven's Lighthouse Point. Once there, she exchanged letters with her family, who thought she was visiting friends. Alone, Oxley met with Dr. Ernest Thomson of New Haven. But the Yale-trained physician had always been expensive, and now he was out of reach.

Having barely survived an abortion charge fifteen years earlier, Thomson was in hot water again. The doctor had been pressured to testify during the community flap about Gertrude Vaughan's hospital. A lawyer, previously believed by Thomson to be his friend, revealed that the doctor had spoken to him privately about performing abortions. The doctor denied everything, and the hearing was about the hospital, not him. Nevertheless, a new cloud attached to Thomson, the rare abortion provider with solid medical training.

This was no time for Thomson to test the limits of his charmed life. In 1883 he'd been expelled from the city's medical association for using the everybody-does-it defense in his abortion trial. He'd also escaped investigation for the sudden death of a key witness in that case—a Black cook, whom he'd attended in her last days. But luck could run out.

Thomson examined Emma and met with Oxley three times, possibly trying to arrange financing that would cover legal risks. If so, the negotiations failed. Oxley, with a depleted wallet, and Emma, with dashed hopes, returned to the train station that evening. The only thing they'd gotten from the Yale-educated doctor was a referral.

Continuing on their southern journey, their next stop was Bridgeport. Arriving at around 8:00 PM, they asked a boy for directions to Gilbert Street. Their short walk from the train station would have taken them down Water Street, past a junkyard and an engraving plant. A night watchman kept guard at the sprawling Wm. M. Terry wholesale grain company, where they would have turned left onto Gilbert.

One of Bridgeport's architectural treasures awaited them at the next corner—the Barnum Institute of Science and History. A fantastical mixture of terra cotta, tile, vaulted barrel, and spire, it housed many of the curiosities discovered by Bridgeport's former mayor, P. T. Barnum of circus fame. Luminaries gave lectures in its auditorium, and an observation deck offered bird's-eye city views.

Oxley and Emma were here for a different Bridgeport attraction. The Barnum Museum still stands in Bridgeport, undergoing renovation, while Gilbert Street disappeared in the construction of a bank plaza. In the summer of 1898, though, a few steps past the museum took the Southington visitors to 51 Gilbert. For years, it had been Nancy's office. Now it was also her hospital and home.

Nancy, still technically a fugitive from the law, had just returned from out of state. The young pair would have met with her on the parlor level, where her medical office was as she'd left it. Upstairs, she was busy outfitting the family living quarters and patient beds. Workmen were installing shades in the rear windows, where the patient rooms looked out on a courtyard shared with a tenement building. There were two such structures on the block, cramming multiple families into tight quarters.

Oxley's conversation with the doctor was brief. Nancy had increased her fee by half, charging $150 per abortion. Henry had left bills behind. Settling with the lawyers and bondsman had cost Nancy dearly. Oxley was told in no uncertain terms that the full amount must be prepaid before surgery. The only alternative was to arrange something cheaper at a New York City boardinghouse, with which Nancy claimed a connection.

That suggested alternative could have been a bluff. Having built a large Connecticut practice, Nancy had little time or need to branch into New York, and the press never found any signs of her there. More likely, this was a wake-up call to a man astounded by her prices. He could pay $150 to this neat, well-dressed New England woman. Or he could get a discount in a filthy back alley of a teeming metropolis.

The only big city with which Harry Oxley was familiar was Boston. He had a friend there who might be able to advance him some money. His older brother Alfred roomed there with their married sister and her family. Although not yet the pharmacist and commercial landlord he'd become, Alfred was already a pharmaceutical salesman and might set up the younger Oxley with some temporary work. The sister and brother-in-law weren't well off but could possibly contribute something.

As an experienced financial counselor, Nancy approved of this plan. Eager to make the 9:00 PM train to Boston, Oxley turned over the entire contents of his pockets to Nancy. Accepting this amount, $65, Nancy agreed to "keep the girl" in his absence. Realizing he'd have nothing left for the train ticket and travel expenses, the youth asked for $10 back. Nancy gave him that amount with no argument.

Leaving Emma at Nancy's, Oxley raced back to the station, arriving as his train was pulling out. For the next one, he had to hang around past midnight, arriving in Boston early the next morning. He immediately met with disappointment: the monied friend was out of town. But Oxley's relatives welcomed him to their house on Yarmouth Street in Back Bay, then a relatively new neighborhood built on landfill.

If Oxley had expected his older brother to be a soft touch, he was sadly disappointed. If there was a man-to-man talk—which is likely, considering that Oxley had planned to return from Boston with money—it didn't produce the desired result. Alfred Oxley had some work for his younger brother, but it couldn't have paid much. There was no money to send to Nancy.

He wired her with an update, writing, "Friend is away. Let me know what you have done." He seemed to be hoping she'd relent about insisting on the whole fee in advance. Her reply told him she was serious. "Nothing, under the circumstances," she wrote, adding, "Don't telegraph, but write."

A young man in a hurry, Oxley found a way around that rule. He enlisted the aid of his sister's husband, with whom he was close. Frederick Durham was a skilled industrial worker, employed by a foundry to create molds for metal parts. Admitted to Oxley's widening circle of male confidantes, Durham composed a message in his own hand and sent it from a telegraph office. Without sending a wire himself, Oxley wanted it known in Bridgeport that he'd arrive in the early morning.

Ringing the doorbell on Gilbert Street, Oxley found Nancy at home but Emma gone. Nancy said she'd examined the girl, finding that surgery was possible, but had done nothing more. Disgusted with the obstacles, Oxley declared himself glad that Emma was back in Southington. He also seemed interested in those less expensive boardinghouses Nancy had mentioned. But, still in possession of his down payment, and sensing his sincerity, Nancy persuaded him to stick with the plan.

Oxley returned to Southington, where he and Emma avoided one another. It was a small town where tongues wagged, and everyone knew one another—or thought they did. Indeed, Emma's parents often shopped at Oxley's store. But, not knowing of her pregnancy and her quest to end it, they were also unaware of a more recent development. Returning from Bridgeport to the house where she was a servant, she'd packed up most of her clothes and left.

She was still in Southington, in a holding pattern, while Oxley did his fundraising. Later, Mr. and Mrs. Pratt, her employers, would say she had voluntarily terminated her employment, which is improbable. More likely, she'd been fired for her frequent absences, which they claimed to have barely noticed, or because she was becoming visibly pregnant.

If the Pratts had shown her the door, Emma must have been ashamed to share that news with her friend Lillian Katzung, the Oxleys' servant. She told Lillian that Mrs. Pratt had given her another week off because she was sick. As close as the two friends were, Emma may never have disclosed her pregnancy to Lillian. As a man, Oxley could unburden himself to his friend and male relatives. Fearing harsh judgment—or hesitant to involve others in her predicament—Emma seems to have stayed silent. Only Oxley shared her secret.

Their relationship at this point eludes easy definition. Despite the shared hotel room in New Haven—probably just a cost-saving measure—they were no longer lovers. Confiding in other men, Oxley invaded Emma's privacy and, given the era's moral standards, doubtlessly degraded her in their eyes. Certainly, he was pressing her to undergo illegal and risky surgery. Still, if she had wanted to force him into a loveless marriage, she might have appealed to his parents, although that would have provoked emotional scenes that they had so far avoided. Instead, she continued her engagement to the traveling salesman, Walt Foster.

If nothing else, Emma and Oxley were trusting coconspirators, each pursuing the same goal, although Emma's reported declaration to Oxley—that she wanted "to have it all over"—indicates fear and hesitation. The two regularly exchanged letters from Boston, Bridgeport, Southington, and even the Waterbury hotel where Emma stayed for a few days. Living at home, Oxley suspected his parents of growing curious about his changing moods and frequent absences. Because he was afraid they might snoop around his room, he gave Emma's letters to his friend, Howard Guernsey, for safekeeping. For some reason, Oxley didn't destroy them immediately.

It would be presumptuous, however, to assume that Oxley kept them out of sentimentality. It's possible that the former lovers didn't trust one another entirely. Oxley could have feared retaliation from Emma at some future time—perhaps after she married Foster—and wanted to keep the letters as evidence. Or the letters could have contained updates on Emma's communication with Nancy that he wished to archive. Apparently, it wasn't unusual then to ask friends to safeguard personal papers. Years before in Massachusetts, Nancy said she'd done the same with letters attempting to blackmail her.

If Emma's employers had noticed her condition, the man who planned to marry her had not. Walt Foster had seen his fiancée in Hartford shortly before her journey to New Haven and Bridgeport. Still off on his sales route, he unwittingly figured into Emma's abortion plans. She told her best friend, Lillian, she'd be spending the last days of summer in Stratford, just east of Bridgeport, at the invitation of "her fellow's sister."

People close to Emma knew Walt Foster as "her fellow," but they knew little about his origins. A resident of Hartford, he was from South Coventry, a different village in a different pocket of Connecticut. He didn't have a sister in Stratford, but Lillian wouldn't have known that.

Emma's cover story was ready, but there was also the matter of Dr. Guilford's busy schedule. Emma found an unsigned letter from Bridgeport awaiting her at the Southington post office, where villagers called for their mail. It said, "If you get this do not come down until Monday. I am busy with my work here. You know what that means. Destroy every line you receive."

Like Oxley, who had circumvented the telegraphing rule, Emma ignored that last sentence. She kept the letter. Nancy's availability on the Monday before

Labor Day was no use to her. Her former lover was still hunting for funds. Although aching for it to be over, Emma still had to wait.

On the Monday that Nancy had cleared for Emma's surgery, money finally materialized from Boston. With the down payment and the money he'd given Emma, this would bring the total payments to $85, and Oxley could promise another ten within a week or so. He thought that would be sufficient to set things in motion.

Wanting Nancy to receive the twenty-dollar bill as soon as possible, Oxley sent it by overnight delivery. The Adams Express Company, a rapid-delivery service, had offices at train stations. To evade prying eyes in Southington, Oxley went a mile south to the Adams Express office at the next stop on the line. The cash and note went into an Adams Express money envelope. A clerk sealed it with wax and stamped it PLANTSVILLE, for the location of the office.

Unemployed, Emma had been staying at the home of Lillian's parents. It must have been a noisy place; Lillian's father worked for the railroad, and their home was near the station. Emma had arranged to meet there with her sister, Clara, who was coming up from New Haven. But the night was dark and rainy, and when Clara tried to find Lillian's house, she walked in the

Emma Gill. *Courtesy of the Bridgeport History Center, Bridgeport Public Library*

wrong direction. Her welcome party waited for her in vain. Emma was angry, thinking that her sister hadn't come. If she'd finally steeled herself to share the secret of her intended abortion, the opportunity was lost.

The next morning at Lillian's, Emma grabbed some underwear and stuffed it in a bag. It was Friday, the start of the Labor Day weekend, and her mother was sick. She was going to stay at her parents' house overnight and then head for Bridgeport.

"Can I have a glass of water?" she asked Lillian, as she left. "I am so dry all the time." Thirst is common in pregnancy, but Lillian didn't seem to make the connection.

Most of her siblings were at her parents' house for the start of the holiday weekend, visiting their ailing mother. Clara was there; having given up on finding Lillian's house, she'd gone to the family homestead. But even if Emma had wanted to unburden herself, there were too many people around. However, she did manage to conceal Nancy's letter in her old bedroom.

To her siblings and parents, she told the same lie she'd told Lillian. She'd be spending Labor Day weekend and a few days more with Walt's fictitious relative. They were to write her in care of J. Jones at General Delivery, Stratford. Any mail that arrived for her in Southington could be forwarded there. It never occurred to Emma that Walt might write while she was away. He was the one person who couldn't possibly buy her story.

Leaving that end untied, Emma left for Bridgeport on the morning of September 3, the Saturday before Labor Day. Having invented a vacation, which would logically start on a holiday, it was best to be on her way. She had the twenty dollars Oxley had given her and assumed he would send more.

Emma arrived at a house that was ready for business. The workmen and commotion were gone, and the window shades in the rear patient rooms were not only up but nailed to the frames. The shared courtyard in the back was a challenge, but one that Nancy could meet. Adjusting the lampshades in the patient rooms, she avoided the possibility of silhouettes. The neighbors surely suspected what she was up to. In fact, one who lived a few doors away, Mrs. Austin, was a former occupant. She had overseen Nancy's conversion of the ground-floor rooms into a medical office with a fake diploma on the wall.

Mrs. Austin had once rattled around in the spacious brownstone. An observer called it a "pretentious-looking building, too large for a family of three." In truth, only mother and daughter lived there. Harry stayed in his ship's cabin most of the time, and Nancy's step-grandson, Willie, was just a visitor. Most of the rooms were intended for paying guests, and a lying-in hospital needed space for staff, including some live-ins.

Recovering from severe financial setbacks, Nancy couldn't hire a nurse. Although her wardrobe was filled with fine clothes, some people in Bridgeport said she was bankrupt. If necessary, Eudora could be her assistant. Certainly, Eudora was accustomed to seeing women in her house, pre- and post-abortion. What she lacked in formal training she made up for in trustworthiness. These were tense times for outlaw practitioners.

Still, there had to be a cleaning staff, and not just for the family rooms. Patient care of this type was messy, with absorbent cotton and gauze needed in abundance. Rubber sheeting had been moved here from the New Haven house, but some of it was nearing the end of its useful life. Nancy had to buy additional rubberized fabric. She could have gotten it at the Howland Company, a few blocks away on Main Street near Cannon Street. Shoppers could find almost anything at Howland's.

Nearby, Nancy found a mother-daughter pair for her housekeeping needs. Rose Drayton and her teenaged daughter, Clara Belle, lived at 230 Cannon. Rose took in washing. Nancy arranged to have her launder her bedding and flat pieces. The family clothing, with all its pleats, buttons, and flounces, would go to a full-service laundry elsewhere.

The employer and her new employee had something in common: narrow escapes from domestic violence. Rose's ex-husband, the father of her children, had fired his pistol twice during a dispute with her. He was tried for assault with intent to kill but acquitted when intent could not be proved. They had split up after that, and he'd left town. But now he was back in Bridgeport with a new family and his old job—he drove a delivery wagon for Howland's.

In the meantime, Rose had suffered other tragedies. Shortly after the break-up of her marriage, she left her three young children alone briefly to talk to a neighbor. When she returned, the oldest, about four years old, was dead. With their father gone, the family had no warm clothes for the cold of January. The girl had gotten too near the fireplace, and her clothes caught fire.

Whether or not Nancy knew all this, she could tell that Rose was hard up for money. Two children had survived the fire that killed their sister. One, Clara Belle, was now fourteen. Because Gilbert Street was so close to Cannon, the mother encouraged Nancy to try out Clara as a live-in servant.

Nancy agreed to put both the Draytons to work. Because they were Black, she almost certainly could pay them less than white domestic workers would accept. Born under slavery in Virginia, Rose Drayton inspired admiration for her strong, clear voice, her habit of meeting people's eyes, and her self-control. Despite the tragedies she'd suffered, she'd kept her two surviving children fed and sheltered. A son, Hannibal, was a year younger than Clara, and the Draytons shared their home with Rose's partner, William J. Philips.

Emma arrived to find a clean house, thanks to Clara, with no other patients in it. As Nancy's don't-come-till-Monday note suggested, the surgical schedule might have been cleared for her. Or it could just have been quiet. After jumping bail in New Haven, Nancy was still quietly spreading the word of her return to Bridgeport. She couldn't just stick an ad in the newspapers.

Obviously, a business of Nancy's sort revolved around biological calendars, not the ones on the wall. Still, with Emma almost certainly in her second trimester of pregnancy—she'd suspected her pregnancy in early June, and it was now early September—Nancy didn't begin the procedure immediately. Despite having told Emma that her schedule was clear, she wanted to press Oxley for that promised ten dollars.

So a few days later, Oxley called for his mail in Southington and received a letter with a Bridgeport postmark. Written in two hands, it was a short message of about ten lines. The first seven, in what Oxley recognized as Emma's handwriting—or thought he did—said she was fine but more money was needed. The last few lines were more direct: "Send me the balance of the money as I am badly in need of it," they said. There was no signature on either part of the letter, but that last sentence was unmistakably Nancy's.

An out-of-town friend, a bartender, had promised to lend him ten dollars. As soon as he could, Oxley left to see if he could get it.

Although always eager for money, Nancy could have just wanted to take the holiday off. With school due to start, Willie's visit to her was nearing its end. He was one of several children born to Henry's son, Herbert, now living with his wife and other children in Atlantic City, New Jersey. Fond of Willie, Nancy had a framed photograph of him in her bedroom. With her office closed for the weekend, as it likely was, she might have taken him for a short excursion. Bridgeport was nicknamed the Park City for its many open spaces.

For outings that included Eudora, Fred Welch would have volunteered his carriage. The son of a Bridgeport alderman, Welch was smitten with the twenty-year-old girl. Evidently aware of her mother's trade and her father's incarceration, the son of a city official didn't care about that. Everyone knew him as Eudora Guilford's admirer.

Attorney Jacob Klein had said that Nancy moved in the "best" Bridgeport society. At the very least, her daughter did. They remained open to all, however. Indeed, their new patient had arrived in a loudly checked blouse with a missing collar. After rushing off, Emma still was waiting for this ordeal to be over with.

She'd told her family to expect her back after the holiday, but that was impossible. So sometime during the long weekend, or perhaps on Tuesday morning, she went to the Stratford post office to mail a letter. It said: "Dear Mother—I can't come home today because I have been very sick with stomach trouble and sick headache. I am going to New Haven to see Dr. Cheney about my catarrh."

No letters addressed to her, in care of J. Jones, awaited her in Stratford, but she knew to expect a rapid response from her family. It couldn't have been easy to worry her mother, who was suffering from a real illness.

No further payments had come from Oxley. However, trusting that he was good for the rest, Nancy began the procedure. Her former patients had testified that surgery was preceded by a day or more of sedation, possibly while the cervix was being dilated to ease access to the uterus. If Nancy followed that pattern, working in two steps, then Emma was sedated on the same day she wrote to her mother.

A bacterial infection of the blood, septicemia, set in at some point. Banned from the patient's room, Clara Drayton watched Eudora move in and out with trays, sometimes carrying coffee, sometimes water. Alternating between chills and high fever, Emma would also have had a racing heartbeat and difficulty breathing. She may have suffered violent spasms, like constant, painful hiccups.

In Southington, Oxley knew nothing of this. After working all of Labor Day weekend, he had a few days off. He surely knew through Lillian, who cleaned his house, that Emma was gone. Still, good as his word, he stuck to his installment plan. He'd picked up ten dollars from a bartender friend. As Emma lay suffering, Oxley filled another money pouch at the Plantsville delivery office. He got a receipt back the next day, signed by Nancy.

The Adams Express driver remembered an "old lady," rather stout, who signed for the delivery. Inside the house, Emma was fighting for her life.

The receipt sent Oxley into a panic attack. If it was routine to send receipts, then where was the one for the larger payment he'd sent earlier? In his haste to send off the first envelope, had he confused the street with the surname, writing "Dr. Gilbert" instead of "Dr. Guilford"? Or, worse, had someone interfered? He dashed off a letter:

> Dear Doctor: Please write and let me know if you have received what I sent the first part of this week, $20, or not. I am all unstrung about it, as I have been away the last two days—thought my folks might have got hold of it. I will be home now for four or five days, and I will send the balance as fast as I can, which will be inside of ten days. It comes hard but can't help it.
>
> Hoping that everything is all right by now, and that you have received the last I sent you. Write right away. Yours, CARL

The code name had been suggested by Nancy. Confused on several points— he'd sent the $20 earlier than his letter indicated—Oxley seemed to think that she hadn't yet operated.

On the day that Nancy received this letter, Emma's condition was grave. In the past, when patients reached this point, she and Henry had asked the family to step in. A decade or two earlier, that had worked like a charm. Long ago in Lynn, Annie Dyer went home to her husband, dying or dead. The case fell apart when the husband declined to talk at the inquest. No one threatened prosecution of the sister who'd accompanied Annie to appointments with Nancy.

But that was long ago. The demand for abortion remained strong, and the public didn't seem to care about it, but the vocal opponents had the upper hand. Moral crusaders had all but shut down the "abortion hotbed" of New Haven, and Bridgeport could be next. What's more, Oxley could easily be forced to testify for the government. After her experience with Charles Ames, the Lynn beverage manufacturer, Nancy had no faith in her patients' lovers. Months in jail couldn't squeeze a word from her old nurse, Mary McLean—now employed by another Massachusetts abortion provider—but these men would squeal in a moment.

Nancy wrote back to tell him she'd received the money he'd asked about. And she added: "Important business. Come down at once." But he didn't come, for the first time ignoring a command from Nancy. Instead, he went through the motions of village shopkeeping, selling penny candy, serving ice cream sodas, and stocking the racks with newspapers.

Dusting furniture in Bridgeport, Clara Drayton didn't need to be told what had happened. Exactly one week after Emma's arrival, Eudora stopped carrying the useless trays of beverages up and down stairs. That meant the patient was dead.

Nancy had already decided what must be done. Emma Gill was dead, and there was nothing she could do about that. The young woman's weekslong quest to determine the course of her life was over. Her travels with Oxley—probably the only adventure in her brief life—had led to this.

It was just bad luck. Even ardent antiabortion crusaders acknowledged that fatalities were rare: an editorial in a Bridgeport newspaper read, "That only occasionally their nefarious work results fatally does not lessen their crimes." This was one of those occasional fatalities, but it couldn't have happened at a worse time for Nancy. She couldn't join Henry in jail and watch their children slide into poverty.

She had to get rid of the body. Marshaling her forces, Nancy sent Clara to fetch her mother from Cannon Street. Rose Drayton returned with her daughter. Someone needed to look after Willie, at least part of the time. That job might have been Clara's. Rose and Eudora were urgently needed for other tasks.

It was Sunday morning, so Harry Guilford wouldn't have been present until late afternoon. He crewed and cooked on the steam yacht *Ceres*, which left New Haven on Saturdays for overnight cruises. As soon as it docked, he'd be off to Bridgeport on his bicycle. Knowing the gravity of her patient's condition, Nancy might have already written her son.

She couldn't wait for him, though. In his letter from prison, Henry might have described Nancy as a "poor, broken-down" woman. But with some female assistance, she managed to move the corpse. It was pulled across a hallway, from the bedroom to the bathroom opposite, and positioned in the tub.

For hours afterward, Nancy would crouch over the body, doing what had to be done with a fine-toothed saw and blade. The others could assist her, but only she knew how to make the expert cuts. This would have been hard work on a table, never mind in a bathtub, but here there was a drain for blood and bodily fluids.

If the procedure had been patterned after an autopsy, ice would have filled the tub, with a "cooling board" laid over it to support the body. However, no one ever mentioned those amenities. Somehow, Nancy managed.

There were six cuts in all, dividing the body in seven pieces. A few harsh critics would pan the work as crude butchery, particularly the severing of the lower limbs from the torso. These may have been the first cuts made, perhaps with a nervous hand that steadied as it proceeded.

Ligatures were tied above the kneecaps to stanch bleeding, and calves and thighs became four parts. Wrapping the parts followed, a job for the less skilled, if not for the queasy. Materials were gathered from throughout the house. Muslin and absorbent cotton, pressed against skin, caught blood and body fluids. An outer layer of rubberized material guarded against drips.

By now, Harry would have arrived. With his own knife and twine, he secured the parcels tightly. With growing confidence Nancy continued her work, including the decapitation. Not bothering to cut off Emma's long auburn hair, she left it loosely braided, as it had been in the young woman's final hours.

Her subsequent work won accolades from the medical community. "Deliberation was used in cutting the body for removal," said one review, adding, "From first to last, method marked the deed." Another saw it as the work of "an expert using a keen knife and a perfect edged saw." A third swore it bore the stamp of another Bridgeport practitioner, a young man known for his surgical skill.

The shadow academies and improvised internships of unlicensed practitioners had served her well. Perhaps some credit was owed to the life-size dissecting mannequins at Dr. Abbie E. Cutter's summer courses at Onset Bay.

"Not a hurried move was made," concluded one admirer, who had to be mistaken. Even with the body in pieces, Nancy had hours of work ahead of her. Tired as she must have been, she had to work quickly. The torso was sawn at the waist. Barely touching the upper portion—arms were left attached to shoulders—she set to work on the lower. All organs except the heart, brain, and lungs were removed with, some later said, the deft technique of someone trained in the art of autopsying. The next step required no special talents, just shovels full of coal. When night fell, the basement furnace roared, fed with corsets, shoes, a loudly checked blouse, a structured purse, and human organs. Remnants of white rubber sheets and black rubber blankets also went in, along with bits of old clothing, torn and stripped. Any leftover packaging materials had to be destroyed. It was a warm September evening, but neighbors would recall that plumes of smoke rose from the chimney.

Upstairs, the bathroom was scoured with liberal use of carbolic acid. Rose went home, her work done. As proven by her vital help, she could be trusted. She even left her daughter in the house with those four ghastly white bundles, done up with string.

Nancy's work clothes had probably gone in the furnace, stained as they must have been. Before going out in the early autumn night, she removed the Oxford tie-up shoes she'd been standing in for hours. Dressed as if going on a house call, she left the house alone and walked two blocks down Broad Street to Isaac Banks's stable.

Banks knew her as someone who customarily rented his livery at odd hours. The fatigue of the day showed plainly on her face. The owner ordered his hostler to ready a rig and bring it around to Gilbert Street. To his customer he said, "Mrs. Guilford, your hair is turning quite gray."

According to his recollection, she answered, "Yes, I am getting too old to perform any more operations. I have had my day. I am done. I am absolutely through. I will never during the remainder of my life do any more of it." At least, that is Banks's reconstruction of what Nancy said. Seeing her face after her remarkable activities, he might well have talked about fatigue and ageing. But if Nancy had wished to confess to her "operations," police headquarters was just down the street.

Nancy returned to Gilbert Street and awaited the hostler. A phaeton, or four-wheeled open carriage, was brought to her, hitched to two horses and topped with a folding hood. Harry waited inside. Two parcels were taken from the house and laid in the bottom of the carriage. The others wouldn't go on this ride. If Nancy were stopped, two bundles were a reasonable load for a woman alone. Ladies often carried packages to or from places. Her son would not be riding with her.

Mounting his bicycle—or "wheel," as it was called—Harry went first, leading the way and scouting for observers. They went north on Water Street along the railroad tracks, turning right at the Stratford Avenue Bridge, a heavily trafficked iron structure. P. T. Barnum had once tested its strength by parading a dozen elephants over it. In their own weird parade, Harry on his bike and Nancy with her packets rode over the span. Reaching the more sparsely populated East End section of the city, they continued down Connecticut Avenue to a place known as the Bishop Avenue cut.

Here, near some railroad tracks, were piles of broken rock left over from street reconstruction. Pedaling from the east on his frequent trips to Bridgeport, Harry must have noticed them. Dismounting, he selected the stones best for his purpose: shaped well for tying rope around them and heavy enough to sink fast. He fastened them well; like his mother, he was good with his hands.

With the bundles weighted, it was even more vital to avoid sharp eyes and probing questions. Nancy turned her horses around. Retracing their route down Connecticut Avenue, she and Harry reached Seaview Avenue. Here, in this lightly settled area, was a long wooden bridge, which, if tested by elephants, would have failed miserably. For this errand, though, it had one unmatched strength: there were no houses within a few hundred feet of its north or south ends.

The bridge spanned a small arm—a thumb, really—of Yellow Mill Pond, which separated Bridgeport's fashionable East Side peninsula from its more remote East End. Nancy's carriage and Harry's bicycle approached it from the south, where three streets converged into a triangular vacant lot. There was a bright electric streetlight here and another at the north end, but no lights on the six-hundred-foot bridge. Cycling ahead to do reconnaissance, Harry saw no other vehicles. The phaeton rattled behind the bicycle until, closer to the north end, he signaled it to stop. Reflecting the electric light, water flowed just four feet under the bridge. This was deep enough.

The bundles hurled over the railing showed white against the dark water, but only for a second. Harry had weighted them well. Swallowed by the pond, they quickly sank six feet to the bottom. Reversing direction once again, Nancy returned to Banks's stable at eleven thirty, left the livery, and walked home alone.

She and her son had parted at the bridge. Pedaling past the quarry again, but picking up no stones this time, he returned to New Haven. He spent hours cycling around the city, hoping to be seen and, hence, establish an alibi. On Monday morning, he was at his usual post, serving breakfast at the yacht club. No one would have guessed what he'd been handling just hours before. He had a full day of work ahead of him, and then he'd bike back to Bridgeport to finish the job.

They'd go back to that same bridge, unless his mother had any objections. That deserted place worked out well.

———————

By day, the Seaview Avenue Bridge had its fair share of traffic. At four o'clock that Monday, some juvenile residents of the area were crossing it when they spied something large and white, nearly covered with water. Reaching the shore at the northern end, they started throwing rocks at it.

School wasn't back in session yet, and there wasn't much else to do. Some of the boys had spent the day swimming, and now they could have a rock-throwing contest. There were two targets, as it happened, one near the shore and one farther out. As the boys played, the water receded around these objects, exposing them completely.

That didn't surprise these children, ages nine to twelve. Almost everyone knew that Yellow Mill Pond was a tidal inlet that drained almost completely at low tide. As they took potshots at the bundles, the water around them receded further, exposing the stones tied to them like anchors. That got the boys' attention.

Johnny Jackson, twelve, waded through the muck to the nearer package and easily dislodged it. Feeling something soft inside, he thought it might be the remains of a dog. By now, he had an audience: a knot of men and boys were watching from the bridge. The boys summoned Johnny's uncle—variously described as a blacksmith or an oysterman—who fashioned a tool to bring the parcel back to the bridge.

The rest of the afternoon's events quickly unfolded. A knife cut the cords around the package, revealing a human foot. Johnny's uncle retrieved the second package. Enough of the wrappings were loosened to identify the contents as the head, with cloth stuffed inside the mouth. More detailed description was left to the medical examiner, the coroner, and the undertaker. The uncle had the good sense to leave most of the wrappings in place and send for the police. An officer was in the vicinity, and he alerted downtown headquarters.

Two men on the bridge decided not to stick around, departing from the southern end. "They didn't seem at all excited," remarked one of the boys, surprised. Or they preferred not to linger at what had now become a crime scene involving a half-dozen police officers, a detective, a police wagon, and a rowboat. Asked to describe the men who left, one boy recalled a brown coat, a derby hat, and a black mustache.

Nearly everyone in Bridgeport had become a possible suspect, it seemed. The wagon took the body parts to John Cullinan's downtown funeral parlor, which did double duty as the city morgue. There, muslin, rubber, flannel, blood and bone would undergo scrutiny to determine the provenance of the bundles, the cause of death, and possible criminality.

To those on the bridge on that early fall afternoon, there was little doubt that something heinous had taken place. As more police arrived, word got out that the head had belonged to a young woman, yet to be identified. But the trunk and arms were missing. With the tide soon to rise, a search began for the remaining body parts.

Borrowing a boat from an area resident, police armed with grappling hooks and a search light launched it in the shallow water. Scores of civilians in rubber boots joined them in the muck. Meanwhile, two men placed an improvised rope harness around twelve-year-old Willie Costello to suspend him from the bridge. Thus lowered and raised, Willie scouted for human remains.

At dusk, with the tide coming in, the police pronounced the search ended. Talk of dredging the pond was abandoned. Every square inch had been explored, yielding no discoveries except a stone weight, separated from the package that enclosed the head.

That was turned over to the police, who had already determined the origin of the sinkers. They could only be from those rock piles on Bishop Avenue, where a railroad had dug up a crossing and built a tunnel. Everybody around here knew that those gray stones with mica were from the Bishop Avenue cut, just as everybody knew about the pond tides.

Harry Guilford wasn't from around here. On that same afternoon, again cycling to Bridgeport from New Haven, he stopped to pick up bits of cobblestone. He and his mother would need sinkers again tonight. They were going to finish the job.

Less than a mile from the piles of distinctive rocks, the water was rising, and the commotion at the Seaview Avenue Bridge was subsiding. Wholly unaware, Harry returned to the Gilbert Street house. Reporters were besieging Cullinan's morgue and peppering the police with questions. Even as the news spread beyond the city limits, it broke too late for the evening editions. However, there were bulletin boards around Bridgeport where the papers posted teasers with the next day's headlines. These were drawing crowds.

An ordinary family might have heard about it from friends or neighbors. But if Nancy and her children had ever enjoyed normalcy, this was not that moment. Eudora and Nancy, together with Rose and Clara Drayton, had spent the day straightening up, scouring the tub, and scrubbing oilcloth in the bathroom. It was an exhausting day, yet someone had tended to Willie.

Nancy was debating what to do about Harry Oxley, who had ignored her mailed instructions to come down at once. A note in her house read, TELEPHONE OXLEY, but she may never have done so. Ads for Cullinan's Funeral Parlor listed the three-digit phone number of its proprietor, but home phones were unusual in Bridgeport. A long-distance call to Southington would have involved a public call box and multiple operators. Skittish about telegrams, Nancy trusted only the mail. It was best to stick to a medium that could burn in a grate.

Adhering to that motto, Nancy and her son repeated their movements of the night before. The only change was an earlier start. Leaving Harry at the house with the bundles, Nancy arrived at Banks's stables around seven o'clock and rented the same phaeton as the day before. In what was now routine, she drove back to her house, where Harry waited with the baggage and his bicycle.

This time, the stones were already attached to the parcels, so there was no need for a detour. The phaeton could go directly to Seaview Avenue and the bridge, where all was tranquil on this Monday night. The police were gone, and so were the legions of rubber-booted explorers. The search rowboat had been returned to its owner, and the boys who'd made the grisly discoveries were home eating dinner. Again, water lapped a few feet beneath the bridge, deserted except for the phaeton.

Sure of themselves this time, the mother and son went a shorter distance before halting. Harry eased one bundle over the rail. Barely able to see it below the bridge, he compensated with the heavier load, flinging it with Olympian vigor. The two bundles were swallowed by the deep—or, more accurately, the temporarily deep. Nancy pulled at the carriage reins to turn the horses around, Harry cycled on, and they were finished. The livery was returned later that evening.

At around 5:15 AM the next day, a young man named Nels P. Larson was biking over the bridge when he spied a white object on the ground below. A news dealer who owned a store on East Main Street, Larson was on his way to deliver the Tuesday morning papers. There wasn't yet a line in them about Bridgeport's big news, but Larson knew all about it. In fact, he'd been present during the search for the missing parts.

Certain of the bundle's contents, but not eager to cast suspicion on himself, he rode on and delivered his papers. Returning to the bridge at six o'clock, he was surprised to find that no one else had sounded an alarm. However, another man about the same age had appeared. Less willing to wade than the boys of the day before, they borrowed a boat and dragged the parcel on board.

The wrapping and stones were like those that had been described. Wanting to see for themselves, they opened the package in the boat, finding the torso, cut from neckline to below the ribs, with shoulders and arms intact.

Not an expert at anatomy, Larson believed the puzzle was now complete. Therefore, he was surprised to spot a second bundle directly under the bridge. This contained the lower torso.

The police came to take charge, and Larson went back to his newsstand. He'd be called to an inquest if needed. A few hours later, stacks of evening papers were left at his store, and his name was all over the pages.

Woman's Body Dismembered with Skill, cried the Bridgeport Evening Post across three columns. One of several subheadings announced, Trunk Found This Morning, Arms and Limbs Yesterday Afternoon." Larson could have corrected them about the arms, but he would have liked the description of himself as "a bright young newsdealer."

It was quite a spread, including detailed descriptions of the body. A Bridgeport illustrator had drawn a macabre sketch of the head, based on a photograph taken at the morgue, with eyes closed and mouth partly open. The New York Journal had a romanticized version. Captioned Who Knows This Woman?, it was the profile of an attractive young woman with long, dark hair and a somewhat prominent nose.

Fifty miles northeast of Bridgeport, another bright young newsdealer was taking delivery of the same papers. Harry Oxley's variety store was the main news distributor in Southington, where almost no one would recognize Emma Gill from those pictures. Oxley did, though.

8 | COMING HOME TO HER FUNERAL

INITIALLY, IT WAS THOUGHT to be murder. Much was made of the so-called gag in the mouth, cut from a bed sheet and stuffed between gold-filled teeth. One of the pictorial newspapers—the tabloids of their day—theorized that the body's dissection began before death. An indentation on the forehead suggested bashing, and strangulation was also suggested.

However, the medical examiner and coroner quickly concluded that the cause of death was blood poisoning, most likely the result of an abortion, and that death had preceded dismemberment. The wad inside the mouth was part of the wrappings. The woman was not gagged, they announced.

But if there was no delicious murder, there was still a delicious spectacle to see. All of Bridgeport was invited—nay, encouraged—to view the head fished from the pond. The police were now sure that the crime had occurred in Bridgeport, but further detective work required an identification of the victim. If she was a local woman, someone would recognize her.

Eagerly joining this civic effort, thousands of men, women, and even children, filed past the head at Cullinan's. For the photo taken the day before, it had been propped up on a table and illuminated by a flashlight. Now it lay in a bucket, submerged in embalming fluid and surrounded by flowing hair. The eyes were closed, but police described them as gray-blue.

Journalists from Milwaukee and other far-flung places had already been in the morgue, where the body parts had been fitted together on an ice-cooled plank—a cooling board, like the one Nancy could have used over her tub before throwing it in the furnace. Only a small board was needed. The dead woman's height was estimated at five foot one. Weighing about 105 pounds, she showed signs of malnourishment. Evidently, Mr. and Mrs. Pratt of Southington hadn't lavished food on their servants. The teeth, though, were apparently well maintained. A newspaper sketch of the mouth showed tiny fillings in the two top incisors, like decorative studs.

The long fingers and elegant arms were mentioned, as well as the thick hair and finely shaped eyebrows. The age was estimated, correctly, at twenty-five. The victim was young, if not quite a beauty. Official descriptions mentioned an underbite and prominent nose—sometimes cosmetically corrected to "aquiline."

While thousands lined up to see the head in the bucket, others told wild stories of what they'd witnessed the night before the torso was discovered. Carriages, they said, had galloped past the north end of the Seaview Avenue Bridge. Red wagons driven by men in slouch hats had stopped for no apparent reason. Police in Matteawan, New York, questioned a stranger carrying a suspicious instrument on the floor of his rented buggy. It turned out to be a bicycle pump.

Leaving journalists to chase those fantastical stories, Police Superintendent Eugene Birmingham assigned a more mundane task to the two detectives on his force, a police captain assisted by a special officer. They were to make a methodical survey of laundries. On some strips of fabric wound around the body parts was a mark made in indelible ink, the kind used by laundry businesses to reunite stray garments with customers. Soiled with mud and body fluids, this mark was difficult to decipher. Some newspapers reported it as C51, while others settled on G51. After the superintendent ordered the remnants washed, G51 appeared with clarity.

The Bridgeport detectives spent the rest of the day carrying ripped men's drawers around New Haven. Superintendent Birmingham had almost immediately connected the pond case to Nancy Guilford of 51 Gilbert Street in his city. But at least one flannel strip came from a large-waisted man's undergarment. The superintendent also knew that Nancy's portly husband, currently a guest of the state, had never lived in Bridgeport.

The Troy laundry in New Haven connected the mark to a former customer, Dr. Nancy Guilford. It was a large operation with steam-driven machines, contracts with local manufacturers, and a connection to the city's telephone exchange. It's unclear why Nancy would use an abbreviation of her Bridgeport address in New Haven. But she'd had offices in both cities simultaneously, and G51 could have been easy to remember.

It wasn't laundry day today at 51 Gilbert Street but rather a day for travel. By late morning, news of the Yellow Mill Pond mystery screamed from every bulletin board. Now fully aware of their botched body disposal, Nancy and Eudora were packing for a vacation.

Their departure may have seemed sudden, but their allies said it was not. Their longtime lawyer and a local pharmacist said it was long in the planning. Someone took Willie home to Atlantic City, just in time for the start of school. Rose and Clara would lose income while the house lay vacant. Nevertheless, they told all who asked that the doctor had previously scheduled her vacation.

They'd both been left with special assignments. Before leaving, Eudora had bullied Clara into killing a cat and smearing its blood on some used women's clothing. At nightfall, Clara was to leave the clothing on a riverbank far from Yellow Mill Pond. The goal was to take the spotlight off Nancy by conjuring the specter of a serial killer.

Other than traumatizing Clara, this intended distraction would have no effect. The police would find the smeared clothing, determine that the blood was an animal's, and keep the matter quiet.

Rose, meanwhile, had to deliver a message that couldn't wait until night. As she boarded a train at the Bridgeport station, she carried no envelope or slip of paper. These words couldn't be recorded anywhere. She'd have to make personal contact.

But she couldn't make direct personal contact. Getting off the train in Southington, Rose stayed close to the depot. She wouldn't venture into the village, where an unknown Black woman was bound to attract attention. Eventually she came across a boy who was willing to run an errand. Of course, he knew where to find Harry Oxley. Everyone bought candy at Oxley's on Center Street.

A young man's nightmarish day was about to worsen. After hours of selling papers trumpeting the head-in-the-pond story, Oxley was summoned to talk to a colored woman awaiting him near the railroad tracks.

Rose didn't keep him from his newspaper vending for long. "Whatever you do, keep mum," she said, not waiting for a reply. There would have been no one to give it to. Nancy was already on the move.

Mum was the word that struck terror into Oxley. He ran to Dr. Thomson in New Haven. The Yale-trained doctor assured him there was nothing to worry about. The body in the pond had absolutely nothing to do with Emma

Gill, the patient he'd referred to Nancy. Oxley need not worry. Thomson had his own way of keeping people mum.

Wanting to believe him, Oxley nonetheless took the precaution of having his friend Howard Guernsey burn all of Emma's letters.

By noon of that day, Nancy and Eudora had walked the short distance to the train station, but they needed someone to bring their baggage. Fred Welch, the alderman's son, volunteered. He was also a willing participant in Eudora's alibi for what she'd been doing on Sunday night. There was a piano on the second floor of Nancy's house, and Fred had spent the evening enchanted by her playing and singing. It couldn't have been sweeter.

Welch's father reportedly disapproved of Fred's engagement, as it was viewed: the papers said the son was Eudora's "accepted suitor." However, the popular politician didn't strenuously oppose the match. Unwittingly, the elder Welch may have helped the Guilfords get away. Alderman Welch operated a thriving food-delivery business, and his son transported the baggage in a wagon.

Before departure, Nancy had gone to her lawyers' State Street office near the county courthouse in Bridgeport. Ignoring Henry's antisemitic tirade, she still relied on Jacob B. Klein, the city's first Jewish lawyer. Klein's longtime law partner, Robert E. DeForest, a former Bridgeport mayor and state senator, was a senior warden of Trinity Episcopalian Church. Henry, a son of a self-educated minister, couldn't touch DeForest's gentile credentials. The Bridgeport lawyer was descended from the Puritan missionary John Eliot.

A journalist from the *Sun*, a respected New York paper, claimed to have been on hand as Nancy briefly visited DeForest & Klein. The reporter wrote that Nancy looked "not at all excited" as she left to see her brother in Wellsburg for what she said was a pre-arranged visit. The reporter continued:

> She said she was tired and wanted rest, but she was in a cheerful mood, and she remarked how glad she was that she had been allowed to make her home in Bridgeport again without having to answer to the old charge at New Haven. She left some legal matters for her attorneys to look after while she was gone.

This was a preemptive move. The police were bound to connect her to the laundry mark, and the papers would remind people of her New Haven bail jump. She and Klein could subtly remind the New Haven County prosecutor that she'd settled the bond. As Henry had written in his letter from prison, that was the deal.

Her lawyers might also find a way to alert Henry and Harry about possible forthcoming interest in their laundered clothing. They were the only members of the family who wore flannel drawers. Her errand done, Nancy left with Eudora for the train to New York City. There, they would get a night train on the Erie Line, arriving in Wellsburg the next morning.

The reporter on the scene said Nancy "looked motherly," adding, "She did not act like a woman who had just been cutting up another woman's body."

The prosecutor assigned to the case agreed, at least in the abstract. In a statement released the day after Nancy's departure, city prosecuting attorney V. R. C. Giddings opined that a woman, even if a physician or a midwife, couldn't have made those clean cuts. Almost admiringly, he saw the culprit as a man, nearly a colleague: "He was a person thoroughly familiar with the holding of autopsies," he said of the person who'd dismembered the body, using male pronouns.

The medical examiner present at this particular autopsy didn't necessarily agree. Dr. F. B. Downs had let slip that he thought a woman was behind this. But when reporters pressed for more, he refused to answer. Downs, who had delivered Rose Drayton's son, could have known more than law enforcers about Bridgeport women and their healthcare providers.

Releasing his statement exclusively to the sensational, hugely popular New York *World*, Giddings put out a cry for help. Speaking of the victim, he said, "A large number of people have viewed the remains." Indeed, the police had been called to Cullinan's morgue the day before when the crowd grew unmanageable. No one had recognized the woman. From this, Giddings concluded that she wasn't from Bridgeport.

He said the photograph of the head would be copied and distributed. Given the technology of the day, not many people would see it. Nevertheless, Giddings wanted the word out, or at least his name in the paper.

He made clear that the victim hadn't been slashed to death. "There is no doubt," he wrote, "that the mutilation of the body was made for the sole purpose of hiding another crime." He added, "It is also shown that the woman had been dead some time, at least an hour, before the body was cut."

He continued, "There is no doubt that a criminal operation was committed. The medical examiner, whose report has been made public, shows us as much. The condition of the vital organs proves all this." A small portion of the uterus had been left in the body cavity, and its examination had led to that conclusion.

But what did it matter? If it were up to the city prosecutor, he'd act as if the woman had been drawn and quartered. From his desk at Bridgeport city hall, Giddings opined that this was a hanging crime. The headline over the piece echoed his pronouncement: "Death resulting from the effects of a criminal operation in this state is murder."

Some of the electrical charge of the piece was lost in euphemisms. More worldly than the scandal-mongering *World*, the Lynn *Daily Item* had regularly printed the word *abortion* for years. Nonetheless, the city prosecutor's meaning was unmistakable.

In contrast to these fiery words, the coroner's inquest was a bore. Boys spoke about finding the head and legs, and the young men recounted their discovery of the trunk. They'd already told these stories to the press.

Journalists were frustrated. The laundry mark connection had yielded a spate of stories about Nancy and Henry. Their past trials and convictions, their different surnames and reputations filled miles of column inches. The sudsy tour through New Haven laundries had continued. More than one had linked G51 to Dr. Nancy Guilford.

The public clamored for a ransacking of Nancy's former dwelling. The Bridgeport police force sent its two detectives to spend the night there after her departure. They let themselves in with a key; an estate owned the building and didn't object to their entry. A photographer took pictures of the rooms, and the cops said they thoroughly searched them, finding nothing but some pieces of cord.

On the same page as the city prosecutor's statement, the *World* quoted Superintendent Birmingham as saying, "I feel confident that Mrs. Guilford had no connection with the case of the woman now at the morgue." Nancy's flight to Wellsburg with Eudora had been widely reported. Indeed, reporters were already combing the western New York village, finding that Nancy had gone into a store to cash a check for $100, drawn on New York's Astor Bank. Chats with old-timer Miles Robert, owner of the livery business near the railroad depot, spawned several how-Henry-met-Nancy features in the big-city dailies. A fascinated public was sure they knew whodunit. Only the Bridgeport police superintendent seemed unconvinced.

Hamlet-like, Birmingham kept the telegraph wires warm with vacillation. Wellsburg fell under the jurisdiction of the Elmira police department. Its chief, Frank J. Cassada, sent him a telegram asking whether the Bridgeport police were interested in the arrival of Mrs. Nancy Guilford in Wellsburg. Birmingham replied, "No." Later, however, the Bridgeport superintendent wired back, "Shadow the house." Then, in complete reversal, "We don't want the party here," followed by—just to clarify—"Woman not wanted here."

It was too late anyway. By the time the last three wires were sent, Nancy had left Wellsburg. Hours after she and Eudora had arrived at his home, her brother drove her to the train station. He said he thought she was heading back to Bridgeport on an evening train; he even named the time and the train number. However, a clerk vaguely recalled selling a ticket to a woman for Montreal. The clerk couldn't describe the woman, but there'd been four diamond rings on the fingers that grasped the ticket.

But the Bridgeport police had lost interest. Harry Guilford in New Haven and his incarcerated father were making a mockery of their soapy detective work. As the coroner's inquest resumed, Harry was tossing reporters some of his collars. All were stamped with the mark G51.

Police Superintendent Eugene Birmingham of Bridgeport.
Marcia Biederman

Thinking to ambush Harry, some reporters confronted him at the New Haven Yacht Club. He said he had just returned from a cruise of several days on the *Ceres* and knew only the broad outlines of the pond case. One journalist informed him of the interest in the laundry mark found on the underclothing.

"What is it?" Harry is said to have asked in "innocent candor."

Enlightened, Harry said, "Why, that's my mother's laundry mark. It's on all our laundry. Why here," he continued, ripping off the collar he was wearing and pointing to an area under the buttonhole. "There it is, G51."

After begging the journalists to wait, Harry went back to his ship cabin, produced two more marked collars, and gave them to his interrogators. "This is a very strange coincidence," one of the newspaper men then remarked.

"Yes, it is," said the young skipper. "You don't mean to say they suspect my mother."

"The Bridgeport police say they would not arrest her if she was in town, but then you know there has been some talk."

Quite reasonably, Harry declined to speak further without a lawyer present. More than cooperative, he let the reporters accompany him on a short

Harry Guilford. *Records of Pinkerton's National Detective Agency, courtesy of the Library of Congress*

train trip to Bridgeport, where Jacob Klein was not at his law office. Reportedly, they passed his mother's house, but Harry didn't enter it. He said he knew she'd gone to New York on a visit. Foiled, the reporters melted away.

At least one of their colleagues had trekked farther on a similar mission. Tricked by a journalist posing as a state detective, the warden of the Wethersfield State Prison located two bags of Henry's clothes in a storeroom. Once the inmates donned stripes, their street clothes were usually sent home, but with no hope of returning to his handsome New Haven residence, Henry had no address other than his cell block.

The mark G51 was stamped on three of Henry's undergarments. Claiming to be working on the case for the state, the "detective"—actually a reporter for the New York *World*—requested an interview. The warden, Col. Jabez L. Woodbridge, prided himself on strict discipline. Nevertheless, he fell for the ruse, and Henry was brought from his job in the prison hospital. At age fifty-five, his hair was mostly white, and he wore gold-rimmed glasses.

The prison roster listed him as Henry F. Gill, physician, but noted in a comments section that his alias was H. M. Guilford. Of course, that annotation was made before the recent burst of press attention. Now his past had been so thoroughly excavated that any casual reader of newspapers knew that Guilford was the real name, and Gill was the alias.

However, names didn't matter much in the Wethersfield prison, where inmates were known by numbers. That practice extended even to the institution's magazine. Declaring itself "devoted to the interests of the inmates," the *Monthly Record* encouraged prisoners to write on their slates and submit work for publication. Reports of debate meets listed team members as "No. 31, 9 and 32." Authorship of published pieces warranted initials, as well as numerals. One recently published poem, "And Ye Visited Me" by No. 197 E. S., asked God to bless prison visitors.

Henry, on the contrary, demanded to know why a state detective had come to bother him about laundry marks. He said he only knew about the body parts found in the pond from newspapers that had been sent to him.

"Down in Bridgeport, there is some talk about your wife's being mixed up in the case," said the journalist, still masquerading as a state investigator.

The chubby, sandy-haired visitor was no match for Henry, who thundered, "You don't mean to say they think my wife was mixed up in such a dastardly piece of business?"

The journalist broached the matter cautiously. "It's a case where the police are jumping at straws; but then the police deny that they are looking for your wife."

Dismissing any suspicions of Nancy as "absurd," Henry unleashed a barrage of gender-based arguments. He said his wife "wouldn't have the nerve for such business," or even to handle a knife or a saw. "She knows nothing about surgery, and this body, you say, was cut up by a skilled hand? My wife never performed an autopsy." What's more, he added, "She's been ill all summer, you know, and she and Eudora, our daughter, are up in the country for rest."

All too familiar with reporters, Henry might have suspected that one stood before him. Whether the man represented the government or the press, here was an opportunity for Henry to protest his own innocence. He seized it, declaring, "I've never committed murder and my wife has never committed murder. I should not be here now. I saved a woman's life and was sent to prison for it."

His interview concluded, the faux detective returned to the warden's office. There, he was introduced to a *Hartford Courant* reporter. Without using false pretenses, this second journalist was also seeking an interview with Henry. Still masquerading, the "detective" advised the warden that Henry was too tired to be bothered by something as trivial as newspaper interviews. Then he left to wire his story to New York.

Despite those machinations, the laundry mark was fading into the category of coincidence. By discussing it openly, the father and son had deflated its impact, and even Superintendent Birmingham called it a "blind clue."

Meanwhile, Nancy's teenaged servant had convinced the police that life at the doctor's house had been boringly routine in the days before Nancy's departure. Questioned at her Cannon Street home, Clara Drayton said she'd slept at 51 Gilbert all the past week—on the same floor as the family—and hadn't seen a sick woman. On Sunday night, the presumed time of the body disposal, Clara had stayed up till 10:00 PM, and the doctor had been there too. Workmen had come nearly every day, and a few lady patients were seen in the parlor. Otherwise, it had all been very humdrum.

It was a convincing performance. Milk bottles left on the stoop indicated that no one had informed the delivery man of Nancy's supposedly long-planned trip. That could have been an oversight, however.

The Bridgeport police were "at sea," as one headline phrased it. The coroner resumed his inquest, calling on an East End man who said he'd seen bundles in a rubber-tired carriage driven by a mysterious man. Meanwhile, several "prominent physicians" had examined the remains and concluded there'd been no abortion after all, and that the viscera had been removed to conceal poisoning. That theory didn't gain traction with the press. Towering sketches of Nancy dominated the pages of the pictorials, and readers were treated to minute details of her personal and legal history.

The police, though, were wavering. "We have absolutely nothing," Detective George H. Arnold told an Elmira paper, "except that the woman was probably murdered."

The detective seemed to forget the message from the prosecutor, by now rolled onto miles of newsprint: abortion *was* murder in Connecticut. Apparently, the cops didn't truly think of it that way. On one point, though, all parties agreed. There could be no resolution to this case until the victim was positively identified.

False identifications had abounded from the start. From towns near Bridgeport and beyond, people swore that the description of the dead woman tallied with a woman of their acquaintance. After the first chaotic day of public viewing at the morgue, the police restricted admittance to those quite sure of making a credible identification. Still, people came, swearing they knew who it was, and some people telephoned. Mostly they used the mail. The Bridgeport police got more than three hundred letters about missing women who could have been seeking an illegal abortion.

As the public then saw it, virtually any woman of childbearing age could have been a candidate—married or single, rich or poor, troubled or free-spirited. Among those named was Bertha Mellish, a daughter of an Episcopal clergyman, who'd gone missing from Mount Holyoke College in Massachusetts. Other possibilities on that social rung included Nellie Loughery, the daughter of a West Haven artist, and a debutante-turned-waitress named Mary Craddock or Cradford, determined to support herself after a dispute with her parents.

There was also Mrs. John Collins, wife of a mechanic who said she'd been missing for several days. The brother of a member of the governor's staff phoned to say it might be a woman he'd met at a Bridgeport boarding house. A woman doctor who visited the morgue identified the head as that of a nurse, Mamie Rourke, who turned out to be alive and well.

Most false leads came from neighbors or landlords. Fewer people were willing to tell the police that a wife, sister, or daughter had sought to end a pregnancy. The new morgue rules required visitors to give their names and reasons for coming. Nevertheless, Isaac Ogden of Seaview Avenue came to check if the remains were those of his missing daughter. Seeing that they weren't, he left.

On Thursday night, another father was admitted to the morgue. Frank W. Perkins of Middleborough, Massachusetts, had read a description of the dead woman in the Bridgeport case and was frantic with worry. One of his seven children, Marion Grace, had been missing for about three weeks. She had been keeping company with a young man, another resident of the town, whose whereabouts were also unclear.

Perkins was asked if there had been anything wrong with his daughter. He said his wife was afraid there was. A railroad engineer, Perkins had limited time and money for his own travel. Some marks described on the dead woman's head corresponded to those of his daughter. Tooth fillings were also described, both the gold ones on the front teeth and others on the molars. For these details, Perkins had borrowed his daughter's chart from the family dentist and telephoned Bridgeport to check for similarities. There was also a telephonic discussion of the condition of the feet.

Arriving at Cullinan's funeral parlor that evening, Perkins regarded the face in the bucket. Certain that he recognized it as his daughter's, he spent an hour in the morgue, sobbing. Leaving a request for the body to be sent home for burial, the father returned to Massachusetts.

Coroner Charles A. Doten was incensed to learn that he hadn't been consulted before the man left Bridgeport. Telling the morgue not to touch the remains without his permission, Doten asked Perkins to come back to Bridgeport. A special session of the inquest was arranged for the next day, Saturday. The coroner wouldn't release a death certificate unless the man swore an affidavit before him. It was a trip of more than 150 miles, but the father said he'd be there shortly after noon.

A small group went to the station to meet Perkins, who was accompanied by a nephew. Cullinan, the undertaker, hooked arms with the grieving father and guided him to the county courthouse. About a dozen officials, all male, were seated around a table for the inquest. Perkins had brought a framed photograph of his daughter, Marion Grace Perkins, known as Grace.

Birmingham, the police superintendent, was present and immediately noted discrepancies. The framed image was of a twenty-year-old woman with a high, broad forehead, not at all like that of the dead woman. The nose was smaller, and there were also differences in the chin and forehead.

Taking the witness chair, Frank Perkins said the pock mark above the dead woman's eye was exactly where Grace had one. The indentation in the head was, he said, the result of an accident with a curling iron.

Perkins had viewed only the head, not the rest of the body. The coroner didn't ask about the alleged foot similarities that the father and the morgue keeper had discussed by telephone. Apparently, the feet found in the pond had corns on every toe, not an unusual consequence of tight women's shoes. The morgue employee, however, thought this a sure sign of a correct identification. However, Doten was more interested in the dental portion of the phone conversation.

Perkins was asked if he'd brought Grace's dental chart, but it was back at the dentist's office. Lacking that, the coroner had to rely on the morgue keeper's memory of the phone call.

Cullinan ticked off several points of similarity, but then he faltered, not sure of the location of a "soft" or composite filling.

Continuing his questioning of Frank Perkins, the coroner was surprised to hear the father say that the general appearance of the face in the morgue, the nose and the mouth, did "not resemble her."

Confirming that his meaning was clear, Doten repeated, "No, not resemble her?"

Perkins replied, "Do not."

The coroner continued, "Are you positive these are the remains of your daughter, Marion Grace?"

Half rising in his chair, the father said, "I am, I am willing to take my— pledge, my life, it was her." The railroad engineer punctuated his declaration with a powerful bang on the table.

Perkins was shown the photograph taken at the morgue soon after the body parts were found. He was asked if he could identify that as a photo of his daughter.

The answer was affirmative, with Perkins insisting that he saw "looks across her forehead and on her cheekbone and down the side of her eyes," that resembled her.

To give the mistaken father his due, the severed head by now was beyond recognition. Time and embalming fluid had taken their toll. The features had been pulled out of proportion, and wrinkles had appeared where there were none before. The starkly illuminated photograph wouldn't have been of much help either. As copied in drawings, it was a death's head resembling no living person.

Doten asked the medical examiner to fill out a death certificate for Marion Grace Perkins. Her father would be permitted to take the body home that day. There was only one small condition. The coroner asked Perkins to have a doctor present when the coffin arrived in Middleborough, to make sure of the identification. The father promised he would. Not dwelling on this crucial point, the coroner took the man at his word.

Lasting less than half an hour, the inquest ended in a foregone conclusion. When the father and nephew returned to the station, the coffin was already there. After initially ordering that no one touch the body, the coroner had reversed himself, allowing the undertakers to start their work even while Perkins was answering questions.

It was only afternoon, but Perkins didn't expect to be home until late that evening. Sealed into a zinc-lined coffin and enclosed in an oak box, the head and body parts would ride in the front baggage car. After a change of trains in Providence, the journey would proceed to Taunton, Massachusetts. A hearse would meet the train to take the casket over ground for the last twenty miles.

Waiting for the train in Bridgeport, Perkins spoke of his daughter Grace, who had failed to come home after going three weeks before to Onset Bay. He said that Charles Bourne, who frequently called on Grace, had also been in that area. Perkins was asked if he knew about the possible links between this case and Dr. Nancy Guilford, who had spent some of her summer in Onset. The father had been told of that in Bridgeport but had nothing to say about it.

However, he did speak highly of his daughter's suitor. Charley Bourne was "an honest man" and "from a good family," said Perkins, before boarding the train.

The wires were already clacking. With Bridgeport's mysterious head finally attached to a name, the press tarnished Bourne's "good family" with scandal. As the father took the slow train, a narrative took shape. A rich boy had run off with the daughter of a working man, and death and mutilation had followed. Newspaper illustrators were soon creating contrasting sketches of the sprawling Bourne "mansion," with its many wings and onion dome, and the "humble" Perkins "cottage."

A story filed from Middleborough for the *Baltimore Sun* offered details of the couple's relationship and absence. An heir to a considerable estate left by his father, Charley Bourne had openly courted Grace Perkins, who worked at a bakery. The association of two such socially disparate families was "somewhat of an anomaly," the report said, and tongues wagged. However, the "aristocratic" Bournes had made no objection.

The stringer for the Baltimore paper had also gone to Onset, finding a Perkins relative named Mrs. Snow. That woman said that Grace had visited her five weeks earlier, saying she was in trouble and needed help. Mrs. Snow, a cousin of Frank Perkins's wife, had advised the girl to go home and talk to her mother. Declining that advice, Grace informed the relative that she and Charley Bourne, who had driven her to Mrs. Snow's house, were engaged to be married. However, "Grace said that she did not know that she cared to be married."

At this point, Grace revealed "certain plans," involving a doctor who had advised Grace to find a trustworthy friend who could house her for a week or so. Mrs. Snow said she'd refused to be a part of any such scheme and wouldn't "harbor" Grace if she went through with it. The conversation ended, and Grace drove away with Charley.

The relative expressed no sorrow about the reports of Grace's tragic end. Instead, she was eager to distance herself from the crime that could have caused it. As a cousin of Grace's mother, she could have gone fifteen miles to stand with her kin at this trying time. But Mrs. Snow chose to stay away from what could now be described as a celebrity funeral.

Grace's image was emblazoned on papers across the nation as Middleborough prepared to bury one of its own. Swamped with orders, a florist turned out piles of immortelles, the long-lasting tributes of dried flowers that were then fashionable. On crosses, mounds, or open books, they stood in his shop window, inscribed GRACE and *REQUIESCAT IN PACE.*

In the village cemetery, not far from the Perkins house, a pile of loam stood by a new excavation. A minister had been engaged to perform the Sunday funeral service.

At least one reporter had boarded the Taunton-bound train to pepper Frank Perkins with questions. Dispatches received at various stations said that

Grace had been spotted, alive, and would be home in Middleborough later that day. Perkins disregarded these messages as heartless hoaxes. Meanwhile, other members of the press converged on the Taunton depot, eager to see the casket of human fragments loaded on the hearse.

But the hearse never arrived. As the Middleborough undertaker began his somber trip to Taunton, an unaccustomed sound reached his ears. People were laughing and pointing at him. He beheld an amazing sight. Grace Perkins, in the flesh, was at the gate of her house. She'd arrived in time to stop her own funeral. A late-afternoon train from Providence had deposited Grace and Charley Bourne at the Middleborough station, where carriages awaited them.

People gathered on street corners, first to cheer and later to exchange gossip. At the cemetery, a gravedigger heard the news and started shoveling dirt back in.

Exchanging the hearse for a regular carriage, the undertaker brought a small group of men to meet Frank Perkins's train. As the father stepped off, the wires were already abuzz with reports of Grace's resurrection. Perkins refused to respond until sighting his own son-in-law in the undertaker's entourage. Then he knew it was true.

Arriving home, he found his wife weeping over their living daughter. Grace, too, had sobbed on the train back from Onset, not mutilated but certainly mortified by the blunder. The parents' joy at seeing her was short-lived. Humiliated by the press and the public—his neighbors thought the girl's return home was a good joke on the New York reporters—Frank Perkins took to his bed.

His wife informed the press that her daughter was now Mrs. Charles Bourne, having been married on Friday in Providence, Rhode Island. After that, the Perkins home ignored the many knocks on the door. Charley was back at the Bourne residence, which was similarly sealed against intrusions.

On Monday, the Perkins parents gave prepared statements to the *New York Evening Journal* only. Now a national laughingstock, Perkins wanted to set the story straight about his family. A reporter was invited into the family home, where the father lay in bed with "limp hands" on the coverlet, presumably recovering from his sudden change from grief to joy. His two days in bed also shielded him from the shouts of passersby, like the man who said he'd made the mistake of the century.

Thanking the *Journal* for its treatment of him, he said the other papers had printed nothing but lies and "cruelties." Evidently, this was a shot at the

Boston Sunday Globe, which suggested that Perkins "took no apparent interest" in Grace on the night of her arrival, ignoring her as she lay sobbing on a couch. As Perkins said, no journalists had been admitted to the house that night. It's possible, however that the *Globe* had gotten its information from a relative who was present.

Certainly, the papers had exchanged their sympathy for smutty suggestiveness and shaming. Grace's mother turned defensive about charges of gold-digging. "While the circumstances of the Bournes are different from ours, Charles has always seemed to court Grace's company. He used to call at the house three times a week," Ellen Reed Perkins told the *Journal*.

Apparently, no questions were allowed during the issuance of these statements. But even the Perkins family's favorite paper wanted something cleared up. The next stop for the *Journal* correspondent was the Clark & Lovell grocery store.

Behind the counter stood Charley Bourne. His deceased father had earned his fortune by selling baked goods, and Charley wasn't too aristocratic to wait on customers. However, his family did have a lawyer, whose hand showed in the answer to an anticipated question.

"I want to deny emphatically that I am married to Miss Perkins," the youth said, or perhaps read from notes. "There is no truth in the statement, no matter what the Perkins folks say. I have come quietly back to work, and the misfortunes of the past two weeks will not affect my plans for the future."

That was all Charley had to say. Asked where he'd spent his vacation, he clammed up.

The press quickly decamped from Middleborough. Days before, one paper had described it as a "typical New England village." It was the perfect setting for a cozy mystery, in which a dead body turns up—in this case, hacked up—but sex and violence are kept out of view. Now, there wasn't a body. The remains were returned to Bridgeport and buried as "person unknown" at the town farm.

All the remains were buried except the head, that is. Even in its distorted condition, it went back on display at the morgue.

The Bridgeport police were back where they'd started. There were many "I told you so's," but none louder than that of Superintendent Birmingham. He said he'd never been in favor of releasing the body to the Perkins father, given all the physical discrepancies.

Perplexed by the father's insistence, Birmingham overlooked the stigma attached to abortion. Mrs. Perkins, who knew that Grace had been pregnant, probably also knew that her daughter had located an abortion provider in Onset. Both bits of information likely came from Mrs. Snow, the mother's cousin. Charley Bourne could have paid for the procedure. If Grace left pregnant, she didn't return that way.

Nancy was in Bridgeport as these events unfolded, but Grace could have found care with another "graduate" of Dr. Abbie Cutter's island-based school. Learning of the notorious Bridgeport midwife's connection to Onset, and knowing why his daughter was there, Frank Perkins could have drawn a reasonable conclusion.

But the blue coats, as the Bridgeport police were called, still didn't want Nancy Guilford. Only the press clamored for her. She was said to be hiding in Montreal, holed up in a hotel under the name N. A. Goodrich. But, as the *Hartford Courant* noted, the Bridgeport authorities, having said she wasn't wanted, made no effort to locate her.

Casting his client as the victim in this case, attorney Klein showed the press a letter he'd received from her. Postmarked Wellsburg and mailed before she left for Canada, it said:

> My heart is almost breaking at the persecution I am being subjected to, and I am being hounded by reporters ever since I left home. . . . They ask me all sort of questions about a horrible crime in Bridgeport of which I know absolutely nothing. What am I to do? If I return, I will be arrested on suspicion and placed in jail, and perhaps held there for months without a trial.
>
> I do not think it is safe for me to return, owing to the prejudice against me. My position is one calculated to drive most members of my sex insane. I know the police of Bridgeport have not the slightest evidence against me for the crime, nor can they ever have.

Begging Klein to advise her, she signed herself "Dr. Guilford." Practically exulting in the Bridgeport police's failures, Klein blamed them for his brokenhearted client's flight from Bridgeport. He said he couldn't advise her to return because of the deal made with Williams, the state's attorney for New Haven County, when she'd forfeited bond to elude trial. He said Williams had said he'd rearrest her on the old charges if her name was ever mentioned again in connection with an abortion case.

Therefore, Klein said, his hands were tied. Although he hadn't the "slightest suspicion" that she was connected to the pond case, he couldn't advise her to return. Rearrest would inevitably be followed by months of incarceration as she awaited trial.

He concluded, "I can produce Dr. Guilford in Bridgeport inside of forty-eight hours, and as soon as the mystery of the Yellow Mill victim is cleared up, Mrs. Guilford will return here."

The lawyer's last pronouncement, coming on the heels of the Grace Perkins debacle, was a sly dig at the Bridgeport police. Even the press was showing signs of fatigue. The scandal sheets had profited from their splashy coverage of Middleborough's runaway couple, but more sober publications were starting to despair.

A few days after the canceled funeral, the *Hartford Courant* wrote, "The police have apparently about exhausted their resources and there is very little new to record. It is the general opinion that the investigation will die out and the mystery never be solved." Other papers joined in the chorus. A week after the discovery of the remains in the pond, Superintendent Birmingham and his men were back to the start line.

Seemingly unbothered, the embattled Bridgeport police chief resumed his plodding pace. As mistaken identifications continued to pour in, he wired detailed descriptions of the body to numerous police departments. Many of these false leads came from the police departments in surrounding towns. Indeed, out-of-town cops seeking missing persons sometimes went to Birmingham's house to wake him up and have him take them to the morgue.

That charming house went under the searchlight as observers asked why Birmingham kept letting Nancy slip away. Again, as in western New York, he vacillated. When she took the train to Montreal, he wired the police there, asking them to watch for her. Hours later, he reversed himself, sending a second telegram to say she wasn't wanted.

Indeed, at one point the Bridgeport police superintendent declared, "I don't want her. I tell you I wouldn't arrest her if she were in this city under my nose."

Later, Birmingham would acknowledge that he feared losing his property in a civil suit. He had his suspicions about Nancy, he said, but "if I had arrested her and she was innocent there would have been a civil suit against me, and I would have lost the little house that it has taken me so many years to acquire."

But Birmingham was suspected of worse than offering that seemingly weak explanation. Charges of corruption flew, with the harshest criticisms coming from the *Boston Sunday Post*. Skewering the Bridgeport cops for chasing bogus identifications while Nancy went free, the Boston paper wrote, "'Dr.' Guilford has boasted many times that if the strings were pulled against her, they would pull down both church and court."

The same paper reported that Nancy had already sailed for England from Montreal, adding, "If she were innocent of the crime, why has she not returned to face her accusers?"

The papers might convict on such proof, but Birmingham needed something stronger. More was at stake than protecting the house. The state had agreed to help, paying for Pinkerton detectives and building a case that could lead to conviction.

Birmingham assured skeptical reporters that his "steady" work had "not been fruitless." He promised them he had "evidence, and good evidence, too, which I cannot divulge, but which will play an important part when the time comes."

No one took much interest as Birmingham sent Detective George Arnold to Meriden. A photograph of someone missing in that area bore a strong resemblance to the head in the morgue. Or, rather, to the head as it had once been. Now embalming fluid had toughened it so much that, as one morgue employee said, it could be thrown over a building without suffering much damage. Criticizing the crude preservation, a paper wrote, "It is unlikely that even the mother of the girl could recognize anything familiar in the gray, shrunken face." But her brother could, as Detective Arnold was about to find out.

9 | LINK BY LINK

MANY IN SOUTHINGTON KNEW the Gill parents were worried sick. After Emma had written them of her plans to see a doctor about her stomach, her father mailed another letter to the Stratford post office. It got a response with her signature, but the handwriting was not Emma's, and it was uncharacteristically written in pencil. The parents had sent a third letter in an envelope requesting its return if not picked up within three days. It came back a week later.

Some townspeople had already started whispering that the body in Bridgeport might be Emma's. However, the newspapers said the dead woman's mouth was small. People in Southington thought Emma's mouth was unusually large, but that could have been just her smile. A local informant described her as a "gay girl" who never lacked for admirers, "though her deportment in public was always above criticism."

Until now, that is.

Among Southington's residents was a stringer, or freelance journalist, who contributed occasional articles to the *Hartford Courant*. Belatedly learning of the Gill family's anxieties, this fellow villager roused the parents from their sleep to conduct a midnight interview. The family was sick with worry. Nearly every detail about the Bridgeport mystery woman pointed to their daughter. The parents shared the letters from the Stratford post office.

With the stringer, a fellow villager, the father was forthcoming. He spoke of the last time that Emma had seen the family. Knowing nothing of her liaison with Harry Oxley, he named Walter Foster as the only man in her life. He also said she'd spent a few summer days at a boardinghouse in New Haven's Lighthouse Point. He believed she had friends there.

The subject of pregnancy didn't seem to come up in that late-night interview. The father would always insist he knew nothing of his daughter's "trouble." However, it hung in the air as the reporter asked, "Why don't you go to Bridgeport and view the head?"

Mr. Gill replied, "I am not going to make a fool of myself as the father of Grace Perkins did. I shall let the matter rest."

His interviewer, however, recognized this as a tremendous scoop. The scribbling neighbor persuaded the family to talk to the police in New Haven, probably because of the Lighthouse Point connection. The New Haven police began developing the case, coordinating with what they called an "agent" in Southington, probably someone on the borough's small law-enforcement staff. The parents lent the police a studio photograph of Emma. Her center-parted hair, curled and anchored by beaded combs, was swept into a topknot. A bib front of lace covered her high-collared gown. The nose, in particular, was highly reminiscent of the now-famous sketch of Bridgeport's morgue photo.

The New Haven cops had planned to develop their clues methodically. They changed their mind on Tuesday afternoon. The Southington agent, they learned, had turned chatty, probably with that stringer for the *Courant*. Precipitously, they caught a four o'clock train to Bridgeport, arriving after the police superintendent had left for the day. However, the desk sergeant agreed to take them to Birmingham's treasured little house.

This was one intrusion the chief didn't mind. "This is the very first suggestion of this clue that I have heard," Birmingham said of the Emma Gill connection. "I am well pleased with your theory." He asked the New Haven department to follow up.

Birmingham also set to work. He sent a telegram to the Gills, asking the father to come to the morgue for an identification. Still hesitant, the father said he'd send his young son Fred. Equally skittish about a possible repeat of the Perkins embarrassment, Birmingham asked for the name of Emma's dentist and wired him a request for her records.

Meanwhile, his visitors from New Haven rode the rails. In Southington, they contacted Emma's former employers, the Pratts. A search of her room yielded a sheaf of letters, some signed by Walter Foster but none from Harry Oxley.

Hastening to pack when she left her job, Emma had forgotten the removable collar of a "waist," as blouses were called. It was a tasteless thing, in the loud checks that Emma preferred when not posed for a studio picture. The New Haven sergeants, William G. Doherty and Michael J. Hayes, would spend wasted hours showing it to passersby around the Stratford post office, hoping someone had seen a woman in a matching outfit.

The New Haven officers also went to Hartford that night. They didn't have an exact address for Walter Foster, but they knew that Emma had once met him there. Foster's employer, Fleischmann & Company, was headquartered in Hartford.

The Hartford police took charge, launching an all-night manhunt for mild-mannered Walter C. Foster. At dawn they found him at a boarding-house where his landlady, Mrs. Albert Yeomans, said that Foster was rarely out late at night, spending much of this time reading in his room. Foster admitted he knew Emma Gill but said he hadn't seen her since before Labor Day.

He said he'd written her many letters but had never been "criminally intimate" with her and had no idea she was in the condition that had been reported. Nevertheless, the arresting officer announced that Foster had made some "startling disclosures," which could not yet be shared with the press.

Detained in Hartford, Foster answered a few questions before refusing to speak further. His interrogators acknowledged that he'd "told a pretty good story" and was "remarkably cool" as they awaited instructions from Bridgeport, where Foster was wanted.

This time, no one could accuse Superintendent Birmingham of inaction. He'd ordered the arrest of Walter Foster for his connection with Emma Gill, but the body hadn't yet been identified as hers.

That afternoon, as Foster languished in the Hartford lockup, Fred Gill came to Bridgeport with two friends from home. Birmingham greeted the young man with a warning. At the morgue, he was to say nothing of which he wasn't positive. Fred said he planned to look for a mole on Emma's neck, which he and his brothers had teased her about. On his own left neck, he indicated a location just below the jawline. Neither the initial descriptions of the body nor the recent, more detailed one had mentioned this mark.

Fred Gill, age twenty-one, thus invented a test of his own credibility. This wasn't something he could have read about in the papers. The mole wasn't even visible in his sister's photograph. Perhaps the teasing had made her sensitive about it; the lacy stand-up collar of her gown concealed her entire neck.

Shown the head in the pail, Fred unhesitatingly pointed to the spot. It was there, shrunken and discolored, right above the line of decapitation. The police and undertaking assistants briefly withdrew to leave the brother alone with his grief.

The father agreed to come the next day with three other sons. If they could corroborate Fred's identification, the coroner would resume his inquest. Just for good measure, a telegram was sent to Dr. E. G. Rosenbluth of Southington asking him for Emma's dental records.

The news spread quickly through the village. Writing this time for the *New Haven Register*, Southington's local correspondent found some doubting Thomases, including the Gill family dentist. Dr. Rosenbluth demanded to know why the preserved head in Bridgeport lacked certain fillings that Emma had. And at a village shoe shop, two clerks swore that Emma's feet were a half-size larger than the police estimation for the corpse.

But Birmingham already had made up his mind. Speaking to the press, he said, "No further proof of the identification should be required than a glance at the brother's face. Every feature which was prominent in the dead woman is duplicated in the features of the brother."

"We'll solve this fiendish crime yet," Birmingham promised. That night, Walter Foster was brought to Bridgeport and locked up. It was discovered that he'd been in that city before, which wasn't surprising. Not restricted to sales anymore, Foster had been substituting for other Fleischmann's employees all around the state and in Massachusetts. He was found to have no sister in Stratford. However, he had friends there. After a long interview with the suspect, Detective Arnold hinted ominously that Foster and these Stratford people were "pretty close" friends at that.

The Gill father and three other brothers visited the morgue and swore affidavits before the coroner, who made out a new death certificate for Emma Gill. The body was not to be released until later, and there was to be no fanfare when it was. The press was warned that the burial site might be kept secret.

Still, the papers had plenty to run with. Emma Gill became famous overnight as a victim. Sketches of her and her upswept hair proliferated. Readers were treated to touching portraits of her father as he testified at the inquest, revealing his British origins with an occasional dropped "h." A less sympathetic report described her as a "wayward girl."

There were also illustrations of Walter Foster, described as five-foot-four with a "drooping black mustache." The press wasn't quite certain why he was being held. Some reports said he'd been charged with complicity in Emma's death, but that was untrue. He was being held as a witness. Detective Arnold said that articles found in the man's room indicated he knew something about the case. A rumor spread that a framed photograph of Emma had been found in Foster's spartan room, but the detective later denied having said that.

It was thin gruel for an arrest. Foster also had company memoranda tracking his recent movements for the past ten days. He'd been nowhere near Bridgeport. Nonetheless, Birmingham had made quite of show of his capture.

"There is our prisoner," the superintendent exclaimed when Foster was brought in. He'd insisted on frisking the man himself before reporters. Foster withstood the ordeal stoically.

In the meantime, more reports placed Dr. Nancy Guilford on the open seas. Birmingham didn't seem to believe that. Energized with his recent infusion of state funds, he posted two Pinkerton detectives in Wellsburg. Eudora was still staying with her uncle, claiming ignorance of her mother's whereabouts. Nonetheless, the press and police had their eyes on her. Birmingham was convinced that Nancy was somewhere within twenty miles of Wellsburg.

Or maybe abortion had nothing to do with Emma Gill's death. The new prosecutor suspected that poison had been administered. Samuel Fessenden, the state's attorney for Fairfield County, asked the medical examiner to reinvestigate that theory, which few took seriously.

As the authorities in Connecticut dithered, a New York reporter took a fresh look at something he'd found in Nancy Guilford's garbage. Soon after Nancy left town, this enterprising reporter had explored the ash heap in her backyard, where trash was burned. The practice was commonplace at the time.

Two documents had escaped total incineration. One was Henry's letter to Eudora from prison, already long outdated. The other was an envelope with nothing in it. The reporter pocketed these items, hoping to file a story about the prison letter. That was before the Grace Perkins escapade eclipsed everything else. Eventually, on a slow news day, an Elmira paper ran the letter on page 5.

The half-burned envelope was from the Adams Express Company, addressed to "Dr. N. A. Guilford." Embossed letters on its broken seal read, "Plantsville, Connecticut." The reporter thought nothing of it. Then the dead woman was identified as Emma Gill of Southington.

The New Yorker may have consulted a map, or perhaps a local enlightened him. One way or another, he realized that Plantsville neighbored Southington, and that both were in Hartford County. Accordingly, he gave the envelope to Detective Walter Smith, the man who'd arrested Foster. Apparently, there was an understanding that the Hartford police would trace the origins of the money order and give the New York journalist an exclusive.

It was a gentlemen's agreement, but the Hartford cops were no gentlemen. As they worked on a trace, so far without success, they told Bridgeport about it. That had not been part of the bargain. Worse, they cut the New York journalist out of the loop, failing to communicate with him about their progress.

The reporter decided to take matters into his own hands. Teaming up with a colleague, he took a train to Plantsville. The Adams Express clerk declined to help the journalists. He would not look in his records without orders from company headquarters in Boston or New Haven.

Phone calls were placed. The New Haven office said it would release the information only to law enforcement. The journalists hopped a train to New Haven, where the captain of the detective bureau gave them a warm reception.

"Great Scott, man!" Captain Henry Cowles reportedly exclaimed. "This is the best thing we've run across! I'll send a man to Plantsville, and I'll get that name if I have to take the whole Plantsville office."

Racing there, the New Haven cops nearly collided with their Hartford and Bridgeport counterparts. Confronted with dozens of brass buttons, the Adams Express clerk opened his record book.

One payment to Dr. N. A. Guilford had originated at a Southington hotel, passing through the hands of several clerks before reaching the Plantsville office. However, other waybills made the name of the sender plain. For the last payment, made by Oxley on the honor system while Emma lay dying, the record book said, "H. A. Oxley to Mrs. Dr. N. A. Guilford, $10." The press corps would dub the charred Adams paper pouch, discovered by one of their own, "the telltale envelope."

The clerk remembered that Howard Guernsey had accompanied Oxley on at least one visit. The Adams Express worker recognized both youths. As retailers, Oxley and Guernsey were local fixtures—Oxley, dispensing newspapers and candy, and Guernsey, a druggist and grocer for his father's business.

Their connection to Emma Gill was a surprise, however. Neither name had been mentioned in the article tarring her as a wayward girl. Instead, there'd been rumors about her link to a former meat merchant. That man had suddenly sold his business, saying he was moving to Boston, only to be sighted living elsewhere in Connecticut. In Southington at the time, those were grounds for suspicion of murder.

Now that that the names were known, the New Haven police left matters to Detective Arnold of Bridgeport and Detective Smith of Hartford. Smith went into the village, hoping to find someone or something to connect these youths with Emma Gill. The detective's presence didn't go unnoticed. Excitement in Southington mounted as Smith entered the Gill home. It had been a trying day for the family, burying their daughter only to learn of the disinterment orders: Birmingham had a dentist make a final identification.

According to the whisperers, Smith found an important clue in Emma's former room, which had already been thoroughly searched. More likely, Smith was enlightened by conversation. As far as the family knew, no man had come into their daughter's life other than Walt Foster, still behind bars in Bridgeport. Of course, they knew Oxley and Guernsey. One or the other of them was in Oxley's store every single day.

And Emma's best friend, Lillian Katzung, worked at the Oxley home. That would have dawned on them.

Lillian was found, probably at her job. At great personal risk—she was betraying her employer—she offered invaluable help. Once, she'd believed Emma's fib about visiting Walt's Stratford sister. Since then, she'd put things together. As a domestic in the Oxley home and Emma's close friend, she could reliably speak of their affair.

She might have also noted that Harry had been a wreck lately. In fact, he'd stayed home from work today, the day of Emma's burial, claiming to have a "hard cold."

The Hartford cop went back with this to Arnold. A telephone call was made, and the two met with the local sheriff on the road from Plantsville to Southington. The sheriff would free up some rooms, and Arnold would question Oxley while Smith took care of Guernsey.

It was late afternoon, and Guernsey was out with a wagon and team, delivering groceries. The sheriff caught up with him on his route. The young boy who carried the packages took over the reins, as Guernsey went back with the sheriff. The youth was allowed to stop first at his father's business, Neale & Guernsey, and the family attorney was alerted.

Detective Walter Smith of the Hartford
police. *The Connecticut Historical Society*

The knock at the Oxley door wasn't a complete shock. Lillian, of course, was partly the cause of it. Her name would be in the papers as police expressed their gratitude to her, not thinking of her job security. However, Lillian wasn't alone in her knowledge. Oxley had confided in at least one of his parents, probably his mother, who'd advised him to tell the truth.

So far, Oxley had ignored that advice. More surprisingly, he'd also disregarded an attorney's guidance. On that first day of the pond findings when the news screamed from the racks in his store, Oxley had consulted a Southington lawyer named Marcus H. Holcomb. Without specifying what advice he'd given, Holcomb said that the young man ignored it. Oxley had not turned himself in.

That was no longer necessary. The Bridgeport cop took him to the sheriff's office, on the same street as the Oxley store. There, he and Guernsey were questioned in separate rooms. At some point in the proceedings, Guernsey was allowed to see his father again. Their family lawyer was none other than Holcomb, whom Oxley hadn't heeded. The lawyer—who would later become a three-term Connecticut governor—agreed to represent both youths.

As the questioning continued for more than an hour, a crowd gathered. According to one report, "consternation reigned" as Southington learned that two of its leading citizens were in custody. Both had been charged with assisting to procure an abortion. When finally satisfied, the cops spirited them away through a back door.

Waiting for the train at the Southington station, the two men made a study in contrasts. The *Courant*'s Southington stringer wrote that Guernsey "took his arrest very coolly," puffing a cigarette "in a nonchalant way." He'd already conferred with the attorney. Meanwhile, Oxley, with his face stark white, "trembled like a leaf" and "walked with downcast eyes."

Detective Arnold, meanwhile, "appeared to be in excellent spirits," reported one paper. Asked whether one or both men were implicated, he said, "One for certain."

The train took the men to Bridgeport. Within hours, the press learned of Harry Oxley's "partial confession," implicating Nancy Guilford for the crime of abortion.

The police needed more. Oxley was the man responsible for Emma Gill's pregnancy, and he had taken her to Nancy Guilford's house. However, he'd only paid the bills, not witnessing the operation, illness, or death. He knew only what he'd read about the mutilation and disposal of her body.

The police could make Oxley sob; reportedly, they'd done just that. But they still couldn't be sure that the crime fell within their jurisdiction. Theories abounded that the body had been carved up in a country house in Stratford. The Bridgeport police had pieces of cord and shreds of rubber sheeting found at 51 Gilbert Street. There were smells and laundry marks, but no definite links to death and dismemberment.

The cops went back to Oxley and finally got what they wanted. He remembered the messenger who'd come to his store after those first-day headlines. The boy had told him to meet a colored woman at the railroad tracks, and she'd said to keep mum. Oxley couldn't tell the police her name, and he didn't seem capable of estimating her age. Clearly, though, Nancy had sent her.

The cops sprang into action. They remembered Clara Belle Drayton's convincing story about her uninterrupted routine at the doctor's house. Less convinced now, they burst into the Draytons' house, searched it from roof to cellar, and marched Clara and her mother to interrogations.

Clara and Rose were "put on the rack," as the press called it, not necessarily implying physical brutality. The phrase would often be used as the Bridgeport police questioned others in this case, including less-than-well-connected white people. But, judging by the scant reporting on tactics, the cops went particularly hard on these women, nearly always described in the press as "colored."

The threat of a murder charge had scared Oxley, the white son of a merchant. One can only imagine the terror it inspired in Clara, who had lied to the police to protect her employer, and Rose, born enslaved and raised in the South. What chance of justice would the Draytons stand in Bridgeport, where, later that year, a newspaper would run the headline NEGROES ARE VINDICTIVE over a report on a Southern white-supremacist riot that left dozens of Black people dead?

Still, the women didn't break down easily. Even if they no longer cared about guarding Nancy and her family, they didn't want to incriminate themselves. The police would threaten them, lie, and even fabricate nauseating "evidence" to show them. Before her ordeal was over, Rose would pass out during one of these sessions. Nevertheless, the police described them as "reticent."

LEFT: Rose Drayton. RIGHT: Clara Drayton. *Records of Pinkerton's National Detective Agency, courtesy of the Library of Congress*

At the end of this banner day, Birmingham assured the press that the crime had happened in the heart of Bridgeport and not in some country house. That was all he had to say for the present. Behind the scenes, though, harsh questioning had opened new avenues for investigation. Clara denied having seen any cutting but could testify to Harry Guilford's presence in the house on the critical days. Regardless of what treatment he'd been getting, the loyal son apparently said nothing.

Above all, they were a family. It wasn't clear what Harry had wanted to take from his mother's house, but Birmingham chose this moment to disclose something his men had found there: a letter to Nancy from Eudora. Written in the summer, shortly after her father's imprisonment, Eudora begged her mother to quit the family business, threatening estrangement if her wishes weren't heeded. "I would rather go to work in a factory any time than be called upon to witness again anything of the kind," Eudora wrote.

For Birmingham, the word *witness* might have seemed to incriminate the writer. But for more sentimental civilians, the plea only provoked sympathy. As revelations of the family's collaboration emerged, charges stuck easily to Harry Guilford, the "hunchback." No one cared whether filial devotion had prompted his actions or his silence afterwards. Eudora, on the other hand, became nearly a figure of worship.

That was true even after Birmingham ordered her arrested, based on information obtained from the Draytons. It would have been his fifth arrest that day, but the order reached Wellsburg too late for that. A few hours past midnight, Eudora lay in her bed as an apologetic constable read her the arrest warrant.

A night in the Wellsburg lockup was out of the question. Its two wooden cells were for tramps and drunks. Instead, Constable Lee Knapp sat in a chair all night, keeping watch over his reclined prisoner. There was an unavoidable lapse of security in the morning when Knapp briefly reported to the police station. Eudora spent the time sewing. As she'd said in the days she was under surveillance, she had no money to flee Wellsburg even if she'd wanted to.

Eudora insisted she had no idea where her mother was, adding that the police would never take her alive. Nancy always traveled with poison, she said, and would choose suicide over capture. However, Connecticut wanted more than information from the so-called comely daughter. As police reconstructed events that had preceded and followed Emma Gill's death, the *Sun* wrote that

Eudora "probably had no hand in the crime." Connecticut authorities weren't so convinced. They prepared extradition orders for the governor to sign.

After hours of interrogation, furnace dismantling, and carriage cleaning, Birmingham triumphantly announced his solution of the Yellow Mill Pond mystery. The bathtub on Nancy's second floor gleamed in the spotlight as Birmingham issued a statement outlining his findings. One newspaper illustrator swiftly produced a sketch of a ghostly apparition hovering over the faucets.

Evidence, the superintendent said, led him to believe that Emma Gill had died in that house, and that her body had been cut up in the tub. He also theorized that Harry had assisted his mother in cutting up the body. Birmingham didn't mention Rose Drayton during these pronouncements. However, his subordinate, Detective Edward Cronan, had "no doubt" that Rose had assisted in the cutting, as he told reporters afterward.

Even more confidently, he retraced the route the carriage had taken to the Seaview Avenue Bridge. One of the prisoners, probably Clara Drayton, had led police to Banks's stables, where Isaac Banks remembered the times and dates of Nancy's recent rentals. The phaeton she'd driven hadn't gotten much of a cleaning. Small blood spots were found on the rug behind the seat, along with fragments of the distinctive mica-specked rock used to weight the packages.

Confidently, impressing even his harshest critics, Superintendent Birmingham said in his statement:

> Mrs. Guilford hired a team at a livery stable. We know that the head and legs were placed in that carriage. I am convinced that Harry Guilford, her son, on his bicycle, led the way while Mrs. Guilford followed in the carriage. I am convinced fully that Harry Guilford rode direct to the Bishop Avenue cut. There the stones that weighted the packages were secured. From the cut, I am convinced that he led the way to the Seaview Avenue Bridge. He rode across the bridge and back again to see if the coast was clear and then signaled to his mother to drive on the bridge. . . . I am convinced that Harry Guilford then lifted the packages from the carriage and threw them into the pond. The same procedure was repeated the next night when the trunk was disposed of in the same way.

The police chief had skillfully resurrected the scene, but not with the help of Nancy's son. There'd been no news of confessions, partial or otherwise, made by the son. Harry Guilford had been charged with assisting with an abortion, but the charges were "only as a formality," a paper wrote. The family's lawyers, DeForest & Klein, were keeping a close watch on his treatment and threatening to file papers of habeas corpus.

Still, Birmingham had managed to reconstruct the scene. Many people had claimed to see suspicious vehicles on the bridge on those fateful nights. Most of those sightings had been misleading or worthless. However, one woman was found to have described the rented phaeton down to the last detail. Fusing her testimony with whatever he'd forced from Clara Drayton, the police chief had his scenario.

Then came the most moving part of his announcement. Just as Emma Gill's body had defied submergence, things she wore had survived an inferno. Nancy's closets had been opened, and its rooms searched. Now, on orders from State's Attorney Fessenden, the furnace grate was removed. Still pursuing the possibility of poisoning, Fessenden had been looking for the victim's stomach and intestines.

Instead, the police found the stubbornly fireproof remnants of a young woman's wardrobe: steel corset stays, hooks and eyes, a buckle, the heel of a shoe, and a handbag frame. Her body was now buried forever—the dentist had made his graveside identification—yet some of her remained. Although melted and twisted by the heat of the furnace, these were the last pieces of her.

"The case is sufficiently advanced to warrant my making these statements public," Birmingham said. "Harry Oxley is the man we want. Howard Guernsey is not guilty. He was Oxley's friend and confidante. He made the mistake of not telling what he knew." Guernsey was released on a bond of $500.

With less fanfare, Walter Foster was also found to be not guilty, and the charges against him were dropped. After returning some books he'd borrowed to a Bridgeport friend, he took an early train home. He said he was considering suing Bridgeport for lost wages and damage to his reputation. He'd spent four days in jail.

Birmingham's statement failed to specify the tools used in the dismemberment, and his men were evasive. Although midwifery instruments had been found in Nancy's office, no saw turned up. Finding a saw on a hook in the Draytons' home, Arnold got creative. The detective brandished this saw before

Rose, claiming that human tissue had been found in its teeth. Measuring six-foot-three, Arnold was said to strike terror in suspects with his "giant physique." A moment later, reporters watched him rush out of the room to get water. His prisoner had fainted.

Later, a different saw was found under an icebox in Nancy's house. Even as Birmingham made his assured pronouncements, the house search was still in progress. Unhappy to hear that the bathtub plumbing had not been inspected, Fessenden ordered the pipes and traps removed and microscopically examined. It was late in the day for this. Someone, probably Harry Guilford, had entered the house since the police first went through it. Burnt matchsticks left near the tub indicated an attempt to cover the smell.

But that was nothing compared to the big unanswered question: Where was Nancy? As Birmingham said, the only thing lacking was her arrest.

Deluged with such questions, Birmingham issued a supplemental statement later that day: "I am positive that Nancy Guilford is not now in Europe and am pretty sure she is at the present time within 20 miles of Wellsburg, NY."

What's more, top officials along Nancy's alleged flight path seemed to agree with him. A Buffalo paper received a telegram from Chief Cassada of Elmira, asserting that, if needed, "Nancy could be reached." The report said that the Montreal police chief had also "had a hand" in that wire. Detectives in

Detective George Arnold of the Bridgeport police. *Boston Sunday Post*

Canada said she'd returned to the states instead of getting on the steamship. The Bridgeport chief was getting global support.

Around Wellsburg, some were convinced they'd seen her. An unknown attendee at an Elmira teachers' meeting seemed to answer Nancy's description. Then there was a stranger, dressed in black, who rented a rig at the train station to visit a prominent family on the city outskirts. Neither was Nancy, but the false sightings showed that she was still viewed as an estimable, middle-class woman. Descriptions of a bloody bathtub scene hadn't tarnished that image.

Openly skeptical of Birmingham's claims, State's Attorney Fessenden was keeping a close watch over the Liverpool wharf. A reporter had gotten on board before the *Vancouver* sailed from Montreal. He wrote that Nancy was on it, registered as "Mrs. Wilbur." It was due in Liverpool three days after Birmingham issued his statement. Fessenden had asked a Liverpool police detective to watch the wharf. He had also wired Scotland Yard to request Nancy's provisional arrest if she set foot on British soil.

The state prosecutor had also sent at least one Pinkerton detective to Great Britain. His Pinkerton man in Wellsburg was now a familiar face in the village. There, Eudora calmly remained under house arrest with her uncle and aunt. She said she'd be willing to appear in Bridgeport even in the absence of extradition orders. However, Connecticut preferred to wait for the cooperation of the New York governor.

Even in her absence, Eudora Guilford was the subject of much discussion at police headquarters. Superintendent Birmingham personally sent for her devoted admirer, Frederick Welch, the alderman's son. The session reportedly lasted three hours, as Welch continued to insist that he'd been at the house on the nights in question. No charges resulted, and the press learned little about these discussions other than "what he told Birmingham did not develop." If asked about Eudora's whereabouts during a body's butchery and disposal, he might have shielded her with a false alibi. Hopelessly smitten, Fred wanted Eudora, and she would have wanted him to lie for her.

A less ethereal view of Nancy's daughter emerged from the continued grilling of Clara Drayton. She told of slaughtering a cat on orders from Eudora, smearing its blood on women's clothes and undergarments, and leaving them on a riverbank for easy discovery. Intended to avert suspicion from Nancy, the ploy hadn't worked. Now, however, Clara's testimony implicated Eudora, at least in the cover-up.

But Birmingham didn't trumpet this new information, and the press made little of it, preferring not to sully the angel in this story. Eudora's good looks, tempered comments, and expensive clothes placed her beyond reproach.

That was not the case with Emma Gill, torn apart yet again. Under the outrageously hypocritical heading POOR EMMA, a New Haven paper wrote, "The deeper the detectives delve into the case, the more unsavory appears to have been the dead girl's career." Her family's grief was regrettable, the paper wrote. However, now that two "good fellows," Oxley and Guernsey, were under arrest, more than one family was suffering. And those other two families, the paper implied, were far more important than the Gills.

Oxley's brother added to the battering. Visiting his brother in jail, Alfred Oxley painted Emma Gill as a liar and fortune hunter. In his version, all her plans for an abortion were set before she asked the younger Oxley to help with the bills.

"She knew Dr. Guilford, and that she could cure her of her trouble by an operation, and she would get out of her trouble that way," asserted Alfred Oxley, negating all the weeks his brother and Emma had devoted to obtaining that information.

From Alfred, the press learned that Howard Guernsey had advised Oxley to marry Emma—if Oxley could be sure he was responsible for her condition, the brother hastened to add. The offer was declined, Alfred said, because this other fellow, Foster, "didn't know her true character" and was "a better catch."

As the yellow press ate this up, Alfred's real purpose for coming to Bridgeport was nearly forgotten. He wanted to assure Oxley that he would be released soon. Howard Guernsey had already been freed on $500 bail, with an agreement that he'd return for arraignment, but Oxley's bail had been set at $1,500. The Oxley family had a store but not much in the way of property, which was then preferred for bail. Nancy knew that well; when she jumped bail in New Haven, her bondsman's property was attached until she covered the cost.

So Oxley stayed in jail until he appeared at his arraignment two days after his brother's visit. He had a heavy growth of beard but a fresh magnolia in his buttonhole. Biting his nails even before the charges were read, he soon had more reason to do so. The charge was now manslaughter, and bail was doubled to $3,000.

Howard Guernsey was also charged with manslaughter, but his bail remained $500, easily paid by his father. It was generally agreed that he was only needed for information. Rereleased, he returned home, leaving his friend in jail.

A call went out for help with Oxley's bail. As one report noted, "Everyone in Southington does not possess of $3,000 of unencumbered real estate." In the meantime, Oxley adjusted to life in the county jail in Bridgeport, later thanking the sheriff for allowing him "unusual liberties."

Then the big news came from over the Atlantic. Nancy Guilford had arrived at the Liverpool wharf. As detectives and journalists pursued her, she took a train to London and vanished into the great metropolis.

In Bridgeport it was Fessenden's turn to be the punching bag. As a member of the police board said, the state had taken the investigation out of Birmingham's hands. But Nancy had managed to elude all the Pinkertons and foreign contacts at the state's disposal.

Harry Oxley. *Records of Pinkerton's National Detective Agency, courtesy of the Library of Congress*

"In all my twenty-seven years' experience in the police business I have never encountered as slippery a woman as Nancy Guilford, and so am not surprised that the detectives lost track of her," Fessenden said. Don't blame it on me, he seemed to say, my quarry has quasi-magical powers. Newspaper readers on two continents had a new folk hero: Old Nance.

10 | TRANSCONTINENTAL DRAGNET

IT HAD BEEN A FRAUGHT VOYAGE FOR NANCY. The *Vancouver* was operated by the Dominion Line, which boasted of protecting its passengers as much as possible from the vagaries of open-sea weather. The company's vaunted "St. Lawrence Route to Europe" took passengers on a picturesque path through the river and gulf of that name before reaching the North Atlantic. From there, it was just two or three days to Liverpool.

But for "Mrs. Wilbur," the anxieties began on the river. Another passenger saw her busy with scissors in the ladies' room, a spacious facility with benches and tables. Extracting from her bag a number of railroad brochures and ladies' shirt collars, she cut them into small pieces. The only railroad schedule spared was for the Canadian Pacific line. Unable to pry a restroom window open, Nancy returned to her compartment and threw the fragments out a porthole.

Traveling on a second-class ticket—between the luxuries of "saloon" class and the humiliations of steerage—she would have eaten with other passengers on hard chairs at a long table. Not her usual conversational self, she was remembered only as a gray-haired woman with a pince-nez and a very pale face. As the passengers crowded onto the deck, waiting to disembark, she wouldn't have been easy to spot. However, an American reporter had enlisted the help of the ship's head steward, who pointed her out.

The press was there to meet her, but not the police. Fessenden had contacted Detective Lamothe of the Liverpool police department, but, lacking the necessary papers to arrest her, the best he could do was to shadow her from a distance.

The reporter, however, wasn't hobbled by the restrictions of international law. Questions of journalistic ethics didn't stop him either. He was on

179

an assignment from the *World*, the publication that had sent a reporter to Wethersfield State Prison in the guise of a state investigator. The *Hartford Courant* had exposed that ruse, an indication that other papers found the tactic unscrupulous. But here again, the *World* seemed up to its old tricks.

The New York paper had found itself a sharp-eyed correspondent. He wrote that the steward had pointed him to a woman with her "lower eyelids swollen and deeply marked." As usual, her jewelry captured attention. Small diamond pendants hung from her ears, and she wore a gold pin, studded with agates, in her collar. The journalist thought the pin "old-fashioned." Leaving the subject of fashion aside, he asked her if she was Mrs. Wilbur.

She flushed as she answered, "Yes, yes, I am." Asked where she was from, she replied, "Los Angeles." Evidently, his pose was convincing. The fictitious Catherine Wilbur could have brushed a reporter off, but she would have had no reason to stymie a detective.

The next question came from Nancy: "Why do you ask?" Given the limits of ship-to-shore communication, she didn't know the progress of the case. She had sailed from Montreal before the body was correctly identified. Knowing nothing of Oxley's arrest, she might have hoped the whole thing had died down by now.

Warming to his role, the man continued, "It is said in New York that the woman who occupied your stateroom under the name of Mrs. Wilbur is Mrs. Dr. Nancy Guilford of Bridgeport, Connecticut. Is there any way you can prove your identity as Mrs. Wilbur?"

Neglecting to say how he'd identified himself, the correspondent wrote, "When the words, 'Mrs. Dr. Guilford' were uttered, Mrs. Wilbur turned almost ashen, her lips quivered visibly, and her teeth seemed almost to chatter."

Certainly, Nancy was rattled. "I don't see why you should ask me," she said. Still, she seemed to think it was best to cooperate. Rattled, she said it was her first trip to England, only to contradict that a moment later. Having gotten what he wanted, the reporter asked a ship official to show him her stateroom. The bed linens had already been changed.

Almost all the passengers were gone now, but Nancy remained on deck. When the reporter reappeared, she asked him her burning question: "What is this Mrs. Guilford charged with?" The hoaxster answered, "The murder of a young girl in Bridgeport, Connecticut." Hearing that, "She blanched and turned away," he wrote. That was her news update.

The pestering continued on shore. The reporter stuck with Nancy as her luggage went through customs. She had a small valise and a wooden trunk with two yellow straps, one broken. There was no name or monogram on the trunk, just a "W" on a slip of paper affixed by the steamship company. These were the days when labels stayed on trunks forever. One of Nancy's was marked "Grand Central Station," dated September 13, the day she'd gone there from Bridgeport and changed to the Erie Line, headed for Wellsburg.

She refused to answer questions about the label or anything else. At this point, she must have seen through the correspondent's guise. At the very least, she knew he had no authority to arrest her.

A special train took ship passengers from Liverpool to the Euston railway station in London. Nancy bought a third-class ticket and boarded. The reporter followed one car behind. The Liverpool detective was on that train as well.

Arriving in London, Nancy had a porter heft her trunk onto the roof of a hansom cab but refused to tell him her destination. The reporter got into a cab behind hers. He watched Nancy crane her neck out a window to give her driver lengthy instructions. This was repeated at every intersection, with Nancy apparently amending the directions while looking to see who was behind her.

The cab carrying the hapless Liverpool detective followed the other two until forced to stop for a long line of pedestrians. Resuming the chase, Lamothe followed a four-wheel carriage for some time before realizing that he was after the wrong party.

The reporter made no such mistake. As his cab hung onto Nancy's despite stops, turns, and doubling back, Nancy got out at a crossing to speak to him. Following people was in this country was unlawful, the wanted woman informed her scribbling countryman. Undeterred, he had his driver stay close until her hansom slowed near a post office, which was guarded by a man in uniform. Fearing she might actually summon a bobby, the journalist had his cabbie fall back. Seizing his chance, Nancy's driver applied the whip to round a corner at top speed.

Nancy was swallowed into the byways of London. Like all cabs in the city, hers had a number. It was a special Great Northern cab, no. 81, but the American correspondent and the Liverpool detective had failed to note that. Otherwise, they could have simply tracked down the cabbie and asked where he'd taken her.

It was an escape worthy of Robin Hood or the yet-to-be-written tales of Zorro. On both sides of the Atlantic, newspapers picked up the *World*'s story. "American reporter teaches the English a Yankee trick or two," crowed a US publishers' trade journal. As with serial fiction, readers eagerly awaited the next installment.

Blustering about Nancy's slipperiness, Fessenden made an ideal foil for her—a powerful figure with all the resources of the state behind him, outdone by a woman armed only with her wits.

After what the British press called "an inexplicable delay," a warrant for her arrest arrived in London. Until then, Fessenden explained, all he could have done was surveillance. As he neglected to add, even that was botched. More than twenty-four hours had elapsed between Nancy's arrival and Scotland Yard's receipt of the warrant. She could be anywhere by now.

Not everyone was rooting for Nancy. Marveling at the impotence of the Bridgeport authorities, newspapers wondered what "mysterious influence" was at work. Abortion and dismemberment were pushed to the side. In America, at least, the story had evolved into a police procedural tinged with hints of corruption.

Fessenden's response was to dig deeper into the state funding earmarked for the case. His hired Pinkertons hadn't yet proved very effective, but the state's attorney still believed in them. To hunt down Nancy, he turned to the head of Pinkerton's European bureau. Frederic Abberline was a former chief inspector for Scotland Yard. He'd been a major player in the Jack the Ripper case of the previous decade, formulating theories that are still discussed today.

Explaining why so many hounds were after this gray-haired lady, the British press wrote quick recaps of her alleged crime. The focus, even in the staid journals, was on the dismemberment of the corpse, a minor infraction. The British papers seemed even more skittish about printing the word *abortion* than their counterparts in the United States, where a few journals used it regularly.

The arrival of the warrant solved the problem. The London papers could simply say that the American authorities had ordered Nancy Alice Guilford arrested for involuntary manslaughter, as worded in the provisional arrest warrant. But was she still in England?

While Nancy baffled police on two continents, Eudora had a visitor in Wells-burg. As she finished breakfast at her uncle's house, there was a knock on the door. The New York governor had signed the papers releasing her to Connecticut. A sheriff had a warrant for her arrest.

Unlike the warrant read to her by the local constable some days before, this one was for manslaughter. Eudora complained of a sudden chill but quickly regained her composure, changing her morning gown for a traveling suit. The press was on hand, admiringly describing her outfit from head to toe, not neglecting the plumed hat and alligator traveling bag.

"I know nothing of the crime," Eudora told a local reporter. "My mother often had visitors I knew nothing about, and I never meddled with her affairs." Declining to say anything further, she accompanied a Connecticut deputy sher-iff to the train. Endorsement of the extradition papers had taken hours. It was past noon when they boarded the train, the deputy sheriff carrying her bag for her.

The besotted Fred Welch awaited her return in Bridgeport. Her bail wouldn't be set until arraignment, but Fred had virtually a blank check to pay it. Unlike Oxley's father, Alderman Wallace Welch owned plenty of property, the ideal form of surety.

Ready to make use of the Welch resources, Klein awaited her for hours at the courthouse. After midnight, he gave up. With no judges remaining on duty, her bail couldn't be set anyway. If she arrived late, she would have to be locked up.

As it turned out, that wasn't necessary. She spent the night at the home of the deputy sheriff who'd brought her in. He lived in Stamford, closer to Grand Central Terminal, and, of course, it had spared her a night in a cell. Arriving in Bridgeport the next morning, she was questioned by police for an hour. It was brief, compared to the four-hour sessions spent with the Draytons, and no one rushed out for a glass of water.

"Miss Guilford has the sympathy of police here," observed one reporter. "They regard her as a person more worthy of respect than those with whom they ordinarily have to deal."

Certainly, they thought her more worthy than Rose Drayton. Apparently, there were some discrepancies between Eudora's story and that told by the Black servant. A few days earlier, Rose and Clara had been transferred to the county jail. Now Rose was brought back to police headquarters for further questioning.

Fred Welch had proven more than willing to recite from any script Eudora provided. But Rose didn't worship at the same altar. Besides, police were pressing her about a more important matter than piano playing. Eudora had suggested that another physician, a man, was responsible for the death and cutting up.

It was a sly strategy, exploiting the doubts about women's abilities and using them to Nancy's advantage. However, Eudora had overlooked one thing: Rose Drayton wasn't her toy.

The next morning, as the others were charged with manslaughter, Eudora wasn't present. The authorities had "relieved her of the embarrassment," said the papers.

No testimony was heard. The case was continued for two weeks. Oxley's lawyer helped to pay his $5,000 bail, and he went free. Harry Guilford and Rose Drayton returned to jail, unable to raise $5,000 and $3,000 respectively. Clara Drayton was still held but not charged. For her, no one threatened to file a habeas corpus complaint.

In Elmira, Eudora had been uncharacteristically cold to reporters, refusing to give them a statement. After conferring with Klein, her lawyer, she turned on the charm again, granting an interview. She said her mother and brother were innocent, and that Harry hadn't even been home. As for herself, she'd been at home with Fred Welch in the room with the piano.

She added, "I played some, and I believe that is the only foundation for the charge against me. I have often heard of the neighbors suffering from piano-playing in a house in their midst, but this is the first time I ever knew a charge of manslaughter to grow out of it."

That clever quip was quickly overshadowed by bigger news: Nancy Guilford was under arrest in London. Printed in big type, the news blared from newsstand display boards. In Bridgeport, crowds gathered to read the bulletin. General satisfaction was expressed, particularly at police headquarters.

"I have felt sure that they would get her and am not surprised, for the case after her was too hot for her to escape," said Birmingham, learning he wouldn't go down in history as the man who'd let Nancy Guilford vanish forever.

It had taken dogged British detective work and Yankee dollars to bring her in. Scotland Yard's chief inspector Frank Froest would remember it as one of the most memorable cases of his remarkable career. Later known as a real-life Sherlock Holmes, Froest found Nancy a worthy opponent.

"She is a most remarkable woman," said Froest after her capture. "She is shrewd, sharp and clever. I have rarely seen her equal. It has been impossible to get anything out of her."

They found her in an attic room of a third-class boarding house, insisting that she was Mrs. McAllister of Chicago, that she had been in London for six months, and that she had never heard about this crime in Connecticut.

"This is an outrage," she said when told the police believed her to be Dr. Guilford. "The charge is untrue. I will see counsel." Taken to Bow Street Police Court, she refused to give her name. She was entered on the charge sheet as "a woman."

It hadn't been easy to get to this point. Froest's diligent detective work laid the groundwork, but Fessenden's liberal spending also played a part. The money that the Connecticut prosecutor had showered on the Pinkertons finally paid off.

The challenge was finding the cab driver. Froest said he spent thirty-six hours interviewing cabbies at the train station, eventually finding one named Henry Baker. Baker remembered the gray-haired American woman he'd picked up at Euston, her nervousness, and her erratic instructions. The *World* reporter interpreted her circuitous route through London as a clever dodge. It was partly that, but she also was genuinely confused.

On one point, she was clear: she wanted to go to a temperance hotel. Nancy told the driver to take her to Tanner's Temperance Hotel in Aldsgate. He drove there but failed to locate it, despite consulting several newsboys and policemen. Thinking that the American must have meant Aldersgate, the driver went there but had no luck.

Consulting a guidebook, Nancy directed the hack to Wild's Hotel in Ludgate Hill. Large letters over the entrance spelled out TEMPERANCE. Learning that the hotel was full, she had her trunk brought to the lobby for safekeeping, paid her cab fare, and went to a nearby restaurant.

There ended the cabbie's story, but Nancy's London tour wasn't over yet. After eating something at the ABC Teashop, she hailed another cab. Again, her trunk was hoisted to the roof, and the hotel search resumed.

The police saw the change of cabs as a wily ploy: it left the first cabbie ignorant of the suspect's final destination. But Nancy was probably just hungry.

It was three o'clock in the afternoon when she had her cake and tea, and she hadn't eaten since morning.

Further canvassing and questioning led detectives to the Midland Temperance Hotel on Guilford Street in Russell Square. The fact that the street name and her surname were identical went unremarked at the hotel desk because she registered under the name Gould. The cops found this out on September 29, also learning she'd checked out a day earlier, saying she was going to Paris.

Another cabbie search was launched, this time with a boost of American enterprise. The Pinkertons printed stacks of handbills with her portrait and description. The American detective agency wanted to speak with anyone who'd driven the woman from Guilford Street, offering a reward of one pound.

It paid to advertise. A second driver stepped down from his box to tell all. The American woman had asked him to take her from the temperance hotel to the Dover station. When they were almost there, she'd had him reverse course. Their trip had ended at Harrington Square, at the cheap lodgings of no. 25. BETRAYED FOR A POUND blared a headline over this news in an American paper, as if the cabbie had violated a confidentiality agreement.

Paying several weeks' rent in advance but never producing the references promised, Nancy had secured the Harrington Square lodgings. She quickly settled into a routine, often out buying morning newspapers. As "Mrs. McAllister" she claimed to be a native of an Aberdeenshire village who'd picked up an American accent through long residence in Chicago. The room was needed only temporarily, she said, while a house was readied for her.

The landlady said her tenant was nervous, often dosing herself with brandy and chloral, a sedative. Apparently, anxiety had pushed Nancy's temperance beliefs to the side. She also seemed afraid to be alone, often ringing for service, then engaging the landlady in conversation.

She burned a large quantity of paper and other things in the fireplace, observed the landlady, and insisted on locking her room when she went out while taking the key with her. The landlady complained that this made cleaning difficult, but "Mrs. McAllister" was insistent. She said that she had some valuable papers, and servants were always so inquisitive.

Two days into Nancy's stay, her landlady had some important visitors. Chief Inspector Froest had come with Abberline, the Pinkerton's European chief. Recognizing Nancy by the description of their suspect, the woman took them to her.

"You lie!" Nancy reportedly said when Froest said he could identify her. Reports of her exact words vary, but that was the gist. He said he could sense her fear of discovery, but that she never lost her self-control. She had only ten dollars in cash, he said, but quite a lot of valuable jewelry.

The chief inspector admired all the work done by Nancy to cleanse her identity. Labels and laundry marks had been snipped off her clothes, names were cut from letters and cards, and the corners were gone from five handkerchiefs. Initials had been scraped off the metal clasp of a purse.

The trunk was taken to the Bow Street police station for further inspection. Nancy was allowed to hold onto her bag of diamonds, but Froest demanded her purse. It had a secret pocket with worthless little mementos in it, and those were her downfall. A gold thimble was engraved "N. A. G.," a silver thimble was inscribed "A. G. from F.," and three teaspoons bore the marking "Dr. G." Predictably, one paper called them "the telltale trinkets."

Police also found what they called a surgical instrument. They identified it as a uterine sound, like the one that had played a central role in the Jennie Peters case in Lynn. There were also some bottles of drugs in powdered and liquid form and a number of medical books.

At the police station, a representative of the American embassy confirmed the warrant for the provisional arrest. Detective Lamothe of Liverpool identified Nancy as the woman he'd seen getting off the *Vancouver* and had followed in London. Presumably he'd found his way to Bow Street more successfully.

Then Nancy was led to a cell. There was no mention of bail.

Relishing the limelight, Froest told the press she'd made one other mistake besides the spoons and thimbles. When he questioned her, he recalled, "Nothing had been said about murder, but she suddenly said, 'There are other ways of death than murder.'"

Nothing had been said about murder on the warrant either. She'd been provisionally arrested for manslaughter, not murder, and she was making a point of that.

———————

Making her first appearance in a British courthouse, Nancy had a new group of followers. Papers all over Great Britain were abuzz over the so-called

Yellow Mill Pond mystery. They also approved of her clothes. As she was placed in the dock at the Bow Street police court before a capacity crowd, a British paper pronounced her "handsomely dressed" in a black silk skirt with matching blouse and a small hat with feathers.

Her courthouse debut was largely uneventful. She'd retained a high-powered London solicitor, but he didn't appear, claiming illness. It was basically a recital of the events surrounding her arrest by the detectives and the embassy representative.

Her arraignment the next day offered a little more excitement. Somber shades still dominated, relieved this time by a striped silk blouse and crimson belt. This was Nancy's costume for a moment of drama. Her solicitor was on hand as she fainted, but was revived with smelling salts.

The case was postponed for a week, and Nancy was taken back to Holloway Prison. She'd been placed in a cell formerly occupied by a duchess who was awaiting trial on contempt charges. The duchess's special furniture had been removed, however, leaving Nancy with the ordinary jail furnishings. Questions were raised about preferential treatment. The response was that the cells ordinarily assigned to women awaiting trial were being renovated. Her meals were brought in from a nearby coffee shop. That was said to be standard practice for pretrial detainees.

But what had suited the duchess wasn't suitable for Nancy, who later said it was vermin-infested, cramped, and limited in its view, with only one window looking out on a dirty alley. She was soon transferred to the prison infirmary, reportedly after a nervous collapse. Anticipating orders for her extradition, her solicitor had supported her mistaken-identity argument, arguing against the use of the Pinkerton flyer as evidence. Now he was about to change his legal strategy in light of new stateside developments.

There'd been talk in Connecticut that Nancy Guilford could get a chance to turn state's witness against another physician, male, who'd done the deed and dismemberment. That hope vanished as the Bridgeport coroner concluded his inquest and submitted his report. He found that Emma Gill had died of septicemia as a result of a criminal abortion performed by Nancy A. Guilford. Calling her act a "felonious homicide," the coroner named Harry Oxley as an accessory before the fact and Eudora, Harry, and Rose Drayton as accessories after the fact.

A grand jury was immediately convened. Testimony was heard from Birmingham, his detectives, the boys who'd found the body parts, and the patrolmen who'd come to the scene. There were also a few new names, including a woman close with the Draytons and the stable hand who'd brought the rented rig to Nancy's house. Testimony was also heard from a doctor whose examination of a bathtub waste pipe had detected traces of blood. A captain and a seaman from the New Haven boathouse testified that Harry had been on land at the times he said he was sailing.

Harry and Rose were already in custody. A warrant was issued for Eudora, who went missing for several hours, and Oxley was brought back from Southington. He went calmly this time, accompanied by the lawyer who had assured him of bail. He kept quiet about the case, saying he would wait for his chance to tell the story. More than one newspaper postulated that Oxley was shielding others ranked higher in society. The clear suggestion was that some other man or men had slept with Emma Gill and used the innocent Oxley to carry money to her.

If the truth came out, wrote a Southington correspondent, "It might not favor the reputation of certain citizens of this place, but ultimately its result would be for the benefit of the town, both morally and socially," the report concluded.

Even Emma's father reportedly didn't want Oxley prosecuted and continued shopping at his store. However, it was also said that Oxley had signed a full confession, which was attached to the papers requesting Nancy's extradition from Great Britain. Those papers, signed by Connecticut's governor, were awaiting approval in Washington.

The grand jury indicted Nancy and the four others on the charge of manslaughter. That was also the charge on the extradition papers that Bridgeport police detective Edward Cronan had taken to Washington. However, Cronan was informed that Great Britain didn't consider manslaughter an extraditable offense. Accordingly, Fessenden called the grand jurors back. The judge informed them that death resulting from a criminal operation could be construed as murder. All five were indicted for murder in the second degree, punishable by life imprisonment.

The four still on American soil appeared to enter their pleas. The *New Haven Evening Leader* described their turns in the prisoner's pen listening to a clerk read the charges. Oxley flushed and shifted from foot to foot. Eudora, in a large plumed hat and a gray dress with gold and crimson accents, kept her hands folded quietly before her. Harry, "undersized" with a "very shallow complexion" leaned on the rail.

Although admiring Eudora's "pretty figure," the *Leader* reserved its highest praise for Rose Drayton. "She stood with defiant eyes looking straight at the clerk as he read the charge which alleges she is a criminal. She is a woman of great control . . . who would rather die than give up a word more than wanted to," said the piece, which, unlike most of the reporting of the case, didn't specify her race.

Drayton's partner, William J. Philips, had come to support her. Seeing him, she smiled. Philips, who was Black, had not been called for questioning. Nonetheless, Detective Arnold asked him if he was married to Rose Drayton. Philips responded, "I don't know as I have to tell you my private business."

All four entered pleas of not guilty. The judge set bail at $5,000 for Oxley. This was a steep increase from the $3,000 previously furnished for him. Again, he'd be the guest of the hospitable Bridgeport sheriff while his lawyer scrambled for the additional amount.

Eudora had avoided a night in prison by hiding at a friend's house. Her bail was set at $5,000. Arguing for a decrease, Klein said that the state had indicated that she didn't bear much responsibility for the crime.

Fessenden bristled at the suggestion. On the contrary, the state's attorney said, "we have letters to show that she wrote to [Rose], calling her 'her dear friend' and advising her on how to prove [sic] an alibi should one be necessary. In my conclusion, she is just as deep in the mud as her mother is in the mire."

Apparently, the police had found more than a saw in the Draytons' house. Yet, even with the letters in their possession, the cops had subjected the Black woman to interrogation when her version conflicted with Eudora's.

Again, Fred Welch came to Eudora's rescue, posting a $5,000 bond provided by his father. "She is innocent. I know she is innocent, and I'm going to stick to her," he said. She spent a few hours in a cell before the bond arrangements were finalized. Then she walked free.

Her less fortunate brother was unable to pay that same amount and was taken back into custody. For Rose Drayton, the bond was $3,000. Klein, now representing her and her daughter, argued that $1,500 would hold her just as well. The judge was unmoved, and with either amount unattainable, Rose was taken back to county jail.

"Mrs. Drayton has got over thinking that the case against her is only a joke," wrote one newspaper, disregarding all the interrogation she'd already endured, along with loss of income and the separation from her children and her partner, Philips.

A rumor spread that Clara Drayton had avoided indictment by turning state's witness, providing the police enough evidence to incriminate her mother as well as all the Guilfords. However, the authorities denied that, saying they needed Clara only as a witness in certain parts of the case.

After four days in jail, Oxley returned to Southington, where a merchant had furnished bond for him. Only Harry Guilford and Rose Drayton remained imprisoned.

In London, Nancy's solicitor announced that his strategy had changed. His client no longer denied that her identity was Dr. Guilford, but she knew nothing about Emma Gill and had fled and assumed other names only to avoid the hounding of the police. He and his client had a new purpose: to fight extradition.

Across the ocean, Klein joined the struggle. He took aim at the prosecutor's last-minute change of the charge against her. Having read the affidavits attached to the extradition papers, which included Oxley's confession, Klein said, "He cannot hope to convict my client of murder, and I think it a queer proceeding to extradite her on an offense of which she is not guilty." The prosecutor, he said, "should not get her here on one charge to convict her on another."

Bolstering his argument, Klein pointed to the recent trial of Elijah Bond, Henry's former partner in electromagnetic cures. Bond had been charged with murder after the death of one of his abortion patients but convicted of manslaughter. The judge in Bond's case had instructed the jury that death resulting from a septic abortion did not rise to the definition of murder.

Indeed, extracting Nancy from London proved no simple matter. Returning from Washington with the papers unsigned, Detective Cronan had to travel up to Hartford again for the governor's signature on the amended documents. The correction was said to be a "formality," but it delayed matters considerably. Edward Cronan, the Bridgeport cop, had been selected to bring Nancy in. He'd had to cancel his steamship booking.

Grudgingly agreeing that "the offense may, perhaps, be best described as accidental homicide," the *New Haven Register* speculated that a competent lawyer could convince a jury that because no regular practitioner would perform an abortion except to save a woman's life, the matter fell to "irregular practitioners who are as greedy for gain as they are desperate and unskillful in method."

Forgotten in the *Register*'s editorial was all the skill displayed in the body dismemberment attributed to Nancy, or the fact that Connecticut law had licensed her as a practitioner. As to whether "no regular practitioner" would perform an abortion, that was a bold observation for a newspaper based in New Haven, where Yale-trained Dr. Ernest LeRoy Thomson had once stood trial for abortion while his lawyer memorably proclaimed that any father in Connecticut could find a way to end a daughter's unwanted pregnancy.

Indeed, as Eudora and Klein fanned those still-smoldering rumors that a man had done the cutting, Thomson's name had come up again. After all, he had met with Oxley and Emma Gill.

At any rate, the New Haven paper was more bothered by what Nancy had allegedly said about "shaking the pillars of the courts, the clubs, and the churches" of Connecticut if she were brought back. The *Register*, an evening paper, attributed the quote to Nancy. So did the *New York Press*, which had printed those words early that morning. But again, as when other publications had named Nancy as the author of similar statements, it was unclear where or when she'd said this.

Even if the quote was apocryphal, reactions to it were revealing. The New Haven paper dismissed it as an "idle threat" by the irregular Dr. Guilford, asserting that "the courts, clubs, and churches of old Connecticut are not so fragile as she evidently imagines." The *New York Press*, by contrast, wrote that its neighboring state was "terrorized by the threat," asserting that "no one doubt[ed]" the depth of Nancy's "knowledge of Connecticut society failings." As proof of those failings, the New York paper pointed to the three hundred letters received by the Bridgeport police "about missing girls believed to be in a condition to meet the fate of Emma Gill." Ninety-two of those letters, the paper said, were from parents in Connecticut with missing daughters. The *New York Press* wasn't the only out-of-state paper to frame the story this way, taking special delight in embarrassing "old Connecticut," viewing the entire state as a conglomeration of villages frozen in colonial times.

In fact, Connecticut had its fair share of urban types, some about to get more worldly. On Columbus Day, Detective Cronan sailed from New York to Southampton on the USS *St. Louis*, carrying the extradition papers and some additional depositions. Both British and American papers had suggested that quirks of extradition law might save the fugitive doctor. Connecticut authorities were confident, however. Accompanying Cronan was Jennie E. Hill, matron of the Bridgeport jail. If Nancy was released, the detective would need a woman to place her under constant surveillance. The slippery woman couldn't be allowed to escape their grasp.

After an eight-day voyage of mostly smooth sailing, the pair arrived in London on a Friday. Cronan submitted the documents, and a court date was set for Monday.

By now, Chief Inspector Froest and Dr. Nancy Guilford were well acquainted. On Monday morning, he came to bring her in from Holloway Prison. Nancy asked who had come to take her, and he told her. Nancy took her place in the prisoners' dock, and her eyes met Jennie Hill's. Nancy knew her to be the Bridgeport prison matron, but she made no sign of recognition.

Cronan was asked to make a positive identification of the prisoner. He approached and did so. She asked, "What have you done with my children?"

Detective Edward Cronan of the Bridgeport police. *Boston Sunday Post*

He told her they were safe, and she said no more. The court accepted the identification.

Nancy's solicitor said he could no longer find a path toward resisting the extradition. At her request, he also denied reports that she'd admitted her guilt. The magistrate ordered her extradition with a fifteen days' grace period to allow for the possible submission of new evidence or the start of habeas corpus proceedings.

Their work finished, Cronan and Hill were at liberty for the next two weeks. London rolled out the red carpet for its workaday guests from an obscure American city, treating them "royally," Cronan said. The Bridgeport detective became a familiar visitor at Scotland Yard, learning about British detective methods and forming a lasting friendship with Inspector Walter Dew, who would later become internationally famous.

Cronan marveled at the "army" of women soliciting men on London streets. He found time to visit London's saloons, as he called the pubs, surprised to see women employed as barmaids and equally amazed that the male patrons seemed to leave them alone. Indeed, he heard no profanity at all in the saloons, which struck him as remarkable.

The detective's colleague found the trip less satisfying. Expecting to be asked to confirm Cronan's identification of Nancy, she wasn't called upon to do so. The only benefit she hoped to gain from the experience was weight loss. She couldn't stand English cooking or tea and found the coffee undrinkable. Hill was more than ready to leave when the grace period expired in mid-November.

Nancy, too, was tired of waiting. Finally, Froest and a subordinate came to escort her from prison on a Sunday morning. Cronan and Hill traveled separately to the Queenstown pier. Officially, Nancy would remain in British custody until handed over to the Americans when the ship was ready for boarding. As the group stood together, she addressed Cronan. "You need not be afraid of me running away, for I am as anxious to get back to Bridgeport as you are," she said.

She also apologized to Jennie Hill for ignoring her in Bow Street police court, explaining that she had to do so for legal reasons. The explanation gratified the prison matron, who also learned that her prisoner had spoken well of her to the Scotland Yard men. Hill was also impressed to see Nancy's eyes mist as Froest spoke of his sick son.

Matron Jennie Hill of the
Bridgeport police. *Bridgeport
Herald*

Again, on the wharf, Nancy expressed agitation about false reports that she'd confessed. In truth, the British press seemed to have lost interest. As her American handlers took her on board the Cunard line's RMS *Lucania*, the big news was about her fellow passengers. The famous opera singer Nellie Melba was on board, as was the American jockey James Forman "Tod" Sloan, fresh from a streak of wins in Britain. Nancy was booked under her maiden name as Mrs. N. Brown, but the curious could have found her.

Instead, a few papers briefly noted that, in honor of Sloan's equestrian victory, there was a horseshoe-shaped floral arrangement in the *Lucania*'s first-class dining room. Nancy and Hill, sharing a forward stateroom, had the right to sit at that table. Courtesy of the state of Connecticut, they were traveling in style on a steamship notable for its velvet curtains, working fireplace, and other marks of Victorian splendor.

However, the anxious prisoner and her minder didn't enjoy the voyage. As the ship churned through rough and foggy weather, both were seasick most of the time. Nancy kept to her cabin for the first five days. The matron felt only slightly better. Both women were suffering psychologically. Hill said she experienced "mental anxiety" as the ship rolled, and Nancy asked constantly about her children, saying, "They must not suffer. They cannot be made to suffer."

The matron had brought an unsealed letter from Eudora. Familiar with its contents, the matron said it was a "sweet" and "comforting letter." Reading it, Nancy teared up, and "I felt sorry for her," said the matron.

Prisoner and jail keeper talked of other things. Although avoiding discussion of the crime of which she was accused, Nancy vented freely about the press. Hill got a quick course in journalism as her prisoner ranked the newspapers in order of fairness, placing at the bottom those that called her "Old Nance."

The weather brightened toward the end of the weeklong voyage, and Nancy took some strolls on deck. Cronan said his prisoner gave him no trouble and that few on board knew who she was. Hill said Nancy won the admiration of the other passengers, "especially Madame Melba." But it's unclear if these admirers recognized their fellow voyager as an accused murderer and butcher.

If not, the reception in New York harbor would have surprised them. About a dozen reporters rushed onto the ship that morning, ignoring the jockey and the opera star to look for Nancy. Cronan had made a shipboard friend who prankishly misdirected the newsmen, identifying an unsuspecting Englishman as the Bridgeport detective.

Meanwhile, Nancy sat on one end of the ship's music room, while Hill controlled entry. Now wise to the distinctions between papers, the prison matron acted as a press agent. "I slighted the *World* and [*New York*] *Journal* reporters, and I told them that they used insulting terms in referring to Dr. Guilford at the time of the murder," she said.

The Fairfield County sheriff, Sidney E. Hawley, met them at the pier. Leaving Cronan to handle the luggage, he took the two women to a restaurant near Grand Central Terminal. They had a meal together, and Nancy asked the sheriff about her children.

The sheriff told her that Harry was in jail "and that he was a good boy." As a pretrial detainee, he was not required to work, but "he prefers doing hall duty to idleness in his cell," said Hawley.

Then came the disappointment. "I told her I had seen Eudora, her daughter, Friday and at the time the young woman told me she was going out of town for a few days. That caused tears to come to Dr. Guilford's eyes," Hawley said.

Eudora had left town as Nancy was expected back! The daughter who'd begged her to go legitimate was turning her back on her. According to Hawley, Nancy recovered quickly and said, "Eudora is a good girl and it's too bad her name has been brought into the case." Noting that Nancy didn't say the same

TRANSCONTINENTAL DRAGNET | 197

of Harry, the sheriff seemed to be buying into the prevailing belief: that the daughter's hands, at least, were clean.

Having finished their meal, the trio took the next train to Bridgeport. The two women were allowed to sit together, with the sheriff behind. There'd been no chaining or handcuffing of the prisoner through her transatlantic transfer, and none started now.

If Nancy had wanted to slip away into a crowd, she might have managed at the Bridgeport train station. Some seven hundred people had gathered to try to catch a glimpse of her. Disappointed earlybirds had watched several trains arrive without depositing her. Finally, the sheriff sent a message to expect her on the 2:20.

There was a rush toward the last car, as word spread that Nancy was there. She kept her black-bonneted head lowered as she got off the train, saying she should have worn a veil. "I hate to be gazed upon like a curio," she told the sheriff. The lower muscles of her face twitched. It was widely remarked that her daughter hadn't come to greet her.

Hill briefly spoke to reporters. "Did she talk?" they asked.

Hill said, "Why yes. She talked freely all during the trip, but no references were made to the affair for which she will be tried. She did not at any time say anything that would incriminate her."

Some friends had come to meet Hill, who said she was going home with them and could take no more questions—at least for now.

A closed carriage took Nancy to the county jail on Bridgeport's North Avenue. She was put in a room, originally a debtor's cell, that had recently been converted to an infirmary. It was on the top floor of the imposing Gothic structure, and one window offered a panoramic view of the city. Rose Drayton, her daughter, and a handful of other women prisoners were held elsewhere. Nancy's son, one of dozens of men in the facility, was not immediately informed of her arrival.

With representatives from the *New York Journal* and other despised newspapers present, Nancy said she wished to see her son and daughter as soon as possible. But for now, she told her scribbling visitors, "my only request is that I be not disturbed for a few days. I am in need of rest." Assuring she would get that, the sheriff showed the journalists out.

Later that day, however, the *Bridgeport Herald* got a story that would turn into a lightning rod. In a shipboard conversation with the matron, Nancy had singled that paper out for praise, rating its coverage as accurate and respectful. That evening, a *Herald* reporter was present as Matron Hill came to the precinct for a debriefing by Birmingham, Arnold, and the city prosecutor, Giddings.

A weekly newspaper with a liberal bent, the *Herald* had covered the Yellow Mill Pond case in magazine-style depth, combining reporting with analysis. Some of its practices were ethically questionable. For example, the weekly attributed a scorching critique of Birmingham's investigation to a specific state prosecutor, said to have vented his frustration to "a Bridgeport man," presumably in confidentiality. This secondhand account appeared in the *Herald* with a disclaimer stating that the quotes couldn't be verified. On the other hand, it printed the word "abortion" and wrote sympathetically about exploited sex workers in Bridgeport's Tenderloin district, centered at Water and Bank Streets.

The *Herald* never used the phrase "Old Nance." It took a far different view of "Mrs. Guilford," as it called her, suggesting she was covering for a male New Haven physician to whom she was tied romantically. According to this theory, Dr. Guilford may have performed the abortion, but a man quartered the body.

Jennie Hill would land on the *Herald*'s front page that week. She spoke of the shortcomings of British cusine, but she also made some statements that would be widely quoted.

"Do you know that I think a jury would be predisposed in favor of Mrs. Guilford?" Hill said. Asked why, she replied, "Well, because of her manner. She doesn't look like a woman who would commit such a crime as the one with which she is charged. She is an educated woman and a pleasing woman to talk to."

None of this was new. Even one of Nancy's most hated newspapers had described her as "simple, dignified, kindly, matronly, confiding"—the very "anti-type of crime."

But now the prison matron threw a match in: "I have known of cases where she has done a great deal of good," she said.

Here, the city prosecutor interrupted. "Be very careful, Mrs. Hill," said Giddings, "that you do not say anything to reporters which would bear directly upon this case. If you have heard anything that would be evidence, do not say anything about it."

The matron denied she'd done any such thing. But her words were potent. Here was a police force employee stating that Nancy was no criminal. What's more, she'd suggested that abortion could be beneficial.

Jennie Hill wasn't alone in her assessment. Public opinion was shifting. People wondered aloud if the punishment faced by Nancy was too harsh. One Connecticut paper described her reunion with Harry as "affecting." Another wrote of the tears that ran down Eudora's "pretty cheeks" when she finally surfaced and visited her mother, now called "a much hunted woman."

With the hunt concluded, the story lost its national luster. The New York papers sent its correspondents to cover crime and scandal elsewhere. Locally, as the shock of the pond's contents faded, so did the thirst for aggressive prosecution. "Old Connecticut," absorbing new waves of immigrants daily, began to view well-spoken, native-born Nancy as one of its own. There were calls for mercy even from the pulpit.

That only galvanized her enemies. One paper had already called for her hanging. Now, it would have company.

11 | A MUCH-PERSECUTED WOMAN

UNDER THE HEADLINE BRIDGEPORT TROUBLED BY SENTIMENTAL GUSH, the New Haven *Evening Leader* skewered its neighbor to the west, writing, "This town is full of a wishy washy sentiment that is surrounding 'Dr.' Nancy Guilford, the midwife charged with the murder of Emma Gill, with a halo of glory. It is the sort of stuff that makes some women take bouquets to wife murderers."

As an example of this "twaddle," the paper offered the remarks of Jennie Hill, ridiculing the prison matron for describing Nancy as a woman of refinement and culture. The *Leader* also took aim at the Fairfield County jailers for giving their new inmate "a fine room with service," meaning a knife and fork, not just the usual prison spoon, and earthenware dishes instead of tin plates. The New Haven paper had made no such criticism when Oxley spoke of the privileges he'd enjoyed in the same jail.

Nancy, it seemed, might need to extend her stay there. Just days after her arrival, superior court was called into special session to enter her plea and set her bail. Klein and his partner, DeForest, wanted the indictment quashed. They argued that the grand jury had been improperly instructed that a death caused by abortion was murder in the second degree.

The surprise session, announced just that morning, was a boon for Nancy, who'd come from the jail unnoticed. On Klein's advice, she declined to enter a plea, and the clerk wrote, "not guilty." On the question of the bond, her lawyer asked for a range between $3,000 and $5,000. The state's attorney asked that it be fixed high enough to ensure her appearance at trial. He also called her one of the most notorious abortionists. It was set at $10,000.

Nancy said that one of Henry's brothers would pay it, but she was probably just putting on a show of confidence. It soon became evident that she had no way to raise that amount.

Meanwhile, one of the Bridgeport papers joined the anti-Nancy chorus. Borrowing some words from the New Haven *Evening Leader*, although crafting them with less finesse, the local *Morning Union* slammed the "maudlin sentimentalists who would surround a notorious abortionist with a halo."

Congratulating Fessenden on his statements in court, the Bridgeport daily characterized abortionists as "ghouls" and "leeches" who "use the knowledge they possess of others' sins in extorting money from the guilty ones." In light of that last statement, it was a wonder that Nancy couldn't make bail. "Should the crime be laid at her door," the piece continued, she'd be "deserving of the gallows."

Was the tide of public opinion turning? Shut up in prison, Nancy couldn't project the carefully cultivated image that had won her so many admirers. When a Boston paper asked for an interview with her at the prison, she agreed. That was a tremendous mistake.

George H. Donohue of the *Boston Sunday Post* came to Bridgeport to do a character assassination, taking straight aim at the halo. He accused Bridgeport's elite of protecting Nancy to save their own reputations. As for the accused woman herself, he found her no more grandmotherly than the wolf of "Little Red Riding Hood":

> Mrs. Guilford looked anything but the poor, broken-hearted mother, as she has been recently pictured in the local papers. She looked more like the keeper of a sailors' boarding house who was about to start to the fish market for the daily dinner. There was none of the "enfeebled step" or the "tear-stained face"; she was just plain Nancy Guilford.

Turning the flame up, he continued,

> The alleged motherly air is particularly noticeable by its continuous absence; the habitual air assumed by "Old Nance" is that of the cold, cruel-hearted, grasping woman, whose single ambition in life is the accumulation of money. Then she has a way of closing her lips as though she contemplated biting the person she is talking to.

The Boston paper devoted two broadsheet pages to Donohue's feature, lavishly illustrated in art nouveau style. The headline read, BRIDGEPORT'S 400 TRYING TO SAVE 'DR.' NANCY GUILFORD FROM A PRISON CELL, but no local socialites were quoted or pictured. Instead, an illustration of Nancy was ringed with portraits of police-force employees. Among them was Jennie Hill, ridiculed for her postvoyage praise of the accused murderer.

Also pictured was Eugene Birmingham, presented as a hero. Entirely ignorant about all the controversy surrounding Birmingham's bungling, Donohue described him as "thoroughly informed in all matters criminal." Puzzled to find that the Bridgeport police superintendent was "rather averse to discussing the strange case" of Nancy Guilford, the Boston reporter attributed this to modesty.

During his admittedly brief stay in Bridgeport, Donohue gathered that Birmingham was under fire. That was true enough, at least in the press. The police board seemed to stand behind its chief, despite his repeated failures to capture Nancy. Jumping to a comically wrong conclusion, Donohue attributed these "abusive articles" to the members of Bridgeport "swelldom," who wanted Birmingham deposed because of his "aggressive measures in the famous case."

In this imaginative version of events, Birmingham had single-handedly "given the people of Bridgeport the woman for which they clamored," only to face criticism from religious and political quarters, while "society in general holds its fair hands in horror and loudly protests that 'He should never have been permitted to bring the poor woman back to Bridgeport.'" As is evident in that fair-hands image, Donohue didn't mean society in general. He meant women.

Buried within this barrage was the text of Donohue's interview with Nancy. His questions were mild. Responding cautiously, cooperative but careful not to incriminate herself, Nancy would have had no sense of a trap being laid.

The Boston journalist began by asking her about public sentiment, to which she replied, "Oh, public sentiment is all right, only not very practical. I need money and a good legal representative more than I care for sentiment."

Other questions unsuccessfully tried to goad complaints from Nancy about her situation, her mental state, and her treatment in jail. Among her bland responses was, "Everybody has their troubles in this world, and I suppose I have mine." However, she was rattled a bit by the question of whether "sympathetic friends" had visited her. As a longtime outlaw, she couldn't afford to have friends.

She replied, "I don't look for sympathy from anybody, and should anyone come to me and offer me sympathy, I should certainly decline to receive them." Incorrectly, the reporter suggested she would be "all right" while she was "under the protection of the state's attorney." In fact, Fessenden was prosecuting, not protecting, her. Nancy answered, "I do not care for protection from anyone; my protection lies in my work." By her work, she meant legitimate medical practice—the only work she'd ever laid claim to. Like her other answers, this was a declaration of self-sufficiency. As a professional with an established career, she didn't need a man for protection.

But Donohue turned the statement against her. Her work, he implied without writing the word, was abortion, and her protection was blackmail. Once again, she was said to have threatened to pull down pillars. Donohue had a slightly different version, attributing this warning to her: "If I am convicted of this crime, let certain people of Bridgeport beware; for the imposition of a sentence upon me means the disclosure of my list of patients since I have been in business in Bridgeport." Donohue wrote that she'd said these words as the sheriff took custody of her, an occasion during which the reporter wasn't present.

Promoting the conspiracy theory already in circulation, the Boston paper hinted at the "mysterious influence" that had supposedly bankrolled Nancy's global adventures. In its most fantastical flourish, the piece continued:

> The police have the names of 406 women of Bridgeport who have sought the kindly services of "Dr." Guilford during the time she was in business in Bridgeport. They have also the names of 838 women who were taken care of by Dr. Gill and his wife at the office in New Haven. Some of the names on these two lists appear at frequent intervals in the society columns of the local papers.

Unsourced, unfounded, and extremely unlikely—why would Nancy give the police anything if not through her attorney?—this tidbit was too delicious to ignore. The *Waterbury Democrat* reprinted that section verbatim, using Bridgeport's nickname in the headline: FUN AHEAD FOR THE PEOPLE OF THE PARK CITY. In western New York, a paper quoted Donohue at length, delighting in his report of "trembling and concern in staid old Connecticut."

The powerful Hearst news syndicate picked up the story the following week, giving it almost a full page of the *New York Journal*, one of the papers on Nancy's enemies list. Slightly trimmed and rewritten, it omitted the paeans to Birmingham, focusing instead on Nancy's alleged threats. Leading with her quote, "My protection lies in my work," the Hearst paper framed that as a ticket out of jail.

The *Journal* repeated Donohue's assertions about the thousand-plus names in Nancy and Henry's little black books. Apparently assuming that its wide readership agreed that abortion was commonplace, the Hearst paper wrote, "Her . . . patients have moved about, married and become part of other families, who will necessarily be disgraced forever by the disclosures of 'Old Nance.' This is an unfortunate position for the guiltless."

Writing that "the traditions of the past still live" in a Pandora's box, to which Nancy held a key, the editorial implied that abortion was, or had been, routine for many affluent young women—almost a rite of passage. Nearly forgotten in the *Journal* piece was Emma Gill's death. What really stirred its outrage was the potential spilling of secrets.

The rich friends and mysterious influences attributed to Nancy didn't spring her from prison. Had Henry wanted to help her, that would have been impossible. Three properties in New Haven were listed in his name, although her income, of course, had also made their purchase possible. All were heavily mortgaged, and now they were facing foreclosure. On Wooster Square, neglect was taking its toll on their former gracious home and the Chapel Street building that had housed Henry's office. A third property in a more modest residential section was also degenerating. Sales of all three would barely pay off the mortgages.

Illness, or perhaps the semblance of it, held Nancy's place in the jail infirmary. As her lawyers readied their arguments to challenge the murder indictment, she lay suffering with grippe but refusing medical attention. Again, as in Sherborn, she'd lost considerable weight. The press described her "metamorphosis" from her former robust self.

On December 25 Nancy got a Christmas gift of sorts from the *Bridgeport Herald*. An editorial titled "Who Created the Demand?" began by accepting Fessenden's description of Nancy as a most notorious abortionist. But, while not directly challenging the laws banning abortion, the *Herald* urged its readers to reconsider the gravity of the crime in light of its widespread practice.

It was a remarkable piece for the era, promoting sex education in schools and the abandonment of prudery. On one point, however, the *Herald* agreed with the papers that were inimical to Nancy. It wrote that the greatest demand for abortion was among the middle and upper classes. A glance at the birth register at any town clerk's office would show "which class of society populates the earth and which class makes [the] most strenuous efforts to depopulate it," the editorial board wrote, adding that the upper classes were always the first to protest the discussion of such facts "in cold type."

The editorial said its purpose was not to defend Dr. Nancy Guilford, but to put the crime of which she was accused in perspective. Calling abortionists a "necessary evil," the editorial noted that "little pills" sold at every drugstore for the same purpose had also caused the deaths of many women, yet no one had called for the prosecution of the vendors. Clearly, this was a reference to abortifacients.

With the trial not expected to begin for months, the *Herald* was careful to say that the issue of Nancy's guilt was still "an open question." In the meantime, the paper agreed with the scandal sheets that public opinion was shifting. According to the *Herald*, "many" now thought of Nancy as just unfortunate for "getting caught in an unlawful act which is being repeated weekly in every city in this state." However, the paper conceded, "There are not many who would go on the record as saying it."

That was evident as the Connecticut state assembly opened its new session in Hartford. In a brief, rushed speech, the Republican leader of the legislative body listed a handful of important issues confronting the state, ending with, "We've got to convict Nancy Guilford down in Fairfield County."

The legislature had no power to do so, of course, but one of the state's most prominent Republicans was prosecuting the case. State's Attorney Fessenden, active in the national party, was said to be considering a run for the US Senate.

The new year, 1899, began on a sour note for Nancy and Henry, both behind bars in separate facilities. Nancy's champion, the *Bridgeport Herald*, did not think much of Henry, printing his name as "'Dr.' Henry F. Gill" with scare quotes around the title, while Nancy was simply "Dr. Nancy Guilford." The paper had also written that the marriage was on the rocks.

According to the *Herald*, Henry's "confinement has rendered his temper uneven, and he is not very pleasant to visitors who go to see him on business. One such recent visitor was a lawyer preparing the foreclosure sales of Henry's properties. Having been burned once by a reporter disguised as a detective, Henry greeted him by bellowing, "Who are you?" This was followed by, "I don't want to hear you," and a refusal to sign or even glance at papers. The visit abruptly ended as Henry walked away.

The foreclosures went forward, and all the horses, carriages, and furnishings left at the Wooster Place house were sold at auction. Meanwhile in Bridgeport, the owner of Nancy's former house on Gilbert Street couldn't find tenants. No one wanted to live in a place where a woman had entered alive but departed in sections. The property became known in real estate circles as a white elephant.

Connecticut, too, had financial worries. The state calculated that the Nancy Guilford case had already cost it $2,307 (more than $80,000 today), and the trial had yet to begin.

In early February, Nancy made an appearance in superior court as Judge George W. Wheeler ruled against quashing the indictment for second-degree murder. The trial would go forward on that charge, which carried a mandatory sentence of life imprisonment. Nancy reportedly showed no sign of disappointment, instead appearing "oblivious of all about her."

A huge crowd filled the courtroom on February 20, when the trial was expected to commence. Women, particularly eager for a look at the accused murderess, flocked to the courthouse singly or in pairs. However, many were stopped at the door. Sheriff Hawley reportedly had banned women from the proceedings.

At any rate, it was a false alarm. The Guilford case had been postponed so that another murder case could be tried first. This was the first of several abruptly announced postponements that would continue into March, drawing in throngs only to send them away, disappointed. One postponement was explained by Nancy's decline into a "mental and physical wreck."

In the meantime, the sheriff came under fire for his unfair treatment of women. At every false start, men filled the seats while women were banished. Denying that his decisions were gender-based, Hawley said he was restricting admission to "persons known to the sheriff or his deputies, to persons interested in the case, and to those introduced by members of the bar." Or so he said. Eventually, it became evident that these decisions were based on gender. Trivializing the issue, a paper wrote that women "will have to content themselves by congregating on the courthouse steps and hating the sheriff, the mean old thing."

When the day finally arrived, Nancy arrived in a fashionable carriage driven by a man in full livery. Sheriff Hawley had escorted her from jail along with the prison doctor and a nurse. After all the false starts, the crowds had thinned, and she faced relatively few spectators. However, the press was on hand to describe her ashen face, stricken manner, and labored movements. It was generally agreed that the last few weeks had destroyed her completely.

Unable to walk unassisted, she was escorted to an easy chair provided for her behind her lawyer's table. As jury selection began, Nancy seemed to retch and faint, falling halfway from her seat. A deputy sheriff ran for water. Stimulants were administered, and there was a short recess as Nancy recovered in a restroom.

The nurse—dressed in purple and mistaken by one out-of-town paper for Eudora—was constantly at Nancy's elbow, appearing to be both attendant and friend. The real Eudora was absent, also claiming illness.

It was a classic Nancy performance, upstaged somewhat by the quiet presence of Emma Gill's mother, who was genuinely ill, and several of her children. One reporter remarked on "the striking resemblance of the young children to the face which so long stared through the sealed glass jar at Cullinan's morgue."

Their Southington neighbor, Oxley, was also there with an impressive legal team. An esteemed Hartford attorney, William C. Case, had joined with Holcomb to represent him. It was murmured that the Oxley parents must have dug deep into their pockets to retain such an eminence as Case.

Nancy looked mostly at the floor, the press wrote. For once, that was probably accurate. If she glanced Oxley's way, it would have been with secret loathing. In her code of conduct, he was the lowest of the life forms: a snitch.

No one contested the fact that the jury would be all-male. That was taken as a given. The process took less time than expected, with eleven jurors chosen from a panel of some forty on the first day. The court dismissed some candidates who said they'd made up their minds about their case, and others were eliminated by challenges from either side. Fessenden objected to the selection of a young, unmarried man, and Klein didn't want the father of five single daughters.

Of the eleven selected, nearly all were farmers, middle-aged or older. Their names were released to the press. Some were well known locally, having held public office or otherwise distinguished themselves. No alternate jurors were chosen.

The jury box was filled—with yet another farmer—by noon the next day. As the trial began, the chief line of defense took shape. It would be admitted that Oxley came to Nancy's Bridgeport home to discuss Emma Gill's medical condition. However, the defense would contend that Emma Gill didn't die at 51 Gilbert Street and wasn't operated on there, but instead underwent treatment from an unnamed physician, and that that person or someone else disposed of the body.

Although no friend of Nancy, the *World* found that argument plausible, noting that it had always been considered remarkable that Nancy, so familiar with Bridgeport, wouldn't have known about the tides of Yellow Mill Pond.

The pond was revisited as the four boys who'd found the body parts took turns at the witness stand. It was SMALL BOY DAY, as one headline said. Dressed in knickerbockers and orange sweaters, and punctuating their testimony with many yes-sirs, the quartet boldly told of fishing up the head and legs. Seeming better today, Nancy took an interest in the proceedings, even asking her cocounsel, DeForest, to move some books that were obstructing her view.

Stephen Kelly, one of the juvenile witness quartet, was sternly asked why he wasn't in school that day. Because there wasn't any school, he answered, eliciting a rare smile from Nancy. Or so wrote one member of the big news syndicates, back in Bridgeport and reporting every tic of the accused's face, apparently unimpeded by her choice of millinery. Always wearing black, she alternated wide-brimmed picture hats with high-crowned ones, always with a full veil.

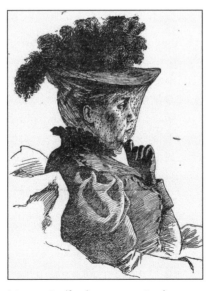

Nancy Guilford in court in Bridgeport.
Bridgeport Herald

Nevertheless, she was said to have averted her eyes from members of the Gill family as they testified tearfully about their last days with Emma. After a sister stood down from the witness stand, Langdon B. Smith of the *New York Journal* claimed to have heard Nancy sigh deeply. "Was it relief?" he asked provocatively.

Imprisonment hadn't stopped Nancy from reading the papers, and she wanted the *Journal* stopped. It was one thing for the press to describe her shriveled face and receding chin—that she could endure. But the Hearst paper was running headlines about the "OLD NANCE" MURDER CASE, which, Klein argued, were prejudicial. Judge Wheeler's initial response was that it was not his place to tell newspapers what to write. However, he had a talk with the reporter.

Langdon Smith, one of the rare reporters to get a byline attached to his work, declared he had no control over the headlines or picture captions that accompanied his stories. He also said that his pieces were routinely rewritten with new introductory paragraphs. However, when the judge asked him to circle the portions that were his, Smith said he couldn't remember.

That prompted a little digging. A clerk at Bridgeport's postal telegraph office provided evidence that Smith had wired the headlines and captions to his newspaper, also giving advice about illustrations. The judge scheduled a contempt hearing for Smith, who didn't appear and stayed away for the rest of the trial.

Fresh from that victory, Nancy swept into court the next week with a defiant look. Monday was dull, as the medical examiner and scientific experts spoke in highly technical language about the condition of the body. Tuesday began in the same tedious way with testimony about the tides. In the afternoon, though, things took a dramatic turn. Harry Oxley got on the stand.

As word spread that Oxley was testifying, the spectators' benches filled to overflowing. This was the centerpiece of the state's case. Oxley's testimony—or confession, as the press called it—was the strongest evidence the government had against Nancy Guilford. Harry Oxley, described as "the good looking, gentlemanly appearing country boy, with never a stain on his character up till today," was pitted against Old Nance.

Things got off to a bad start. Trembling, Oxley spoke in a voice so low it was barely audible. Starting at three o'clock and continuing for three hours, he admitted he was responsible for Emma Gill's pregnancy. The young shopkeeper spoke of accompanying her to Nancy's house in Bridgeport and leaving her there after making his first payment toward the negotiated price. He told of returning to find her gone and seeing her for the last time in Southington before she went back to Bridgeport, never to return.

It was an affecting story of two young people desperately seeking to change the course of their lives. That's not, however, how many in the audience heard it. The parts that caused a commotion were Nancy's warnings to "write, don't telegraph" and "whatever you do, keep mum." Interspersed were her constant demands for money.

Nancy's genteel image lay in shreds. These were the words of a criminal. The next day, visibly frightened but evidently well coached, Oxley withstood the fire of cross-examination. Klein tried to present him as an untrustworthy witness who was tailoring his answers to the needs of the state. However, Oxley denied having made any deals to avoid prosecution.

Scared as he was, Oxley could not be rattled over minor discrepancies in his testimony and an affidavit he'd given police months before. Failing in that, Klein tried to use the state's witness to promote his own other-physician theory—that his client may have seen Emma Gill but didn't perform surgery or dissect the body. Here was a golden opportunity. Oxley had testified about seeing Dr. Ernest Thomson in New Haven.

Klein asked, "Did Mrs. Guilford say anything about operating at all?"

Oxley answered, "I believe she did."

"I don't want any 'believes,'" Klein said. "This is too important a matter for guesswork."

Pressed further, Oxley said twice that he didn't remember whether the word *operate* was used in any of his conversations with Mrs. Guilford.

"Then I don't want you to use it," said the defense lawyer, reminding the witness that he'd been indicted for a murder.

In another exchange, Klein asked Oxley about his new lawyer, the prestigious and presumably expensive William C. Case.

"Did you hire Mr. Case?" Klein asked. The answer was inaudible. Oxley had been repeatedly asked to speak up but rarely did.

"Don't you know that Dr. Ernest Thomson of New Haven employed Mr. Case to defend you?" Fessenden objected, but the court allowed the question.

"No, sir," was the answer. This could have opened a new field for press investigation. Instead, Klein's tactics earned little notice.

The day belonged to Oxley. "He was not without sympathy in the courtroom," wrote one paper, also noting that he was "directly implicating Mrs. Guilford."

However, the case was far from closed. Fessenden had promised a murder conviction within ten days, but the trial continued into April. The prosecution produced a wide array of witnesses, ranging from medical experts to express-delivery clerks. Detectives testified about the smell of the bathroom and the contents of the furnace, plumbers spoke of removing pipes, and disputes raged about the photographs taken of the interiors of Nancy's house.

There were no new revelations, however, and the benches thinned as the trial slipped into tedium. Parts of Emma Gill's body were exhibited in test tubes, and days were devoted to establishing her identity, as Klein milked the Grace Perkins blunder. The defense lawyer also grabbed hold of a rusty buckle found in the Gilbert Street furnace as proof that the clothing burned there was not Emma Gill's. How could rust have formed in a matter of months? One glaring weakness of his other-physician theory was to posit that the body had been carved up in one location while the clothes were destroyed in another.

Oxley continued to attend but spent most of his time in the sheriff's office, emerging only when called. As the trial dragged on, empty seats were plentiful. Still, a local paper observed, "As women are not allowed in the courtroom, they [must try] . . . to get a glimpse of the accused doctress by loitering outside the entrance to the courtyard each evening at the conclusion of the day's proceedings."

Behind the railing where the lawyers and witnesses sat, Eudora finally appeared to sit behind her mother. It was her first time in court, despite earlier reported sightings of her. Harry was still in the North Avenue jail, as unable to make bail as Rose Drayton.

Months earlier, the press had confidently announced that everyone in the case had turned state's witness except for Nancy's children. But only Oxley seemed to have reached a deal thus far. Clara Drayton, although not indicted, by now had spent a significant part of her adolescence behind bars. If Fessenden was still holding her as a witness, why hadn't he called her? But the press had forgotten about the Draytons.

Handwriting experts dominated the first few days of the new month, as the unsigned letter telling Emma to come to Bridgeport was parsed against scraps of paper written in Nancy's hand. Reflecting the general sentiment, a paper wrote, "The state is drawing its web closer about Dr. Nancy Guilford each day," but "thus far there have been no fireworks, no dramatical or oratorical fights."

Then came a juror's collapse. On Wednesday, the sixty-year-old man who occupied seat no. 4 of the jury box dragged himself to the 10:00 AM session. George Gregory, a Darien farmer, knew he wasn't well but tried to fulfill his duty. He happened to be the father of a judge. Soon, though, he announced that he couldn't continue.

The other jurors were dismissed until 3:30, and the doctor and nurse were pulled from Nancy's side to attend to the sick man. Because his home was at some distance, a closed carriage took him to Sheriff Hawley's living quarters at the county jail. A tentative diagnosis was made. The jurors reconvened to learn that the trial was adjourned until the following Tuesday.

Rumors flew about the pace of the juror's recovery. Speculation continued about the evidence the defense would present. It had already been reported that Nancy would testify in her own defense. It was also said that the state might call up Dr. Thomson, who was now in Europe or some other faraway destination.

For all their supposed scoops, the press missed the behind-the-scenes meetings in the courtroom. One was still in progress as the jurors took their places on Tuesday morning. The judge was talking to Fessenden and Dr. Banks, the prison physician who had been caring for the sick juror. It was pneumonia, the doctor confirmed, and Juror no. 4 could not be expected to return to duty until the May session of criminal court.

Fessenden thought that four weeks was too long for the jury to retain its grip on the evidence. Klein had offered to move forward with eleven jurors, but the state's attorney declined. However, recognizing how much this case had already cost Connecticut, Fessenden had been open to a different deal. Judge Wheeler approved it and gaveled in the session.

Those fireworks were coming, after all. Fessenden got to his feet and said, "Your Honor, in the case of the *State v. Guilford*, I have decided to accept with Your Honor's approval, a plea of guilty of manslaughter."

Judge Wheeler approved, giving his reasons for doing so, almost chiding Connecticut for being out of step with the times. A crime of this type in many, if not most, states would be manslaughter. "In this state," he said, "it is murder in the second degree." However, he thought it was important to recognize that, in nearly all such cases in Connecticut, "jurors are wont, if they find conviction, to find the accused guilty of the lesser offense, manslaughter rather than murder."

The judge added that "especially in the case of a woman," that would be the probable outcome. In light of that and considering the expense and disruption that a new trial would cause, he had approved the change of plea.

Nancy was asked to stand up. The clerk said to her, "To the indictment which has been read are you willing to change your plea?"

After a slight hesitation, Nancy said, "I am guilty of manslaughter."

The judge asked her if she had anything to say. She was silent. Her cocounsel, DeForest, made a plea for leniency.

That wasn't granted. The judge sentenced her to ten years in prison, the maximum possible, and fined her one dollar. He said the state had left no question that a criminal operation had been performed.

She was satisfied. The juror's illness had made it possible for Klein to drive a tough bargain. Fessenden had agreed to drop all charges against her son, her daughter, and Rose Drayton.

Before the juror fell ill, the judge hadn't even wanted to talk about reducing the charge to manslaughter. Now, she had a deal to take the heat off Rose and her children. The state wouldn't pit her family against itself. There'd be no snitching.

She released a statement to the press that made the bargain clear: "I am satisfied with my sentence, for now I know that those who are dear and near to me will be given their liberty. That is the reason, the only reason, why I pleaded guilty to manslaughter."

A proud adherent to her code, she said, "I played no part of the sneak as did Oxley, who was more responsible for the death of Emma Gill than any other living person." She said she was tired of hearing that women couldn't hold their tongues when "in cases like these, men are generally the sneaks and cowards." Clearly referring to Oxley, she said, "Those to whom I intended to do a favor and to save from disgrace were the ones who had caused my children and myself so much anguish and suffering."

She indicated that things could have gone easier with her if she'd turned snitch, too, but "I have kept inviolable all professional secrets and this, too, in the face of the fact that I was implored to connect others with this offense." There were those "others" again, the phantom physicians who did the whole thing elsewhere. This was a guilty plea but not a confession.

She praised the judge for his fairness, her lawyers for being her protectors and her counsel, and the jury, wishing they could have tried the case "for many things could have been made public then that favored me." But of the state, she said, "They got no Oxleyized statement from me and never would," suggesting that the prosecution had crafted its star witness's testimony.

Some papers in distant cities announced the news under headlines like SHE-WOLF CAGED. But locally and even in New York, her act was viewed as motherly devotion. The *Bridgeport Herald* ran the story under the banner EUDORA CANNOT GO ON THE WITNESS STAND.

Nancy would be transported to Wethersfield State Prison the next day. Henry was still there with some four hundred other men. A small cell block held about a dozen women. This was bound to be worse than her experience at Sherborn in Massachusetts. Connecticut had an active prison-reform movement, which for years had tried to establish a separate women's facility, arguing that segregated quarters were essential for women's safety. But plans for a potential Hartford site were scrapped when the neighbors objected.

Women's cell block, Wethersfield State Prison. *Courtesy of Wethersfield Historical Society*

Eudora visited Nancy on her last night at the county jail, accompanied by Rev. Russell of the South Congregational Church. The former leader of Eudora's Bible-study class had become known as Nancy's spiritual adviser.

Sheriff Hawley made only vague announcements about the travel plans to Wethersfield, wanting to avoid the curious hordes. But nobody was waiting outside the North Avenue jail when he and a prison matron took Nancy to the station. They'd catch the 8:30 AM train to Hartford and hire a hack for the last four miles to Wethersfield.

The press was busy with its own postmortem, interviewing detectives about how they'd brought the guilty woman to justice. Reminiscing about their part in the Adams Express money-envelope escapade, the New Haven and Hartford cops also basked in the glow. As the sheriff and two women took their seats on the morning weekday train, nobody paid attention to them.

AFTERWORD

VISITORS OCCASIONALLY ASKED TO SEE Nancy in the women's section of the Wethersfield prison, where women were allowed to use their own tea-cups and arrange pictures on the walls of their cramped cells. The new warden had stopped forcing prisoners to march in lock-step, and prisoners could earn special privileges through a grading system. However, it was a harsh place, and there were no more reports of Nancy languishing in an infirmary. Female inmates worked in the laundry that defrayed the institution's expenses.

She spent her first month behind bars waiting for the state to keep its part of the bargain. Weeks passed while Nancy's children and Rose Drayton still faced murder charges. In the meantime, Alderman Welch put up another bond of $5,000 to bail out Harry, the prospective brother-in-law of his son. Even with the mother convicted, the popular politician—just reelected by a wide margin—lent a helping hand.

As he'd said of Eudora before, "If she loves my boy Fred, and he loves her, why I'll be glad to dance at the wedding."

A few weeks later, the state came through and dropped all charges against the Guilford children and Rose Drayton. Rose had spent almost eight months in jail. Presumably, Clara had been home for some time, but, again, no one paid attention. On the same day, Oxley saw the terms of his deal fulfilled. Charges against him were also dropped. Fessenden said the state was satisfied with the work it had done in convicting Nancy Guilford.

A few days earlier, Emma Gill's mother had died. Some papers attributed this to heartbreak, but she'd been sick for some time.

Alderman Welch didn't dance at his son's wedding to Eudora. No longer under the cloud of indictment, she'd returned to Wellsburg, where she spent long hours with another young man named Fred. In late August, she mar-ried Frederick Gibbs, an aspiring professional violinist with a taste for playing popular songs like "The Lost Chord" and "In the Gloaming." He'd had a few bookings on the vaudeville circuit. Hoping for more, the couple moved to a boarding house in lower Manhattan.

Within a year, the young couple was back in the Wellsburg area, living in the home owned by Fred Gibbs's mother. Soon after, Eudora gave birth to a son. They'd name him Henry Guilford Gibbs after his maternal grandfather.

Henry was released from prison around the time his namesake was born. Sentenced to three and a half years, he'd gotten out six months early for good behavior. One of his first stops after his release was a reunion with Eudora in Bridgeport, where she was staying. First, though, he had some business to attend to in Hartford.

Despite his testiness about the New Haven foreclosures, Henry hadn't emerged from the prison gates entirely lacking in resources. Trading in his prisoner number for his old alias, Dr. Henry F. Gill, he quickly established a practice in Hartford, advertising for patients as far away as Middletown, almost twenty miles south. Medical specialists had grown in number since he first opened shop, decades ago at his father's health-lift gym. But Henry remained an outlaw physician of the old school, billing himself as a jack-of-all-trades while meaningfully capitalizing that he could treat all FEMALE DIFFICULTIES, and that ladies could write to him "in the strictest confidence, terms moderate."

By 1904 Nancy had served more than half her time. Her ten-year sentence had been commuted to nine years for good behavior. She requested a pardon that year but quickly withdrew the request. Two years later, she tried again, arguing on her own behalf and through Klein, still her lawyer. The pardon was denied.

By that time, Henry was the proud owner of an automobile. One of only seventy-seven thousand car owners in the entire country, he took a druggist for a spin. Prospering in his practice and real estate investments, he nonetheless was full of resentments. He complained to his passenger that the local medical establishment didn't reciprocate the respect he paid them. The Hartford Medical Association didn't count him as a member, and his name didn't appear in a Connecticut registry of physicians. However, the American Medical Association still included him in its directory as a medical school grad, licensed in Connecticut.

While thus feeling aggrieved, he played an elaborate trick on Nancy. Without fanfare, the state had commuted her sentence again, shaving two years off in all. As the date of her release approached, Henry wanted nothing to do with her personally or financially. To protect his assets from her, he faked insanity and had himself confined to a private mental hospital. The plan was to place his estate under the control of his first child, Herbert, who evidently had agreed to keep it away from Nancy.

Learning about this while still in prison, Nancy joined Eudora and Harry in a lawsuit. For Nancy, this was a heartbreak and a violation of the family code. Henry had manipulated Herbert, the stepson she had lovingly raised and the father of Willie, once her adored little houseguest in Bridgeport.

It was an elaborate scheme, started well in advance of her discharge from Wethersfield. Anticipating a court battle for which he'd need witnesses, Henry told a select group of people, including a policeman, that he heard voices and saw visions about indecent sexual "hijinks" and murderous acts—some involving dismemberment—in the house next to his. According to the medical crony who signed his commitment papers, Henry's obsession with these hallucinations made him a potential public menace.

The matter came before a judge. Henry's lawyer argued that an individual, preferably Herbert, should be appointed conservator of the estate. The attorney for Nancy and Eudora wanted a bank to take control. Herbert was said to have a hostile relationship with his half-siblings and stepmother.

Several witnesses said they'd heard Henry's ramblings about the alleged indecencies next door. Nevertheless, they thought that the doctor's shrewd business dealings proved him to be a man of "powerful mind" and "retentive memory," rather than unsound or dangerous.

Foiled by his own success, Henry saw the court appoint a bank as conservator. Rallying in a miraculously quick recovery, he was discharged from the sanitarium. Declared sane again, he ended the conservancy and took back control of his assets. He couldn't shield them from Nancy, or at least not through that scheme.

A short time later, Nancy was released from Wethersfield State Prison, where she'd spent eight years in one of the curtained cages of the women's section. That event went unnoticed. Only a Swedish-language newspaper seemed to have realized that her twice-commuted sentence had ended.

Henry offered to pay her $150 a month in support on one condition: she had to stay away from him. Both parties agreed.

Geographically, however, they remained close for more than a decade. Nancy settled in the Hartford area, adopting the name Alice Gibbs to match the surname of her daughter and little grandson. Eudora divorced Fred Gibbs, the violinist, soon after Nancy's release. Mother and daughter, both newly single, raised the child in a female-run household.

Eudora began to work as a nurse. It's not clear how she got her training. Years later, filling out an application form, she skipped the question about her professional school but cited longtime employment through the Hartford nurses' registry. The support payments from Henry would have helped the household, too, but those proved unreliable.

A few years after the agreement was signed, the payments ceased altogether. Nancy went to court and attached Henry's property. Until then, she had kept her name and alias out of the papers. At age sixty, she had finally heeded Eudora's advice and gone legit. Or so it seemed.

However, Henry, several years older, was still a well-known abortion provider. That became evident in 1915, when Henry testified in a breach-of-contract case brought by a pregnant woman whose lover refused to marry her. The plaintiff said the man had taken her to see Henry about an abortion, which she didn't want. Placed on the witness stand, Henry said he'd told the woman to consult a lawyer.

Attacking Henry's credibility, the defendant's lawyer asked about Henry's jail time in Wethersfield. This was ruled inadmissible. The lawyer also asked if Henry maintained rooms for female patients where, it was suggested, he paid women to perform abortions. Henry answered that he specialized in chronic illnesses.

There's no way of knowing if he'd replaced Nancy in the manner the lawyer was hinting at. Soon, though, he replaced her in his personal life. At age seventy, he married a forty-year-old woman named Bertha Gearing, his former nurse and housekeeper, without bothering to divorce Nancy first.

The May-December pairing of Henry and his new bride caused a small stir. Impressed by this show of geriatric virility, the medical establishment finally tipped its hat to Henry. "Everything is possible," announced a professional journal, describing how Henry, "nattily attired" in a black-and-white checked suit and carrying a silver-tipped cane, took his vows at a Massachusetts ceremony attended by three of his nieces.

The rest of his family, effectively erased, was not in attendance. Applying for a Massachusetts marriage license under his birth name, Henry M. Guilford, the groom had declared himself a widower. Apparently, it was impossible for Dr. Henry Gill to marry anywhere, since he couldn't prove his existence. Connecticut papers announced the joyous event, explaining the doctor's dual identities and recounting the Yellow Mill Pond murder mystery. According to the *Bridgeport Farmer*, Nancy had been dead for several years. In fact, she was very much alive.

But Henry's new wife was the one who saw him through a 1918 trial. A married Hartford woman was found to have had an illegal abortion, and the evidence led to him. Unable to post $5,000 in bail, Henry spent two months in jail awaiting trial. His business acumen may have failed him, or his penchant for gambling could have swallowed his gains. His fees for abortions had also dropped steeply since his days in New Haven. Down payments as low as $25 were accepted, perhaps due to increased competition.

As a physician opposed to abortion wrote ruefully around that time, "The more civilization progresses, the more frequent does artificial abortion become. And it is nowhere punished because the operators are sheltered by the sympathy of the community."

In fact, Henry was convicted and sentenced to six months in prison. But in consideration of his age, seventy-four, he was allowed to serve his time in a mental hospital.

Perhaps not coincidentally, Eudora finally left Connecticut to begin an entirely new life in Poughkeepsie, New York. Now a hairdresser, she opened a beauty salon near the Vassar College campus. After years of bouncing from one Hartford rental to another with her mother, she was living on her own. Her eighteen-year-old son, Henry G. Gibbs, joined her there once she was settled.

Nancy stayed behind in Hartford. Still known as Alice Gibbs there, she'd acquired a reputation as a quiet, law-abiding citizen and frequent churchgoer.

Then a woman ended up in a New Britain hospital, an illegal abortion was detected, and Nancy was arrested. Bail was set at $1,500, and the case was continued until the following week.

At the *Hartford Courant*, some of the old-timers remembered the Yellow Mill Pond case. Old clippings were pasted together for a front-page piece titled NANCY GUILFORD IN TROUBLE AGAIN AFTER MANY YEARS. Trying to breathe new life into an old tale, the *Courant* sent a reporter to knock on the apartment door of "Alice Gibbs" on Linden Place and ask for Mrs. Guilford.

Two women took turns coming to the door. The hapless journalist— undoubtedly too young to remember the notorious "Old Nance" of decades before—described one as "tall" and "well built" but didn't estimate ages. The second woman could have been Nancy.

"You're a reporter," she said before slamming the door and lowering the shades.

Times had changed, and Nancy now had a telephone that the press could use to hound her. It rang, but she didn't pick up.

Looking far less assertive the following week, she hobbled into Hartford police court. Her lawyer asked for a reduction of bail, asserting that prison food would exacerbate her diabetes. Instead, it was raised to $2,500. She went to jail while the case was bound over to superior court.

The patient in the case had also been charged, but those charges were dropped. The woman was expected to be the chief witness against Nancy. The prosecution maintained that the woman had subjected herself to an abortion "out of ignorance," and the press couldn't agree on her name or place of residence.

The woman may have vanished, taking the state's case with her. Nancy's brief return to the front pages was over. All coverage of the case was dropped.

The family's long journey through the underworld ended. Its new boss was Eudora. Three generations of Guilfords lived under her roof in Poughkeepsie, where she'd bought the building that housed her hair salon. The 1925 New York state census found Nancy and her grandson there, as well as her son, Harry, and his wife, Minna.

Nancy, undoubtedly to everyone's relief, had no occupation. She didn't need to work. Thriving at her original location in the Arlington section of Poughkeepsie, Eudora opened a second salon downtown. The short-hair craze, permanents, and finger waves kept the cash registers ringing.

Henry died in 1928. The funeral was held at his home in Hartford, and his remains were cremated in Springfield, Massachusetts. His native state had once banished him, but, having allowed him to return for his illegal marriage, it now accepted his remains. He was eighty-three.

Nancy died at Eudora's home eight years later. After all the reports of her physical breakdowns and many displays of illness, she survived to age eighty-four, having been "old" for more than three decades.

In the year of Nancy Guilford's death, Margaret Sanger came to the Vassar Alumnae House in Poughkeepsie to talk about birth control.

ACKNOWLEDGMENTS

THIS BOOK COULDN'T HAVE BEEN WRITTEN without the generous and knowledgeable assistance of many individuals and institutions. I'm particularly grateful to Catherine Perreault of the Massachusetts Archives, who made it possible for me to access Nancy Guilford's inmate records remotely when the archives were closed to the public. I'm indebted to Judith O'Blenes of the Lynn Public Library, whose patience and technical expertise brought faded newspaper pages into focus. Many thanks also to Jeannie Sherman of the Connecticut State Library, who steered me toward many invaluable documents, including the original coroner's report of Emma Gill's death, and to Dominique Winn of the Woburn Public Library for locating an obscure poem written more than a century ago.

Thanks also to the Bridgeport History Center of the Bridgeport Public Library. I spent many of the happiest days of my youth in that library, and it was a thrill to revisit it as an adult. The Wethersfield Historical Society and the Connecticut Historical Society provided me with valuable photographs and other materials. The New York Public Library's interlibrary loan service and research databases gave me a ticket to time travel.

I'm also grateful to the Special Collections Research Center of the Syracuse University Libraries and the Warren Hunting Smith Library of Hobart and William Smith Colleges for helping me check into Henry M. Guilford's claims about his medical education. I also thank Ron Keene, the town historian of Barton, New York, for his efforts to substantiate press reports of Henry's practice there. Coming up with nothing can be the most useful result of all. Any errors or omissions are mine alone.

This book couldn't have been published without the support of my literary agent, Amanda Jain, and my editor, Jerome Pohlen. Copyeditor and fact-checker Joseph Webb asked thoughtful questions, and Chicago Review Press managing editor Devon Freeny shepherded my work through production with skill and courtesy.

Cheering me on were the Women's Nonfiction Author group led by Christine Yared and two offshoots of the Biographers International Organization: the women's round table organized by Sara Fitzgerald and the science round table led by Gabriella Marie Kelly-Davies. It would have been hard to make it to the finish line without them.

Above all, thanks and much love to those who listened and responded to my endless Nancy and Henry stories: Phyllis and Alan Biederman, Michael and Jonah Quinn, and Paul DuCett.

NOTES

Prologue

"and I saw a foot": "Coroner's Inquest Fails to Aid Police," *World* (New York), September 15, 1898.

"rolled out": "A Foul Murder," *Evening Leader* (New Haven, CT), September 13, 1898.

"aquiline" nose: "'C51' the Fatal Marks That Silently Point to the Slayer of This Girl," *New York Evening Journal*, September 13, 1898.

"wealth of hair": "Foul Murder," *Evening Leader*.

Fatefully, a small bit: "Dr. Guilford to Testify," *New Haven (CT) Register*, March 28, 1899.

"criminal operation" . . . DEATH RESULTING FROM CRIMINAL PRACTICES: V. R. C. Giddings, "Death Resulting from Criminal Practices Is Murder in Connecticut," *World* (New York), September 15, 1898.

"slender and graceful in figure": "Has Gone to Canada," *Elmira (NY) Telegram*, September 18, 1898.

"impelling force": K. Sellers Kennard, "Criminal Depacage," *Medico-Legal Journal* 41, no. 5 (September–October 1924): 136.

"diseases of women": "Dr. N. Alice Guilford" (advertisement), *New Haven (CT) Register*, July 21, 1897.

"best society": "Threat to Tell All She Knows," *Elmira (NY) Daily Gazette and Free Press*, December 5, 1898.

"pillars of the courts": "Kinks in the Law May Save Nancy," *New York Press*, October 10, 1898.

"move in the best society": "Another Arrest Made," *New Haven (CT) Morning Journal and Courier*, March 7, 1898.

1. Before Henry Met Nancy

"appeared to be sent": Mark Fernald, *Life of Elder Mark Fernald* (Newburyport, MA: Geo. Moore Payne and D. P. Pike, 1852), 301.

"We make no boast": Simon Clough, *The Rise and Establishment in Five and Twenty Years in the United States of America of 1000 Unitarian Congregations Under the Denomination of Christians; Together with a Detailed Statement and Defence of the Their Opinions* (London: R. Hunter, 1831), 7.

"Religion appears to be": H. P. Guilford, letter to the editor, *Christian Herald and Journal* (Exeter, NH), February 20, 1840.

"a voluntary criminal": "Mary Rogers—Another Warning to Youth," *Christian Herald and Journal* (Exeter, NH), January 5, 1843.

"small struggling band": James Montgomery Bailey, *History of Danbury, Conn., 1684–1876* (New York: Burr Printing House, 1896), 318.

"Rev. H. P. Guilford, formerly": "Religious Intelligence," *Zion's Advocate* (Portland, ME), April 24, 1857.

"landsman": Historical Data Systems of Kingston, Mass., Comp. U.S., Civil War Soldier Records and Profiles, 1861–1865, Ancestry.com, 2009.

"the ward-room": William B. Avery, "Gunboat Service on the James River," in *Personal Narratives of the War of the Rebellion*, third series, no. 3 (Providence, RI: Rhode Island Soldiers and Sailors Historical Society, 1884), 21, https://babel.hathitrust.org/cgi/pt?id=hvd.hx4u37&view=1up&seq=125.

"unruly men": Michael J. Bennett, *Union Jacks: Yankee Sailors in the Civil War* (Chapel Hill: University of North Carolina Press, 2004), 81.

in listings: Henry is listed under the alias he later used, Henry F. Gill, with his graduation record in E. Eliot Harris, M.D., ed., *The Medical Directory of New York, New Jersey, and Connecticut*, vol. 1 (New York: Trow Directory Printing and Bookbinding Co., 1899), 40, and American Medical Association, *American Medical Directory* (Chicago: American Medical Association, 1911), 1440.

2. Creating a Doctor

"belle": "Nancy Guilford's Story," *Baltimore Sun*, September 20, 1898.

"a tinge of the romantic": "Left Wellsburg in Haste," *Boston Globe*, September 16, 1898.

"nice girls" . . . *"He did not like him"*: "Nancy Guilford's Story," *Baltimore Sun*.

"sedentary and anemic young ladies": Editor's Table, *Sanitarian* 4, no. 34 (January 1, 1876): 48.

"To those who cannot come": "Something About the Health-Lift" (advertisement), *Fall River (MA) Daily Evening News*, May 20, 1876.

"The Rev. Mr. Guilford": The City, *Fall River (MA) Daily Evening News*, June 3, 1876.

"Dr. Guilford returned this morning": The City, *Fall River (MA) Daily Evening News*, July 26, 1876.

"by mutual consent": "Dissolution" (advertisement), *Fall River (MA) Daily Evening News*, January 11, 1877.

"control the business entirely": The City, *Fall River (MA) Daily Evening News*, May 5, 1877.

"Yesterday we bled everyone": J. Winthrop Spooner, "The Relations of the Fellows of the Massachusetts Medical Society and the Homeopaths," *Boston Medical and Surgical Journal* 107, no. 4 (July 27, 1882): 77.

Under the heading of *"Physicians"*: Charles R. Tuttle, ed., *New England Official Directory and General Hand-Book for 1878–79* (Boston: Jewett & Tuttle, 1878), 250–259.

"The Lame Walk!": "Magnetic Healing of the Sick" (advertisement), *Fall River (MA) Daily Evening News*, December 19, 1876.

"complaints peculiar to females": "Dr. Guilford" (classified advertisement), *Worcester (MA) Daily Spy*, January 19, 1878.

"Dr. Guilford, Psychomatic": "Dr. Guilford" (advertisement), *Fitchburg (MA) Daily Sentinel*, January 21, 1878.

"is not a traveling quack": "Dr. Guilford" (advertisement), *Fitchburg (MA) Daily Sentinel*, January 30, 1978.

"physician, surgeon, and accoucheur": "Ladies or Gentlemen" (advertisement), *Worcester (MA) Daily Spy*, May 1, 1879.

"newly and elegantly furnished": "Dr. Guilford, Physician and Surgeon" (advertisement), *Worcester (MA) Daily Spy*, September 19, 1878.

"persons of either sex" . . . *"afternoons devoted to lady patients"*: "Notice to the Public" (advertisement), *Worcester (MA) Daily Spy*, March 29, 1879.

"The married woman": Ely Van De Warker, *The Detection of Criminal Abortion and a Study of Feticidal Drugs* (Boston: James Campbell, 1872), 7–8.

"physician and surgeon" . . . *"female diseases"*: "Naomi" (advertisement), *Fall River (MA) Daily Evening News*, October 1, 1874.

"high moral" and *"Christian"* character: "The Terry Correspondence," *Boston Herald*, October 24, 1891.

"Mrs. Dr. Guilford, the accomplished daughter": "Wellsburg Items," *Elmira (NY) Daily Advertiser*, August 14, 1879.

3. Lynn, Lynn, City of Sin

"a profusion of diamonds": "Lynn's Last Sensation," *Boston Post*, January 4, 1886.

"gentleman of culture": "Henry F. Gill, MD" (advertisement), *Waterbury (CT) Republican*, January 3, 1889.

MRS. DR. ALICE GUILFORD: "To Ladies" (advertisement), *Daily Evening Item* (Lynn, MA), October 12, 1881.

"Flamboyant" signage: "Mrs. Guildford [*sic*] Was in Prison," *New York Herald*, September 18, 1898.

"immense number": "Lynn's Latest Sensation," *Boston Sunday Herald*, January 3, 1886.

"a well-dressed, rather good-appearing": "Dr. Ford of Brockton," *Boston Globe*, January 4, 1886.

"as a therapeutic agent": "Home for Invalids" (advertisement), *Boston Evening Transcript*, May 29, 1883.

"Parturition Without Pain": "Lecture" (advertisement), *Boston Evening Transcript*, February 18, 1884.

"Cause and Cure of Nervous Prostration": "Lecture" (advertisement), *Boston Globe*, February 15, 1884.

"spirit forms": "Funeral Services by Spirits," *Boston Globe*, April 8, 1887.

"folks" who might "make trouble": "Victim Jennie Peters," *Boston Globe*, May 18, 1886.

"would do no good" . . . *"Come when you have the money"*: "The Guilford Case: Dr. Alice Guilford Testifies in Her Defense," *Daily Evening Item* (Lynn, MA), May 17, 1886.

"give her away": "Victim Jennie Peters," *Boston Globe*.

"feeling no better": "Guilford Case: Dr. Alice Guilford Testifies," *Daily Evening Item* (Lynn, MA), May 17.

"bringing some people around": "Guilford Case: Dr. Alice Guilford Testifies," *Daily Evening Item*.

"Everyone knows who I am": "The Victim as a Witness," *Boston Herald*, May 18, 1886.

"breaking down of the" . . . *"extreme case"*: Frank A. Stahl, "Some Expressions of Abortive Attempts at Instrumental Abortion," *Journal of the American Medical Association* 31, no. 27 (December 31, 1898): 1561–62.

"small body": "Guilford Trial," *Daily Evening Item* (Lynn, MA), May 18, 1886.

"take care of it": "Conviction Improbable," *Boston Herald*, May 19, 1886.

"a sick girl out on the street": "Victim as a Witness," *Boston Herald*.

"Lynn, Lynn": Linda A. Fisher and Carrie Bowers, *Agnes Lake Hickok: Queen of the Circus, Wife of a Legend* (Norman, OK: University of Oklahoma Press, 2012), 85.

"in very bad condition": "Victim Jennie Peters," *Boston Globe*.

determination "to try her luck": "Attempted Suicide," *Daily Evening Item* (Lynn, MA), July 8, 1884.

"evidently did not get completely sober": "Mrs. Dyer Again," *Daily Evening Item* (Lynn, MA), July 9, 1884.

"peculiar cases": "The Guilford Case: Arguments of the Counsel for the Defense," *Daily Evening Item* (Lynn, MA), May 19, 1886.

"Mrs. Dyer continued to show fight": "A Fighting Pair," *Daily Evening Item* (Lynn, MA), August 28, 1884.

"lively and interesting" battle: Police Court, *Daily Evening Item* (Lynn, MA), June 19, 1879.

"very suddenly": "Sudden Death," *Daily Evening Item* (Lynn, MA), August 10, 1885.

"under circumstances which": "Mrs. Dyer," *Daily Evening Item* (Lynn, MA), August 11, 1885.

"in each case that no one": "Inquest Findings," *Daily Evening Item* (Lynn, MA), March 6, 1886.

4. Lethargy

"Ladies wishing to employ the doctress": "To Ladies" (advertisement), *Daily Evening Item* (Lynn, MA), October 12, 1881.

"large": International Publishing Company, *Industries of Massachusetts: Historical and Descriptive Review of Lynn, Lowell, Lawrence, Haverhill, Salem, Beverly, Peabody, Danvers, Gloucester, Newburyport, Amesbury, and Their Leading Manufacturers and Merchants* (Boston: International Publishing Company, 1886), 55.

"matter of general comment": "The Lynn Malpractice Case," *Boston Herald*, January 2, 1886.

"beautiful, pre-possessing blond": "Middlesex County," Lowell (MA) *Daily Courier*, January 7, 1886.

"she had just returned": "Lynn Malpractice Case," *Boston Herald*.

"to be careful" . . . "he had done": "They Met at a Dance," *Boston Globe*, January 24, 1886.

"near enough" . . . "staggered": "They Met at a Dance," *Boston Globe*.

"a fine appearing" . . . "an extensive lot of the more approved instruments": "Lynn Malpractice Case," *Boston Herald*.

"Mournfully, tenderly, we have laid": Deaths, Woburn (MA) *Advertiser*, December 31, 1885.

became a "bed" . . . "was one of the most disagreeable": "Lynn Malpractice Case," *Boston Herald*.

"alleged medical firm": "Lynn's Last Sensation," *Boston Post*, January 4, 1886.

"of the old school": "In Her Father's Arms," *Boston Globe*, January 2, 1886.

"unenviable reputations": "Arrested for Malpractice," *Boston Post*, January 2, 1886.

"of doubtful character": "Criminal Malpractice," *Daily Evening Item* (Lynn, MA), January 1, 1886.

"extravagant": "Lynn's Last Sensation," *Boston Post*, January 4, 1886.

CONFLICTING OPINIONS: "Conflicting Opinions as to Where and When Susie Taylor Died," *Boston Globe*, January 4, 1886.

"not correct" . . . "incensed with her": "Middlesex County," Lowell (MA) *Daily Courier*, January 7, 1886.

informal "reception": "Guilfords Again in Court," *Boston Globe*, January 9, 1886.

"important witnesses" . . . *"All he had to say was"*: "Susie Taylor's Friends Dissatisfied," *Boston Globe*, January 12, 1886.

"ladylike": "Mrs. Iveston's [*sic*] Illness," *Boston Globe*, January 22, 1886.

"seemed unconcerned" . . . *"My daughter said that Mrs. Guilford"*: "Her Last Request," *Boston Globe*, January 17, 1886.

"miscarriage" . . . *instruments of "common use"*: "From the Old Farm to Her Death in the City of Lynn," *Boston Globe*, January 16, 1886.

"ribbons, feathers, and furbelows": "Mrs. Iveston's [*sic*] Illness," *Boston Globe*.

"case of this magnitude": "Mrs. Iveston's [*sic*] Illness," *Boston Globe*.

"ready for business": "At a Dance," *Boston Globe*, January 23, 1886.

"bright" . . . THEY MET: "They Met at a Dance," *Boston Globe*.

"if this affair can't be proven": "Criminal Malpractice," *Daily Evening Item*.

5. The Salem Trials

"I don't think any twelve men": "The Guilford Case: Arguments of Counsel for Defense," *Daily Evening Item* (Lynn, MA), May 19, 1886.

"you won't give me away": "The Guilford Case: Dr. Alice Guilford on Trial for Criminal Malpractice," *Daily Evening Item* (Lynn, MA), May 17, 1886.

"Who was the cause of your trouble?" . . . *"Was any man in the habit of making visits"*: "Guilford Case: Dr. Alice Guilford on Trial for Criminal Malpractice," *Daily Evening Item* (Lynn, MA), May 17, 1886.

"Charles E. Hall was not the cause": "Victim as a Witness," *Boston Herald*.

"for which he": "Conviction Improbable," *Boston Herald*.

"Miscarriage": "Guilford Trial: Dr. Alice Guilford Testifies," *Daily Evening Item* (Lynn, MA), May 18, 1886.

"nervous trouble in Lynn" . . . *"Have you any unkind feeling"*: "Guilford Trial," *Daily Evening Item*.

"diseases peculiar to women": "The Guilford Case: Arguments of Counsel for the Defense," *Daily Evening Item*.

"were troubled with that" . . . *"into trouble"*: "Guilford Trial: Dr. Alice Guilford Testifies," *Daily Evening Item*.

trying to "blacken" . . . *"Who can say"*: "The Guilford Case: Arguments of Counsel for Defense," *Daily Evening Item*.

"It is revolting": "Stop: Women" (advertisement), *Salina (KS) Herald*, October 7, 1892.

"Would this Peters woman" . . . *"but this is left for your decision"*: "The Guilford Case: Arguments of Counsel for Defense," *Daily Evening Item*.

"There was no hope of conviction": "Conviction Improbable," *Boston Herald*.

"The result is a surprise": "Mrs. Guilford Guilty," *Daily Evening Item* (Lynn, MA), May 19, 1886.

"The woman is notorious": "Guilty of Abortion," *Rocky Mountain News*, May 23, 1886.

"his client has not been mixing up": "Charles E. Ames Surrendered by His Bail and Locked Up," *Daily Evening Item* (Lynn, MA), May 24, 1886.

"human evidence is not absolutely certain": "Mrs. Guilford Guilty," *Daily Evening Item*.

"did what was plainly his duty". . . *"To rid the state"*: "The Guilford Case: Mrs. Guilford Gets Six and One-Half Years, *Daily Evening Item* (Lynn, MA), March 1, 1887.

6. New Haven, Hotbed of Abortion

"Sherborn is run by Mrs. Johnson": "They Fight Like Men," *Boston Globe*, April 25, 1890.

"common nightwalkers": Massachusetts Board of Commissioners of Prisons, *Annual Report of the Commissioners of Prisons of Massachusetts*, vol. 17 (Boston: Wright & Potter Printing Company, 1888), 113.

"lady of independent means": Alfred Webb, "The Sherborn Massachusetts Reformatory Prison for Women," *Journal of the Statistical and Social Inquiry Society of Ireland* 10, pt. 77 (1896–1897): 326, http://www.tara.tcd.ie/handle/2262/7847.

"temperate": Inmate Registers, 1878–1965, box 1, Nancy Alice Guilford, no. 3490, HS 9.06/series 824, Massachusetts Archives, Boston.

than at arrival: Prisoners Physical Description Register, 1877–1916, HS9.06/series 294X, March 1, 1887, Massachusetts Archives, Boston.

"certain people": "Mrs. Dr. Guilford," *Daily Evening Item* (Lynn, MA), February 3, 1888.

"come to have the nonsense" . . . *"To be reformed"*: Webb, "Sherborn Massachusetts Reformatory," 327.

"drag others down": Massachusetts Board of Commissioners, *Annual Report*, 99.

"woman who for three weeks": "Trouble at Sherborn," *Boston Globe*, February 27, 1888.

"The year has been marked" . . . *"There has been no change"*: Massachusetts Board of Commissioners, *Annual Report*, 81.

listing "cranks" as an illness: "A Skilful [sic] Diagnosis," *Boston Daily Advertiser*, February 27, 1889.

Nancy survived: "They Fight Like Men," *Boston Globe*.

"Bond pleases to call himself": Henry Ford Gill [Henry M. Guilford], "A Card," *Waterbury (CT) Evening Democrat*, December 10, 1888.

"Board and nurse for patients" . . . *"Married and single ladies"*: "Dr. Henry F. Gill" (advertisement), *Waterbury (CT) Evening Democrat*, December 12, 1888.

"We are ever mindful": Massachusetts Board of Commissioners of Prisons, *Annual Report of the Commissioners of Prisons of Massachusetts*, vol. 20 (Boston: Wright & Potter Printing Company, 1891), 114.

"hotbed of abortion": "Decision in Vaughan Case," *New Haven (CT) Morning Journal and Courier*, July 11, 1898.

"strong evidence": "New Haven Sensation," *Meriden (CT) Daily Journal*, December 31, 1894.

"There is scarcely a father in Connecticut": "New England in Dun Colors," *Des Moines (IA) Register*, April 6, 1883.

"anything to do with Dr. Gill": "Board of Health Hearing," *New Haven (CT) Morning Journal and Courier*, June 21, 1898.

"board and care": "Dr. Gill" (advertisement), *Evening Leader* (New Haven, CT), March 16, 1898.

"well and favorably known" . . . *"mental and physical wreck"*: "Another Arrest Made," *New Haven (CT) Morning Journal and Courier*, March 7, 1896.

"ladies suffering": "Dr. N. Alice Guilford" (advertisement), *Free Public Library, New Haven, Connecticut, Bulletin*, October 1897.

"young, beautiful and handsomely gowned" . . . *"with wild words"*: "Pointed His Shotgun" *Boston Globe*, July 26, 1897.

"Old Reliable Specialist": "Dr. Gill" (advertisement), *Meriden (CT) Daily Journal*, January 3, 1898.

"out of the way": "Cold Blooded Compact," *Morning Record* (Meriden, CT), March 17, 1898.

"was no refusal": "Board of Health Hearing," *New Haven Morning Journal and Courier*, June 21, 1898.

"incriminate or disgrace her": "Dr. Gill on Trial," *New Haven (CT) Register*, May 4, 1898.

"terror of evil doers": "Judge and Attorney Biographies," CT State Library, accessed September 22, 2022, https://libguides.ctstatelibrary.org/law/judge-attorney -biographies/w#s-lg-box-11345896.

"met his Waterloo": Editorial, *Waterbury (CT) Democrat*, May 6, 1898.

"persecution": "Decision in Vaughan Case," *New Haven (CT) Morning Journal and Courier*, July 11, 1898.

"these dreadful Jews" . . . *"There is nothing too small"*: "Letter Written by Dr. Gill in Prison," *Elmira (NY) Daily Gazette and Free Press*, September 21, 1898.

7. Road Trip

"keep the girl": "Harry Oxley Testifies," *Chronicle* (Southport, CT), March 30, 1899.

"Friend is away": "Mrs. Guilford's Furnace," *New Haven (CT) Register*, March 30, 1899.

"*Nothing, under the circumstances*": "Harry Oxley's Confession," *New Haven (CT) Register*, March 29, 1899.

"*to have it all over*": Associated Press, "Guilford Trial Begins Third Week," *Buffalo (NY) Evening News*, April 3, 1899.

"*her fellow's sister*": "Midwife's Son Accused," *Sun* (New York), September 25, 1898.

"*If you get this do not come down*": "Oxley Testifies Again," *Hartford (CT) Courant*, April 5, 1899.

"*Can I have a glass of water?*": "Midwife's Son Accused," *Sun*.

"*pretentious-looking building*": "Murderer's Second Trip," *Sun* (New York), September 14, 1898.

"*Send me the balance*": "Guilford Juror Was Ill," *New Haven (CT) Register*, April 5, 1899.

"*Dear Mother—I can't come home*": "Murdered Girl Was Emma Gill," *Evening Leader* (New Haven, CT), September 21, 1898.

"*Dear Doctor: Please write*": "Harry Oxley Faces Old Nance Guilford," *World* (New York), March 29, 1899.

"*abortion hotbed*": "Decision in Vaughan Case," *New Haven (CT) Morning Journal and Courier*, July 11, 1898.

"*That only occasionally their nefarious work*": "Punish Them," *Morning-Union* (Bridgeport, CT), November 23, 1898.

"*Deliberation was used in cutting*": "Body Cut Up to Hide Crime," *Milwaukee Journal*, September 16, 1898.

"*an expert using a keen knife*": "Story of the Crime," *Elmira (NY) Telegram*, September 18, 1898.

"*Not a hurried move was made*": "Body Cut Up to Hide Crime," *Milwaukee Journal*.

"*Mrs. Guilford, your hair*": "Forging the Chain," *Boston Herald*, September 26, 1898.

"*They didn't seem at all excited*": "Small Boy Day at 'Old Nance's' Trial," *New York Journal*, March 23, 1899.

"*bright young newsdealer*": "Woman's Body Dismembered with Skill," *Bridgeport (CT) Evening Post*, September 13, 1898.

WHO KNOWS THIS WOMAN?: *New York Evening Journal*, September 15, 1898.

8. Coming Home to Her Funeral

"*Whatever you do, keep mum*": "Harry Oxley's Story of Bargain He Made with Nancy Guilford," *Meriden (CT) Morning Record and Republican*, March 29, 1899.

"*accepted suitor*": "Eudora Guilford Bailed Again," *Sun* (New York), October 8, 1898.

"*not at all excited*". . . "*She did not act like a woman*": "'G.51' Only a Blind Clue," *Sun* (New York), September 16, 1898.

"He was a person thoroughly familiar" . . . *"Death resulting from the effects"*: Giddings, "Death Resulting from Criminal Practices."

"I feel confident that Mrs. Guilford": "Mrs. Dr. Guilford Disappeared When Body Was Found," *World* (New York), September 15, 1898.

Birmingham replied . . . *"Woman not wanted here"*: "Dr. Guilford Escapes by a Police Blunder," *New York Journal*, November 30, 1898.

"What is it?": "'G.51' Only a Blind Clue," *Sun.*

"No. 31, 9 and 22": "Debate Meeting," *Monthly Record* (Wethersfield, CT), March 31, 1899, 72.

"Down in Bridgeport, there is some talk": "'Convict Says His Wife Is Innocent, *World* (New York), September 18, 1898.

"at sea" . . . *"except that"*: "She Is Coming to This City," *Star-Gazette* (Elmira, NY), September 15, 1898.

"not resemble her" . . . *"an honest man"*: "Stuck to Identification," *New York Herald*, September 18, 1898.

"humble" Perkins "cottage": "Strange Story of Grace Perkins," *New York Journal*, September 18, 1898.

"somewhat of an anomaly": "Grace Perkins' Home": *Baltimore Sun*, September 17, 1898.

"Grace said that she did not know" . . . *Mrs. Snow said she'd refused*: "Clearing a Mystery," *Baltimore Sun*, September 17, 1898.

"limp hands": "Perkins Better and Makes a Statement," *New York Evening Journal*, September 19, 1898.

"took no apparent interest": "Dead Alive," *Boston Sunday Globe*, September 18, 1898.

"While the circumstances" . . . *"There is no truth in the statement"*: "Perkins Better and Makes a Statement," *New York Evening Journal.*

"typical New England village": "Grace Perkins' Home," *Baltimore Sun.*

"My heart is almost breaking" . . . *"I can produce Dr. Guilford"*: "Nancy Guilford Heard From," *Bridgeport (CT) Herald*, September 18, 1898.

"The police have apparently": "Various Missing Women Who Are Thought to Resemble the Dead Girl," *Hartford (CT) Courant*, September 20, 1898.

"I don't want her": "Scotland Yard Lays Hands on Old 'Dr.' Nance," *Times* (Pawtucket, RI), October 1, 1898.

"if I had arrested her": "Dr. Guilford Escapes by a Police Blunder," *New York Journal*, November 30, 1898.

"Dr. Guilford has boasted" . . . *"If she were innocent"*: "The Guilford Woman," *New Haven (CT) Register*, October 11, 1898.

"steady": "Middleboro Wild with Amaze," *New York Press*, September 18, 1898.

"It is unlikely that even the mother": "Potter's Field," *Boston Post*, September 20, 1898.

9. Link by Link

"gay girl": "Murdered Girl Was Emma Gill," *Evening Leader* (New Haven, CT), September 21, 1898.

"Why don't you go to Bridgeport": "Bridgeport's Murder," *Hartford (CT) Courant*, September 21, 1898.

"This is the very first suggestion": "Link by Link the Chain Is Forged," *New Haven (CT) Register*, September 22, 1898.

"criminally intimate" with her: "The Doctors [*sic*] Name Known," *Evening Leader* (New Haven), September 22, 1898.

"told a pretty good story": "Solving Problem," *Hartford (CT) Courant*, September 22, 1898.

"No further proof of the identification": "Bridgeport Case Solved," *New York Times*, September 22, 1898.

"We'll solve this": "An Arrest Made Today," *Standard Union* (Brooklyn, NY), September 21, 1898.

"pretty close": "The Doctors [*sic*] Name Known," *Evening Leader*.

"wayward girl": "Link by Link," *New Haven Register*.

"There is our prisoner": "Nearing a Solution," *Baltimore Sun*, September 22, 1898.

"Great Scott, man!": "Dr. Nancy Guilford the Murderess and Mutilator of the Bridgeport Victim!," *Evening Times* (Pawtucket, RI), September 24, 1898.

"consternation reigned" . . . *"walked with downcast eyes"*: "Nearly Solved," *Hartford (CT) Courant*, September 24, 1898.

"One for certain": "Gill Murder Mystery Solved, Dr. Guilford's Guilt Alleged," *Evening Leader* (New Haven, CT), September 24, 1898.

"put on the rack": "Telltale Evidence," *Baltimore Sun*, September 26, 1898.

NEGROES ARE VINDICTIVE: "Negroes Are Vindictive," *Morning-Union* (Bridgeport, CT), November 18, 1898.

"I would rather go to work": "Telltale Evidence," *Baltimore Sun*.

"probably had no hand" . . . *"The case is sufficiently advanced"*: "Oxley the Man Say the Police," *Meriden (CT) Daily Republican*, September 24, 1898.

"giant physique": "Captain George H. Arnold Dies: Famous Officer," *Bridgeport (CT) Evening Farmer*, January 7, 1918.

"I am positive" . . . *"Nancy could be reached"*: "Bridgeport Victim Was Cut Up By 'Nance' Guilford": *Buffalo (NY) Sunday Morning News*, September 25, 1898.

"what he told Birmingham": "Police Find a Saw," *Chatham (NY) Courier*, September 28, 1898.

POOR EMMA: "Gill Murder Mystery Solved," *Evening Leader*.

"She knew Dr. Guilford": "Every Detail of 'Old Nance' Guilford's Crime Fully Exposed," *Boston Post*, September 27, 1893.

"Everyone in Southington does not possess": "Eudora Guilford Silent," *Evening Leader* (New Haven, CT), October 1, 1898.

"unusual liberties": "Oxley Is Silent," *Evening Leader* (New Haven, CT), October 8, 1898.

"In all my twenty-seven years' experience": "Hidden in London," *Star-Gazette* (Elmira, NY), September 30, 1898.

10. Transcontinental Dragnet

"lower eyelids swollen" . . . *"She blanched and turned away"*: "Like 'Dr.' Nancy," *Boston Globe* (© *New York World*), September 28, 1898.

"American reporter teaches the English": "American Enterprise," *Fourth Estate* (New York), October 27, 1898, 7.

"an inexplicable delay": "'Old Nance' Held in London," *New York Journal*, October 4, 1898.

"mysterious influence": "Police Lying Low," *Boston Globe*, September 17, 1898.

"I know nothing of the crime": "Eudora Taken to Bridgeport," *Star-Gazette* (Elmira, NY), September 29, 1898.

"Miss Guilford has the sympathy": "Miss Guilford in Bridgeport," *Brooklyn (NY) Times Union*, September 30, 1898.

"relieved her of the embarrassment": "Nancy Guilford Arrested," *New York Times*, October 2, 1898.

"I played some, and I believe": "Miss Guilford Talks," *New York Press*, October 2, 1898.

"I have felt sure that they would get her": "The News in Bridgeport," *Meriden (CT) Daily Journal*, October 1, 1898.

"She is a most remarkable woman": "'Old Nance' Held in London," *New York Journal*.

"This is an outrage": "Mrs. Guilford Arraigned," *Daily Standard Union* (Brooklyn, NY), October 3, 1898.

Betrayed for a Pound: "Old Nance's Long Fight Is Ended," *New York Journal*, November 20, 1898.

"You lie!": "Dr. Guilford in Jail," *Fall River (MA) Evening News*, October 3, 1898.

"the telltale trinkets" . . . *"Nothing had been said about murder"*: "'Old Nance' Held in London," *New York Journal*.

"handsomely dressed": "Dr. Guilford in Jail," *Fall River Evening News*.

"felonious homicide": Charles A. Doten, "Cause of Death of Emma Gill," coroner's report, *Fairfield County Coroner Records*, October 5, 1898, vol. 12, 270, Judicial Records, Connecticut State Library, Hartford, CT.

"It might not favor the reputation" . . . *"She stood with defiant eyes"*: "Oxley Is Silent," *Evening Leader*.

"I don't know as I have to tell you": "'Some Killing Is No Murder,'" *Bridgeport (CT) Herald*, October 2, 1898.

"we have letters to show": "Oxley Will Tell All He Knows So Says Counsel Judge Holcomb," *Evening Leader* (New Haven, CT), October 8, 1898.

"She is innocent": "Eudora Guilford Bailed Again," *Sun* (New York), October 8, 1898.

"Mrs. Drayton has got over thinking": "Rose Drayton Indicted," *New Haven (CT) Register*, October 7, 1898.

"He cannot hope to convict": "'Old Nance' Held in London," *New York Journal*.

"the offense may, perhaps, be best described" . . . *"the courts, clubs and churches"*: "The Guilford Woman," *New Haven (CT) Register*, October 11, 1898.

"terrorized by the threat": "Kinks in the Law May Save Nancy," *New York Press*, October 10, 1898.

"What have you done with my children?": "Dr. Guilford Behind Jail Bars," *Bridgeport (CT) Herald*, November 20, 1898.

"mental anxiety": "Old Nance's Long Fight Is Ended," *New York Journal*, November 20, 1898.

"sweet" and "comforting" . . . *"especially Madame Melba"*: "Old Nance Now in Jail," *Evening Leader* (New Haven, CT), November 21, 1898.

"I slighted the World": George H. Donohue, "Bridgeport's 400 Trying to Save 'Dr.' Nancy Guilford from a Prison Cell," *Boston Sunday Post*, November 27, 1898.

"Eudora is a good girl": "Dr. Guilford Behind Jail Bars," *Bridgeport Herald*.

"I hate to be gazed upon": "Safe in Jail in Bridgeport," *Star Gazette* (Elmira, NY), November 21, 1898.

"Did she talk?": "Dr. Nancy Guilford, Charged with Murder, in Bridgeport Jail," *Boston Sunday Globe*, November 20, 1898.

"my only request": "Safe in Jail," *Star Gazette*.

"Do you know that I think": "Dr. Guilford Behind Jail Bars," *Bridgeport Herald*.

"simple, dignified" . . . *"Be very careful"*: "Dr. Guilford Behind Jail Bars," *Bridgeport Herald*.

"affecting": "Her First Sunday in Jail," *Morning Journal and Courier* (New Haven, CT), November 21, 1898.

"pretty cheeks": "Met in Prison," *Evening Gazette* (Norwalk, CT), November 22, 1898.

11. A Much-Persecuted Woman

"This town is full of a wishy washy sentiment": "Old Nance Now in Jail," *Evening Leader*.

"maudlin sentimentalists": "Punish Them," *Morning Union* (Bridgeport, CT), November 23, 1898.

"Mrs. Guilford looked anything but" . . . . *"The police have the names"*: George H. Donohue, "Bridgeport's 400 Trying to Save 'Dr.' Nancy Guilford from a Prison Cell," *Boston Sunday Post*, November 27, 1898.

"trembling and concern": "Threat to Tell All She Knows," *Elmira (NY) Daily Gazette and Free Press*, December 5, 1898.

"My protection lies in my work": "Bridgeport's 400 Trying to Save," *Boston Sunday Post*; "'Old Nance' Guilford's Threat to Tell All She Knows," *New York Journal*, December 4, 1898.

"metamorphosis": "Nancy's Metamorphosis," *Boston Globe*, December 19, 1898.

"Who Created the Demand?" . . . *"There are not many who"*: "Who Created the Demand?" *Bridgeport (CT) Herald*, December 25, 1898.

"We've got to convict Nancy Guilford": "In the Seats of the Mighty," *Bridgeport (CT) Herald*, January 22, 1899.

"I don't want to hear you": "Foreclosure on His Property," *Bridgeport (CT) Herald*, January 22, 1899.

"oblivious of all about her": "Nancy Guilford's Case," *Brooklyn (NY) Times Union*, February 4, 1899.

"mental and physical wreck": "Nancy Guilford a Wreck," *Buffalo (NY) Commercial*, March 14, 1899.

"persons known to the sheriff": "Guilford Trial Wednesday," *Naugatuck (CT) Daily News*, March 4, 1899.

"will have to content themselves": "City Briefs," *Naugatuck (CT) Daily News*, March 7, 1899.

"the striking resemblance": "The Guilford Trial," *Hartford (CT) Courant*, March 22, 1899.

"Was it relief?": Langdon Smith, "Emma Gill's Sister upon the Stand as a Witness Against Old Nance," *New York Journal*, March 24, 1899.

"the good looking, gentlemanly appearing": "Harry Oxley's Confession," *New Haven (CT) Register*, March 29, 1899.

"write, don't telegraph": "At Guilford Trial," *Meriden (CT) Daily Journal*, March 30, 1899.

"Did Mrs. Guilford say anything": "Harry Oxley Testifies," *Chronicle*.

"Don't you know that Dr. Ernest Thomson" . . . *"He was not without sympathy"*: "Harry Oxley's Confession," *New Haven Register*.

"The state is drawing its web": "Dr. Guilford Case," *Evening Gazette* (Norwalk, CT), April 5, 1899.

"jurors are wont": *Evening Leader* (New Haven, CT), n.d., as quoted in "Fessenden Complimented," *Stamford Daily Advocate*, April 17, 1889.

"I am guilty of manslaughter": "She Plead [*sic*] Guilty," *Evening Gazette* (Norwalk, CT), April 12, 1899.

"I am satisfied with my sentence" . . . *"They got no Oxleyized"*: "Eudora Cannot Go on the Witness Stand," *Bridgeport (CT) Herald*, April 16, 1899.

SHE-WOLF CAGED: "She-Wolf Caged," *Grand Rapids (MI) Herald*, April 12, 1899.

Afterword

"If she loves my boy Fred": "Old Nance Caught in London," *New York Evening Journal*, October 1, 1898.

"in the strictest confidence, terms moderate": "Dr. Gill" (advertisement), *Middletown Penny Press*, July 3, 1903.

"powerful mind": "Gill Hearing Comes to Close," *Hartford (CT) Courant*, February 5, 1907.

"Everything is possible": Notes and News, *Lancet-Clinic*, 116, no. 11 (September 9, 1916): 264.

"The more civilization progresses": B. S. Talmey, "The Limitation of Offspring: By Abortion or Prevention of Conception—Which?" *American Journal of Urology and Sexology* 12, no. 8 (August 1916): 341.

"tall" and "well built": "Nancy Guilford in Trouble Again After Many Years," *Hartford (CT) Courant*, September 28, 1920.

"out of ignorance": "Nancy Gill [*sic*] Held Under $2,500 Bail," *Hartford (CT) Courant*, October 6, 1920.

INDEX

Page numbers in *italics* denote illustrations.
KEY TO INITIALS: EG = Emma Gill; HG = Henry Melancthon Guilford; NG = Nancy Guilford

Abberline, Frederic, 182, 186
abortifacients, 8, 37, 114, 206
abortion, 8, 25, 28, 31–32, 132, 151, 205–206
abortion procedures, 28, 37, 38–39, 131
abortion service fees, 27–28, 41, 123
Adams Express Company, 127, 165, 166
affluence, 205
aliases, use of, 32–33, 78, 99, 218
Allen, Leonard, 56–57
American Medical Association, 15, 32, 39, 218
Ames, Charles E., 49–58, 60, 61–62, 64, 68, 87–88, 90
Ames, Mary Ellen Heald, 50
Arnold, George H., 151, 164, 165, 167, 169, 173–174, *174*
Austin, Mrs., 128–129

baby farms, 103
Bacon, Francis, 113
Baker, Henry, 185
Banks, Dr. (prison physician), 213
Banks, Isaac, 135, 172
Barnum Institute of Science and History, 123

Birmingham, Eugene
  arrest of Walter Foster ordered by, 163
  and body identification, 153, 157–158, 162, 164, 167
  and laundry markings, 142, 150
  and NG, 146–147, 159–160, 184
  portrait of, *147*
  public statements made by, 171–176
blackmail charges, 74, 77–80, 82–86, 204
boarding services, necessity for, 28, 109
body identification attempts, 151–155
body removal playbook, HG's, 54, 56, 112–113
Bond, Elijah A., 99, 100, 102, 104, 191
Boston Globe, 62–63, 64, 82, 89, 93, 96, 97
Boston Herald, 59, 82, 86
Boston Sunday Globe, 157
Boston Sunday Post, 160, 202–203
Bourne, Charles "Charley," 154–155, 156, 157
Bridgeport, CT, 2, 101, 123
  police investigations in, 2–4, 146–147, 151, 157–159, 169–170
Bridgeport Evening Post, 140
Bridgeport Farmer, 221

241

Bridgeport Herald, 197–198, 205–206, 215
Broad Street location (Waterbury, CT), 101
Brockton, MA, 32–33
Brooks, John P., 24
Brown, Horace (NG's father), 20, 72
Brown, Maggie (NG's sister), 28
Brown, Nancy Alice, 19, 21, 27, 29–30. *See also* Guilford, Nancy Alice (née Brown)
Brown, Stephen (NG's brother), 28, 33, 147
Brown, Stephen H. (NG's grandfather), 20
Buchanan, John, 80

cab drivers, search for, 185, 186
Callaghan, P. J., 121
Carr, Frank P., 107, 108
Case, William C., 208
Cassada, Frank J., 147, 174
Chapel Street office (New Haven, CT), 102, 109, 205
Christian denomination, 7, 8, 10, 12
Christian Herald and Journal, 7–8, 9
Clair, Naomi, 28–29
clambake rally, 9, 11
class status, 84, 86, 192–193, 206
Colgate, Donald K., 57, 68
Colgate, Mary Lizzie, 57
collars, removable, 131, 148, 162–163
Collins, Mrs. John, 151
Connecticut
legal status of abortion in, 151, 213–214
litigation costs of NG case in, 207
medical licensing in, 101, 107
prison reform in, 215
religious reform efforts in, 115

Connecticut State Assembly, 206
corruption, 103, 160, 182
Costello, Willie, 138
courthouses
public attendance at, 61, 64, 66
women banned from, 207, 212
Cronan, Edward, 172, 189, 191, 193–194, *193*
Cullinan, John, 152, 153
Cullinan's Funeral Home, 2, 138, 139, 152
Cutter, Abbie E., 34–35

Daily Evening Item (Lynn, MA)
coverage of Annie Dyer story by, 42, 43–44, 46–48
on HG & NG arrest and trial coverage, 58, 82, 85, 86, 90
on NG's petition for prison release, 95
use of term abortion by, 146
Danbury, CT, 10
DeForest, Robert E., 144, 201, 214
dilation and curettage (d&c) procedures, 28, 39
Disciples of Christ Church (Danbury, CT), 10
Doherty, William G., 163
Donohue, George H., 202–204
Doten, Charles A., 152, 153–154
Downs, F. B., 145
Drayton, Clara Belle
assists with clean up procedures, 139
bullied into participatory role, 143
holding of, in county jail, 183–184, 212
interrogation of, 175–176
as live-in servant, 129–130, 131
photograph of, *170*
police questioning of, 150, 170–171, 191

Drayton, Rose
  background of, 129–130
  charges dropped against, 214, 217
  cleanup assistance provided by, 133, 135, 139
  court appearances and return to jail, 190–191
  indictment of, 188
  meeting with Harry Oxley, 143
  photograph of, *170*
  police questioning of, 170, 173–174, 183–184
Durham, Frederick, 124–125
Dyer, Annie J., 42–48, 132
Dyer, George, 44–45, *44*, 47, 48

Egan, James H., 104–106, 108
electrical therapy, 34–35
endangerment, of a mother's life, 38–39
Exchange Place (Waterbury, CT), 121

Fall River, MA, 18, 21–24
Fall River Daily Evening News, 23
Fessenden, Samuel
  indictment of NG by, 189–190
  international pursuit of NG by, 175–179, 182
  and jury selection, 208
  at prosecution trial of NG, 211–214, 217
  prosecutorial orders issued by, 165, 173, 174
  Senate run consideration by, 206
Fleischmann & Company, 163
Foster, Walter C., 120, 126, 163, 164–165, 173
Fredericton, New Brunswick, 12
Froest, Frank, 184–185, 186–187, 193, 194

Gale, William B., 88
Gearing, Bertha, 220, 221
Geneva Medical School, 15–16
Gibbs, Alice. *See* Guilford, Nancy Alice (née Brown)
Gibbs, Frederick, 217–218
Giddings, V. R. C., 3, 145–146, 198
Gilbert Street location (Bridgeport, CT), 4–5, 109, 117, 123, 128–129, 207
Gill, Clara (EG's sister), 127–128
Gill, Emma
  burial of, 157
  death of, 133, 141, 188
  delay by NG to attend to, 130
  dismemberment and disposal, 133–137, 139
  family life of, 119
  and Lillian Katzung, 119, 125
  news coverage on, 140, 161–162, 164–165, 176
  photographic portrait of, *127*
  physical description and features, 119, 141–142, 163
  procedure performed on, 131–132
  relationship with Harry Oxley, 120–126
  travel to Bridgeport by, 126–128
  trial, 208–213
Gill, Fred, 163–164
Gill, Henry Ford. *See* Guilford, Henry Melancthon
Gill, Mr. (EG's father), 161–162, 164
Gill, Mrs. (EG's mother), 208, 217
Glen House location (Lynn, MA), 32
Globe Hotel, New Haven, 122
grand jury indictments, 68, 189, 201
Gregory, George, 213
Guernsey, Howard, 121–122, 124, 167, 168, 169, 173, 176–177

Guilford, Alice. *See* Guilford, Nancy
    Alice (née Brown)
Guilford, Annie (HG's sister), 10
Guilford, Ellen Eudora (HG's sister), 9
Guilford, Eudora "Dodie" (HG & NG's
    daughter)
    adoration for, 34, 72
    appearance at mother's trial by, 212
    arrest of, 171, 175, 183–184, 189–190
    birth of, 26
    claims ignorance of mother's where-
        abouts, 165, 171
    and Clara Belle Drayton, 143
    life after divorce, 220, 221, 222
    marriage of, 217–218
    at Onset Bay, 117
    origin of nickname for, 27
    portrait of, *111*
    reunion with mother, 199
    as teenager, 101–102
    utilized as nursing assistant, 129, 131,
        133
Guilford, Frank (HG's brother), 10
Guilford, Helen M. (HG's first wife),
    17, 18
Guilford, Henry Brown "Harry" (HG &
    NG's son)
    and bail money, 106, 184, 191, 212
    boating skills acquired by, 34
    in Bridgeport, 101–102
    and laundry markings, 147–149
    at Onset Bay, 117
    participation in body disposal by,
        135–137, 138–139
    photographic portrait of, *148*
    physical disability endured by, 22
    reunion with mother, 199
    as suspect, 171, 172–173
Guilford, Henry Melancthon
    aliases used by, 33

arrests and charges brought against,
    221
arrests for criminal malpractice, 59,
    113
body removal playbook of, 53–55,
    112–115
and Charles S. Hamilton, 110
childhood of, 9–10
credentials presented by, 23–28, 107
death of, 222
and Elijah Bond, 104
and health-lift center, 21–22
and Iva Marsh, 40–41
and laundry markings, 149–150
life after release from prison, 218
marriages, 17, 18, 20–21, 29, 220–221
military service, 12–15
name change to Henry Ford Gill, 99,
    218
physical features, 19–20
portrait of, *26*
practices established by, 32–33, 99,
    101, 102
and quackery practices, 35, 100–101
rape allegations against, 77, 82, 83, 85
relationship with children, 98–99
relationship with NG, 41, 106–107,
    116, 218–219
relocation to Connecticut, 99–101
reputation of, 33, 39
as shoe factory agent, 19
and Susie Taylor case, 61, 62, 64, 68,
    71–72, 89–91
temperament while imprisoned,
    206–207
testimony in breach of contract case
    by, 220
Guilford, Henry Pittman "H. P." (HG's
    father), 7–12, 14, 18, 21–23, 46

Guilford, Herbert (HG & NG's son), 17, 18, 98, 219
Guilford, Lester (HG's brother), 9, 14
Guilford, Lucy Wells (HG's mother), 8, 9, 18
Guilford, Minna (HG & NG's daughter-in-law), 222
Guilford, Nancy Alice (née Brown)
  as Alice Gibbs, 219–220
  and Annie Dyer, 46–48
  and Annie Reynolds, 105
  arrests and charges brought against, 59–62, 68, 106, 113, 184–188, 201, 207–208, 221–222
  body disposal by, 135–137, 139
  as Catherine Wilbur, 175, 179–180
  and class status, 41–42, 131
  death of, 222
  determination of, 30, 35
  Donohue interview of, 203–204
  and EG, 131–135
  at Emma Taylor trial, 114
  extradition of, 195–197
  fugitive reports about, 165
  and Harry Oxley, 123–125, 130–131
  health issues, 205, 207–208
  and Iva Marsh, 40–41
  and Jennie Peters, 36–40
  at Jennie Peters trial, 71, 72, 78–82, 86–87
  journey across the Atlantic by, 179
  life as Alice Gibbs, 221–222
  at Massachusetts Reformatory for Women, 94–95, 96–97, 100
  plea bargains made by, 89–90, 214–215
  portraits of, 30, 209
  practices established by, 4, 27, 31–32, 101–102, 126–127
  pursuit of, by reporter in Liverpool, 180–181
  relationship with HG, 41, 106–107, 116, 218–219
  search for, 174–175, 177
  and Susie Taylor, 52
  as suspect in Grace Perkins inquiries, 158
  wardrobe and jewelry preferred by, 31, 50, 64, 105, 180, 188
  at Wethersfield State Prison, 217, 218, 219
  See also Brown, Nancy Alice
Guilford, Willie (HG & NG's grandson), 117, 129, 133

Hall, Charles, 36, 40, 74
Hall, Margaret, 36, 37–38, 40, 74–76
Hamilton, Charles S., 110, 111
Hartford Courant, 158, 169, 180, 221
Hartford Medical Association, 218
Hartford police investigations, 163, 166, 167
Hawley, Sidney E., 196–197, 207, 215
Hayes, Michael J., 163
Heald, Otis, 52, 62, 87
Heald, Stephen C., 50, 62, 64, 87–88
Health-Lift Company, 21–22
health-lift movement, 21–22, 23
Hill, Jennie E., 193, 194, 195–197, 195, 198, 203
Holcomb, Marcus H., 168, 208
Holloway Prison, 188
Home for the Infirm (Onset Bay, MA), 34–35
Hurlburt, Henry F., 66, 71, 77, 79–82, 84–85, 88, 90, 91

Ivester, Mary, 55, 56, 63, 64–65, 66, 67

Jackson, Johnny, 1, 2, 137
Johnson, Clifford, 112, 113, 114
Johnson, Ellen C., 93–97, 100
Johnson, Frederick W., 78
Journal of the American Medical Association, 39

Katzung, Lillian, 119, 125, 128, 131, 167–168
Kelly, Stephen, 1, 209
Klein, Jacob
    antisemitic screed by HG against, 116
    as attorney for the Draytons, 190–191
    as defense attorney for HG, 114
    as lawyer for NG, 105–106, 131, 144–145, 158–159, 191, 201, 208, 210–213, 218
Knapp, Lee, 171

Lamothe, Detective, 181, 187
Larson, Nels P., 139–140
laundry markings, 142, 146, 147–148, 149, 150, 187
Law and Order League (New Haven, CT), 103, 122. *See also* Smyth, Newman
Lewis Street infirmary (Lynn, MA), 36, 38, 40, 43, 58–59, 63
Lighthouse Point (New Haven, CT), 122, 161–162
Lincoln Street infirmary (Worcester, MA), 27–28
Lynn, MA, 17, 31–32

maceration, 39
Main Street offices (Worcester, MA), 27
Marble, Samuel, 20
Market Street location (Lynn, MA), 31, 32, 36, 59, 73

Marsh, Iva, 33–34, 39–40, 41, 71, 76–77, 82, 103
Massachusetts
    abortion case trial in, 28–29
    abortion laws in, 25
    medical practitioner licensing in, 99
Massachusetts Reformatory for Women (Sherborn), 93–94, 95–97
Massasoit (USS), 13
Matthewman, Charles B., 105
McLean, Mary, 37, 63, 66–67, 88, 132–133
medical practitioners, licensing of, 23, 99, 101, 107
Medico-Legal Journal, 4
Melba, Nellie, 195
Mellish, Bertha, 151
Meriden, CT, 101, 109, 112
Meriden Daily Journal, 112, 121
Mix, Eli, 113
Monthly Record, 149
Morning Union, 202
Moulton, Henry P.
    as defense attorney for HG & NG, 61, 65
    as defense attorney for NG, 71, 72–74, 77–80, 81, 83, 89, 90

Nelson, Wilmont D., 58, 60, 64, 107, 108
New Haven, CT, 102, 103–104
New Haven Evening Leader, 105, 189–190, 201
New Haven police investigations, 105, 162–163, 166
New Haven Public Library bulletin, 109
New Haven Register, 164, 192
New York Journal, 140, 156–157, 204–205
New York Press, 192
New York Sun (the *Sun*), 171–172

New York *World* (the *World*), 145, 146,
179–180, 209
newspaper advertisements, 4, 25–26, 27,
28, 81, 105, 109
North Christian Church (Swansea,
MA), 9

Ocean Cottage location (Lynn, MA), 32
Ogden, Isaac, 152
Onset Bay, MA, 34, 117
Oxley, Alfred, 119, 124, 176
Oxley, Harry
arraignment of, 176–177, 190
bond posted for, 191
charges dropped, 217
at jury selection for NG's trial, 208
meeting with Rose Drayton, 143–144
payment arrangements made by, 127,
130, 131–132, 166
photographic portrait of, *177*
questioning of, 168–169
recognition of EG in newspaper
coverage, 140
relationship with EG, 119–126
testimony of, 210–212

peritonitis, 48, 52, 60, 65
Perkins, Ellen Reed, 157, 158
Perkins, Frank W., 152–154, 155–157
Perkins, Marion Grace, 152, 156–159
Peters, Jennie, 36–40, 41, 68–69, 71,
73–74
Philips, William J., 130, 190
Pinkham, Joseph G., 59
Pinkham, Lydia, 25
Plantsville, CT, 127, 132, 166
Portsmouth, NH, 10
Poughkeepsie, NY, 221–222
Pratt, James, 121, 125

prostitution, 84, 103
public opinion, 95, 199, 206

quackery, 23–24

Reynolds, Annie, 104–105, 107–108
Roberts, Miles, 20
Rosenbluth, E. G., 164
Rossiter, Charles, 22, 23
Russell, Rev., 216

Sanger, Margaret, 222
Searle, George, 71, 75–76, 78–79, 82,
89, 90
Seaview Avenue Bridge, 136, 137
septicemia, 131, 188
sex work, 84, 103
sexual assault, 77, 82, 83, 85
Sherborn. *See* Massachusetts Reformatory
for Women (Sherborn)
Sisk, J. H., 88
Sloan, James Forman "Tod," 195
Smith, Langdon, 210
Smith, Walter, 166, 167, *168*
Smyth, Newman, 103, 115
Snow, Mrs., 155
sound (medical instrument), 37, 39, 187
Southington, CT, 119, 121, 161, 169
stoppages, 8
Storer, Horatio, 32
Stratford Avenue Bridge (Bridgeport,
CT), 135
Superior Criminal Court of Essex
County, 68
Swansea, MA, 10

Taylor, Eddie, 55, 67–68
Taylor, Emma, 112–113, 114
Taylor, John, 53–55, 56, 58, 60–61,
62–63, 65

Taylor, Lucy "Lulu," 55–56
Taylor, Susan Ella "Susie," 50–57, 60, 63–68, 88–90
Taylor, William Henry, 112–113
Terry, Charles C., 28–29
Thomson, Ernest LeRoy, 103–104, 122–123, 144, 213
Tidd, John, 58, 64
Tripp, Benjamin A., 56

USS *Massasoit*, 13
uterine sound (medical instrument), 37, 39, 187

Vaughan, Gertrude, 102–103, 104, 115, 122
Vaughan's Maternity Hospital, 102

Waterbury, CT, 99, 101, 121
Waterbury Democrat, 101, 107, 115, 204
Waterbury Medical Institute, 99
Weis, Conrad, 116
Welch, Frederick "Fred," 131, 144, 175, 183–184, 190
Welch, Wallace, 144, 183, 217

Wells, Lucy Ann, 8, 9, 18
Wellsburg, NY, 19, 21, 147
Wethersfield State Prison, 149, 215, *215*, 217
Wheeler, George W., 207, 210, 213–214
Wilbur, Catherine. *See* Guilford, Nancy Alice (née Brown)
Wilkin, Anna, 95, 98
Williams, Annie. *See* Dyer, Annie J.
Williams, David, 46
Williams, Robert, 43
Williams, William H., 114, 115, 116
Windship, George Barker, 21–22, 23
Winsor, Frederick, 60, 65
Wolfe, Isaac, 106, 114, 115
women doctors, preference for, 84
Woodbridge, Jabez L., 149
Wooster Place lying-in hospital (New Haven, CT), 108–109, *108*, 111, 205, 207
Worcester, MA, 25, 26–29
Worcester Evening Gazette, 26

Yellow Mill Pond, 1, 136–137
Yeomans, Mrs. Albert, 163